Freud and Forbidden Knowledge

Freud and
Forbidden Knowledge

Edited by
Peter L. Rudnytsky and Ellen Handler Spitz

NEW YORK UNIVERSITY PRESS
New York and London

The coeditors of this volume wish to express sincere appreciation to Kitty Moore, Jason Renker, and Despina Papazoglou Gimbel.

NEW YORK UNIVERSITY PRESS
New York and London

Library of Congress Cataloging-in-Publication Data
Freud and forbidden knowledge / edited by Peter L. Rudnytsky and Ellen
   Handler Spitz.
       p.   cm.
   Includes bibliographical references and index.
   Contents: "And Rebecca loved Jacob," but Freud did not / Yael S.
Feldman — Promethean positions / Ellen Handler Spitz — The Oedipus
Rex and the ancient unconscious / Martha C. Nussbaum — Sophocles'
Oedipus Tyrannus : Freud, language, and the unconscious / Charles
Segal — The Oedipus myth / Vassilka Nikolava — Recognition in
Greek tragedy : psychoanalytic on Aristotelian perspectives /
Bennett Simon — Freud and Augustine / Peter L. Rudnytsky — The
architecture of sexuality : body and space in The Decameron /
Richard Kuhns — On Hamlet's madness and the unsaid / André Green.
   ISBN 0-8147-7437-7
   1. Psychoanalysis and literature. 2. Knowledge, Theory of, in
literature. 3. European literature—History and criticism.
I. Rudnytsky, Peter L.   II. Spitz, Ellen Handler, 1939-
PN56.P92F72   1994
809'.93353—dc20   93-25137
                    CIP

New York University Press books are printed on acid-free paper, and
their binding materials are chosen for strength and durability.

Manufactured in the United States of America

10 9 8 7 6 5 4 3 2 1

To Paul E. Stepansky and Gladys Topkis

Contents

viii   Contents

Contributors

YAEL S. FELDMAN is Associate Professor of Hebrew and Judaic Studies at New York University. She is literary editor of *Hadoar* and associate editor of *Prooftexts*. She is the author of *Modernism and Cultural Transfer* (1986) and coeditor of *Approaches to Teaching the Hebrew Bible in Translation* (1989).

ANDRÉ GREEN is a member and past president of the Paris Psychoanalytic Society and has held the Freud Memorial Chair at University College, London. His books include *The Tragic Effect: The Oedipus Complex in Tragedy* (1969), *Hamlet and "Hamlet"* (1983), *On Private Madness* (1986) and *Révélations de l'Inachèvement: à propos du Carton de Londres de Léonarde de Vinci* (1992).

RICHARD KUHNS is Professor of Philosophy at Columbia University. His books include *Structures of Experience* (1970), *Psychoanalytic Theory of Art* (1983), and *Tragedy: Contradiction and Repression* (1991).

VASSILKA NIKOLOVA is Senior Lecturer in Latin at the Medical University of Sofia. She is the author of *The Aphorisms of Hippocrates* (1989).

MARTHA C. NUSSBAUM is University Professor of Philosophy, Classics, and Comparative Literature at Brown University. She is the author of *Aristotle's De Motu Animalium* (1978), *The Fragility of Goodness: Luck and Ethics in Greek Tragedy and Philosophy* (1986), *Love's Knowledge:*

Essays on Philosophy and Literature (1990), and *The Therapy of Desire: Theory and Practice in Hellenistic Ethics* (1993).

PETER L. RUDNYTSKY is Director of the Institute for Psychological Study of the Arts at the University of Florida and a Corresponding Member of the Institute of Contemporary Psychoanalysis in Los Angeles. He is the author of *Freud and Oedipus* (1987) and *The Psychoanalytic Vocation: Rank, Winnicott, and the Legacy of Freud* (1991). His edited books include *The Persistence of Myth: Psychoanalytic and Structuralist Perspectives* (1988) and *Transitional Objects and Potential Spaces: Literary Uses of D. W. Winnicott* (1993).

CHARLES SEGAL is Professor of Greek and Latin at Harvard University. Among his books are *Tragedy and Civilization: An Interpretation of Sophocles* (1981), *Dionysiac Poetics and Euripides' "Bacchae"* (1982), *Interpreting Greek Tragedy* (1986), and *Lucretius on Death and Anxiety* (1990). His *Oedipus Tyrannus: Tragic Heroism and the Limits of Knowledge* is forthcoming in the Twayne Masterworks Series.

BENNETT SIMON is a Training and Supervising Analyst at the Boston Psychoanalytic Society and Clinical Associate Professor of Psychiatry at the Harvard Medical School. He is the author of *Mind and Madness in Ancient Greece* (1978) and *Tragic Drama and the Family* (1988).

ELLEN HANDLER SPITZ is Lecturer of Aesthetics in Psychiatry at New York Hospital-Cornell Medical Center and a Special Member of the Association for Psychoanalytic Medicine. A 1989-90 Getty Scholar, she is the author of *Art and Psyche* (1985) and *Image and Insight* (1991).

Freud and Forbidden Knowledge

Introduction

Peter L. Rudnytsky

Anyone who knows your science has veritably
eaten of the tree of paradise and become
clairvoyant.
> —Jung to Freud, May 30, 1907

Psychoanalysis is a discipline that seeks to understand and alleviate human suffering. Its practice is therefore an inherently dangerous activity. The psychoanalyst dares to explore the most intimate recesses of the human soul, to throw open long-barred doors, and to confront the monsters that may lie in wait. This is indeed a heroic enterprise, but if the analyst acts precipitately and fails to provide an atmosphere of safety in which the patient's process of self-discovery can go forward, he or she will become an intruder, a trespasser, a dragon rather than a dragon slayer. The frame of transference is designed to impart a fictional quality to the analytic quest, but even illusory sparks have been known to detonate real explosions.

Despite his scientific *Weltanschauung,* Freud was aware of the atavistic sources of his identity as a soul healer and consistently turned to literature and myth to illuminate both the methods and findings of psychoanalysis.

I thank Deborah Anna Luepnitz and Ellen Handler Spitz for their discerning readings of this preface.

Works of art are therefore not merely external objects to which psycho-analysis can be *applied,* but themselves constitutive of psychoanalytic knowledge. In asserting the sexual and infantile origins of all intellectual curiosity, moreover, Freud implicitly acknowledged the transgressive na-ture of his own lifelong quest to unravel the riddles of the human psyche.

The papers assembled here, by a distinguished array of analysts and humanistic scholars, pursue the theme of forbidden knowledge as it is articulated in canonical works of the Western tradition from the Hebrew Bible to Shakespeare's *Hamlet.* This theme is crucial to the myths of Oedipus and the Fall—those primal narratives of Hellenism and Hebra-ism—the conjunction between which served as an organizing principle of my earlier edited volume, *The Persistence of Myth: Psychoanalytic and Structuralist Perspectives* (1988). Perhaps unsurprisingly, three of the present nine chapters concern themselves with Oedipus, who retains his hold on the psychoanalytic imagination. But Ellen Handler Spitz and I have invited the contributors to look upon the rubric of forbidden knowledge as an evocative and not a restrictive one, and they have re-sponded by producing a series of wide-ranging meditations on the tragic dimensions of human experience, which cumulatively invite reflection on what might be meant by knowledge forbidden *to* Freud.

Yael S. Feldman strikes a keynote by simultaneously deploying and interrogating psychoanalysis in " 'And Rebecca Loved Jacob,' but Freud Did Not." Feldman argues that Freud's oedipal model of intergenera-tional masculine conflict is not well suited to the Hebrew Bible, where fathers rarely express aggression and the most acute conflicts are those between siblings. Although I think that the weakness of biblical fathers might be more amenable to psychoanalytic explanation than Feldman allows, she performs a valuable service by drawing attention to a possible limitation in Freud's vision and to the widely varying assumptions about familial and gender roles that prevail in diverse cultures.

Like Feldman, Ellen Handler Spitz effects a displacement of perspec-tive, from the Sophoclean figure of Oedipus (by whom Freud was mes-merized) to the Aeschylean Titan Prometheus. Spitz's essay, "Promethean Positions," carries forward the project of her path-breaking *Image and Insight* (1991) by seeking to forge a closer bond between psychiatry and the humanities. Since the clinician's "principal task is to listen attentively to the voice and words of another human being," and to discern both the private and culturally encoded meanings that resonate therein, he or she cannot afford to neglect the masterworks of the manifold traditions we inhabit, which even today derive in large measure from ancient Greece. Spitz sifts Freud's scattered allusions to the Prometheus myth before offering her own reading of Aeschylus' tragedy, which highlights the masochistic quality of Prometheus' "script-writing tendencies" and the analogy between his immobility and that of an analytic patient.

Martha C. Nussbaum and Charles Segal are two of America's most eminent classicists, and their divergent perspectives on *Oedipus the King* and psychoanalysis form the centerpieces of this volume. In "The *Oedipus Rex* and the Ancient Unconscious" Nussbaum evinces skepticism about the applicability of Freudian categories to an ancient text, arguing that Sophocles' play is less concerned with sexual desire than with reversals of fortune and that it can be better understood with the aid of the dream book of Artemidoros and Epicurean philosophy than through a Freudian lens. Nussbaum's elucidation of the culturally specific meanings given to dreams and sexual behavior in Artemidorous (and, by extension, in Freud) is both witty and authoritative, yet a classical Freudian might question whether incest is really as incidental to the tragedy of Oedipus as her reading makes out. Nussbaum, in any case, ends by calling not for a rejection of psychoanalysis but rather for a turn to object relations theory, which, she holds, in its concern with the fears and aggressions of infancy more closely corresponds to ancient psychology than does unreconstructed Freudianism.

In contrast to Nussbaum's principled skepticism, Charles Segal in "Sophocles' *Oedipus Tyrannus*: Freud, Language, and the Unconscious" breathes new life into a Freudian approach to the play by showing how it can continue to generate fresh and profound insights. Segal addresses the objection of Jean-Pierre Vernant that Oedipus cannot be said to have an "Oedipus complex" because his putative oedipal feelings would be directed toward Merope, the Corinthian queen whom he believes to be his mother, rather than toward Jocasta. But, as Segal demonstrates, Oedipus' relations with both sets of his parents are caught up in the "processes by which the unconscious is displaced into language." Far from rehearsing previously established conclusions, Segal's reading itself enacts a process that embodies the open-ended and scrupulous spirit of the best psychoanalytic inquiry.

Both the essays of Vassilka Nikolova and Bennett Simon use the thought of Aristotle to connect Greek tragedy and psychoanalysis. In

"The Oedipus Myth: An Attempt at Interpretation of Its Symbolic Systems," Nikolova, a Bulgarian classicist, takes Aristotle's concept of catharsis as a point of departure for her exegesis of the changing ideological functions of the Oedipus myth in ancient culture. Nikolova argues that the myth arose from a synthesis of the disparate motifs of the Sphinx, the exposed child, and the riddle and that—in common with other myths—it gradually became a vehicle for expressing a scientific view of the world. Simon's "Recognition in Greek Tragedy: Psychoanalytic on Aristotelian Perspectives" moves from a nuanced discussion of the meanings of recognition (*anagnorisis*) in Aristotle's *Poetics,* to reflections on several ancient and modern tragedies, to the presentation of compelling clinical material. Like those of Spitz and Segal, Simon's essay provides a standard by which the potential for cross-fertilization between psychoanalysis and the humanities can be measured.

My own "Freud and Augustine" juxtaposes its protagonists as autobiographers, theorists of forbidden knowledge, and proponents of definitive interpretations of the myths of Oedipus and the Fall. I first undertake a psychoanalytic reading of the *Confessions* as a whole, then treat the episode of Augustine's theft of the pears as a reenactment of the Fall that constitutes a screen memory for two casually mentioned incidents involving his parents and raising the specter of incest, and finally contrast the pessimism of Augustine and Freud, on the one hand, with the more optimistic outlooks of Aristotle, D. W. Winnicott, and Heinz Hartmann on the other. While granting the power of both the Freudian and Augustinian versions of the doctrine of original sin, I strive to maintain a critical attitude toward their ideological implications.

The final two essays are by Richard Kuhns and André Green. In "The Architecture of Sexuality: Body and Space in the *Decameron*," Kuhns uses the metaphorical equation between bodies and buildings to explore the somber undertones of Boccaccio's comic masterpiece. Concentrating on the three notable tales of Masetto (Day 3, Story 1), Guiscardo and Ghismonda (Day 4, Story 1), and Rineiri and Elena (Day 8, Story 7), Kuhns in each case unearths a hidden meaning of philosophical import. Creativity for Boccaccio is shown to be a sexual as well as a spiritual process that requires a judicious balancing of both sides of our divided natures. One of France's most renowned intellectuals, Green, like Simon, is a medically trained psychoanalyst of exceptional humanistic erudition. "On Hamlet's Madnesses and the Unsaid" unravels the tangled knots of representation, incest and patricide, and madness in Shakespeare's tragedy. Green's divination of the "unsaid" culminates in an avowedly speculative reconstruction of "the plot of the play that Shakespeare *did not write,* but about which he would have dreamed before writing the tragedy which bears its mark." His provocative reading of *Hamlet* should be set beside that of Stephen Dedalus in James Joyce's *Ulysses,* to which he makes reference.

As I have indicated, the works and authors taken up here are all indubitably canonical in the Western tradition. That tradition is now, with good reason, under increasing pressure from feminist and postcolonial critics. But the canon can be opened up not only by adding hitherto neglected texts but also by reexamining already established texts with altered eyes, thereby making them new. Such a transformation of the past through re-vision is integral to psychoanalysis, in both clinical and cultural practice, and to the project of *Freud and Forbidden Knowledge.*

ONE

"And Rebecca Loved Jacob," But Freud Did Not

Yael S. Feldman

Isaac loved Esau because of the game he fed
him, and Rebecca loved Jacob.
—Gen. 25:28

That the force of passionate love with all its adverse and tragic ramifi-
cations is one of the high points of the Jacob story is well known. And
it is precisely this romantic feature that has made Jacob so accessible to
modern literary reworkings, from Thomas Mann's *Joseph* trilogy (the
first volume of which is devoted to "The Tales of Jacob") to Harold
Bloom's recent hermeneutic fiction, *The Book of J* ("Before I became
convinced that J was a woman, I tended to believe that Jacob was J's
signature, a kind of self-representation" [1990, 209]).

Less obvious is the fact that this ostensibly sudden effusion of passion

The ideas presented here were originally developed in my classes at Columbia University
and formalized in my "Recurrence and Sublimation: Toward a Psychoanalytic Approach
to Biblical Narrative" (1989). Earlier versions of this essay were presented at the 1990
meeting of the Society of Biblical Literature, a 1991 Columbia University Seminar on Israel
and Jewish Studies, and a 1992 New York University Seminar on Psychoanalysis and the
Humanities. I would like to thank the participants at these meetings, particularly at the
University Seminars, for their helpful comments and challenging criticism.
Translations from the Hebrew are the author's.

is not as unpredictable as it may at first seem. Although unprecedented in the earlier portions of Genesis, it is subtly rationalized within the psychology of the Jacob cycle itself, which offers a compact but complete economy of family dynamics.

It should come as no surprise that at the core of this economy we find a proliferation of the verb *'ahav* (love). As we shall see, this single Hebrew root covers a variety of affects and appetites that range—in the language of modern psychology—from transference and maternal love, bonding and attachment, to gluttony and dependence, desire and lust. This semantic field is further reinforced by a set of antonyms, denoting hate, derision, and jealousy (*satam, sana', baz, kine'*), as well as by a relatively high density of other expressions of emotions—kissing, hugging, and weeping.

Surprisingly, these latter expressions are all an exclusively *male* prerogative (not only in this story, but in the David cycle as well); and unlike other traditions (the Homeric or the Far Eastern, for example), where male tears function mostly ritualistically, here they signal a personal experience. When Jacob is carried away to the point of weeping (upon setting eyes on Rachel for the first time; Gen. 29:11), the contemporary Western reader is likely to raise an eyebrow. According to our norms, this is a rather unexpected "feminine" behavior. This cultural divergence (among others) may perhaps be helpful in delineating the boundaries of the issue at hand—the difference between the psychological models implied by biblical narrative and the psychoanalytic models devised for us by Freud and his disciples.

This issue is not new. Several contemporary critics have commented on the disparity between Oedipus and Isaac, who represent, respectively, filial aggression and rebellion in contrast to passivity and submission (Wellisch 1954; Bakan 1966; Shoham 1976). But it is not only Isaac who does not fit the oedipal mold. As I have pointed out elsewhere, "there can be no doubt that Freud could not identify with Isaac. Nor could he have identified with Abraham in that famous episode [the binding of Isaac], for he was just as 'bound' by his heavenly father as Isaac was" (Feldman 1989, 79).

Implied in my statement is the claim that there is of necessity a certain lack of fit between the two systems under discussion; that if Freud was—consciously or unconsciously—searching for a masterplot that would represent the Romantic defiance of authority which he saw as the motive force of his life (and which he generalized for the experience of secular modernism at large), he could not have found it in a monotheistic tradition that made the *Akeda* or "binding of Isaac" (Gen. 22) its centerpiece. Greek mythology, with its constant "vertical" generational struggle, with its potential and actual infanticides and patricides, offered a better fit. Even here, we should recall, Freud had to perform a little cosmetic surgery, ignoring Laius' initial action against his son and—like Sophocles (Rudnytsky 1987, 254–56)—locating his own starting point for the drama in Oedipus himself. Biblical narrative, on the other hand, particularly at the height of its stylistic austerity in the *Akeda* episode, could offer no such resource. Despite its dramatic potential (developed more fully in the various midrashic retellings of the story; see Spiegel 1950; Ginzberg 1913, 271–86), its textual repressions seem to be too successful to allow a full psychoanalytic interpretation, namely, a meaningful analysis of unconscious fantasy and instinctual desire (Feldman 1989, 79–80).

But what of the other patriarchal stories? Couldn't the Jacob/Joseph story, with its profusion of affective states and a viable maternal presence, fill the gap? Why, then, didn't the family dynamics of this story attract Freud's attention? And why, in the final analysis, should we care?

Deferring this last question to the close of my essay, let me start by stating that I have not found any new evidence to corroborate my claims. As far as we know, Freud identified—in a rather awkward manner—with Moses, the giver of the new law, but also the object of patricide, as *Moses and Monotheism* (1939) clearly argues (although this runs completely counter to the plain sense of biblical narrative; Yerushalmi 1991, 61 et passim). Similarly, his so-called identification with Joseph, the favorite young son (Shengold 1979), was marked by ambivalence, as he made every effort to distance himself from the interpretive techniques of his ancient precursor (Frieden 1990). The first three patriarchs, however, do not figure at all in his writings (except, of course, when he refers to his father, whose name was Jacob, an irony to which I shall return). So my question about Freud's lack of love for Jacob is for the moment a rhetorical one—a heuristic ploy to explore the peculiarity of biblical psychology vis-à-vis our contemporary, post-Freudian sensibility. This sensibility, I would argue, may be the culmination of a long Western tradition, but—contrary to prevailing perception—does not necessarily derive from biblical narrative. A close reading of the latter should at least put into question the popular (and facile) equation of the Freudian nuclear family with the biblical family.[1]

To begin with, let us look at the family structure. By equipping Isaac and Rebecca with twins rather than a single son, the biblical narrative circumvents a fundamental presupposition of classical psychoanalysis—the triangularity of all family dynamics. "Squaring the triangle," so to speak, the Jacob story forestalls, at least on the surface, the pitfall of internal conflict imputed by Freud to any son in the oedipal position. Rather, the neat distribution of loyalties, in which each child is aligned with one parent, allows for some dyadic object relations, resulting in bonding rather than conflict.

This avoidance of "vertical," intergenerational conflict is further reinforced by the paternal position. Orally fixated by his gluttony (or "love" of food) and blind, Isaac is too weak and dependent to arouse filial defiance. In fact, the text compulsively emphasizes his craving for Esau's delicacies (ch. 27), thereby retrospectively making sense of the unique expression "ki tzayid befiv" (literally: "for [there was] hunt in his mouth" [Gen. 25:28]). Playing off its closest analogue, the description of Noah's dove returning to the ark "(ve-ʿaleh zayit) taraf be-fihah" (literally: "[and an olive-leaf] plucked [rent?] in her mouth" [Gen.8:11]), Isaac's view of his son activates the synonymic paradigm tzayid = teref (hunt, prey, food, nourishment), thereby conjuring the image of the parental animal or bird of prey feeding its young. If we add to this chain of intertextual associations the resonance of Proverbs' Woman of Valor who "brings food [lit. 'prey'] to her family" ("va-titen teref le-veitah" [Prv. 31:15]), the reversal of roles becomes more apparent: Isaac's partiality toward Esau is what psychoanalysts call "anaclitic love," the dependent attachment a child forms toward his mother or other providers of nourishment and similar needs. (Hence my translation, in the epigraph to this chapter, "because of the game he fed him.") This reversal casts Esau, in his turn, in an unexpected light, implicating him in a second reversal, that of gender roles—an intriguing issue to which I shall return.

One can hardly imagine such a paternal figure serving as the source of a Freudian castration threat or of a Lacanian " 'No' of the Father"—the necessary condition, according to classical psychoanalysis, for the resolution of the son's Oedipus complex. By the logic of this theory, without a strong father image the boy is unable to pass the test of civilization—the renunciation of his instinctual desires, or, in Lacan's formulation, the relinquishing of the preoedipal, maternal Imaginary. In such a position, the son will have difficulty in internalizing the "Law of the Father," that process which produces Freud's superego (the conscience or morality principle) or, in Lacan's scheme, allows him to enter the symbolic order, namely, the law of language and other social institutions (Lacan 1957–58, 39). That this structure comes closer to the classical Freudian position on the *female* oedipal (non)dissolution should come as no surprise.[2] This is one more ironic clue to be followed up later.

For the moment, let me highlight the paradox of my insinuation. From a Freudian perspective, Isaac's progeny risk losing what has always been viewed as the Bible's greatest contribution—the moral principle. Following this paradox to its logical conclusion, we may perceive that they in fact do repeat their father's early trauma, albeit under different circumstances: Jacob/Israel, despite narrative declarations to the contrary ("You strove with God and with men, but you prevailed" [Gen. 32:29]), is unable to "say no" to his sons, with rather disastrous results (see the infamous Dinah episode, ch. 34). And if we allow ourselves a glance into the future, we notice that David, that fearless warrior-leader, evinces a similar policy of noninvolvement where his sons are concerned (Amnon and Absalom are the paramount cases [2 Sam. 13–19]). On the other hand, the blatant exception to this rule—Saul's violence toward David and even Jonathan, his son (1 Sam. 18–20)—is rationalized in the text as an aberration, the result of an "evil spirit" visited upon him by God (1 Sam. 18:10).

Biblical fathers, it would seem, are not made for the Freudian masterplot. Rarely expressing aggression, they seem to avoid conflict rather than arousing (and resolving) it. This does not mean, however, that conflict totally disappears. It is recreated on the "horizontal" level, in the relationship between the brothers, thus highlighting one of the major ways in which the patriarchal stories diverge from Freud's interests: their focus on intragenerational sibling rivalry rather than on filial rebellion.

There is no need to review here the ubiquity of this conflict throughout Genesis (and beyond). What is of importance is the peculiar mode of representation used in shaping it, and the way it differs from the Freudian model. And here we would do well to remember that, although *in practice* Freud's life was marked (both privately and publicly) by constant feuds and rifts, which in fact were "actings out" of sibling rivalry—his inability to tolerate any competing theory is by now a matter of public record, while his jealousy of his younger brother was privately admitted by him and has been probed by his biographers and commentators (Jones 1961, 7; Gay 1988, 11; Rudnytsky 1987, 19 et passim; Yerushalmi 1991, 92)— he showed relatively little *theoretical* interest in the subject. None of his papers is specifically devoted to this issue, nor did he coin a special term for it ("sibling rivalry" does not appear in the index of his works, nor does any other related concept). Moreover, despite the prominent role attributed to the death of his brother Julius in his self-analysis, his probing led to the discovery of "Oedipus," not "Cain" (Rudnytsky 1987, 71; Yerushalmi 1991, 92).

Setting the irony of this discrepancy aside, let us hear the evidence of a latter-day practitioner:

The conflict with siblings does not have the same kind of repressive, utterly forbidden quality that the oedipal struggle does. But as a source of poignancy and pain, this area of human relationship has perhaps been underestimated in comparison with the problems of the child-parent situation. (Zeligs 1974, 88)

The speaker is Dorothy Zeligs, a devout Freudian of the old order. Her tone here is uncharacteristically critical, yet the critique is carefully hedged. And no wonder. She questions nothing less than the centrality of the Oedipus complex—the cornerstone of classical Freudian theory— and this not in the context of contemporary post-Freudian revisions (Kleinian object relations, feminist, or other anti-Oedipus critiques), but from within the framework of an otherwise orthodox Freudian analysis.

Not surprisingly, the occasion for Zeligs' tacit revaluation is her study, *Psychoanalysis and the Bible*. And it is perhaps worth noting that this revaluation appears only in the book, published in 1974, but not in her earlier articles published in *American Imago* throughout the 1950s (Zeligs 1953; 1955a; 1955b). We can surmise, then, that her conclusions were made possible not only by the specific material she was working with, but also by the changing climate within the psychoanalytic establishment, a change that is evidenced by collections of essays and several books on sibling rivalry that were published mostly in the 1980s (see *The Psychoanalytic Study of the Child* 1983, and *Psychoanalytic Inquiry* 1988).[3]

Furthermore, that Zeligs arrives at her conclusion only by the end of her third chapter, after imposing the oedipal plot on Abraham, Jacob, and Joseph, is also quite predictable. Sibling rivalry reaches its fullest orchestration in the Joseph story, so that the strain on her oedipal model becomes unbearable. Thus, she is obliged to acknowledge the *harmony* underlying Joseph's relations with his "father figures" (1974, 89), without actually recognizing that his is only the most extreme case of a general pattern. The other factor standing in her way is her inclination to treat isolated "personalities," thereby missing the centrality of sibling rivalry in the overall narrative structure of Genesis.

Indeed, the Bible's mythological first murder by no means corroborates Freud's patricidal reconstruction of the primal horde. Rather, a case of fratricide—the only one actually carried out in the text—is the primal scene (and sin) of Genesis.[4] Yet if there is no brotherly love lost in the Abel and Cain story (Gen. 4), brotherly aggression comes to be increasingly held in check. In contrast to René Girard's insistence on the universality and ubiquity of scapegoating and (sibling) violence (1972; 1982), in Genesis this basic human impulse goes through a series of representations in which the potential outburst is always mitigated, neutralized, or deflected, usually by means of physical separation (e.g., Abraham and Lot, Isaac and Ishmael, and finally also Jacob and Esau) or other compromises (Rachel and Leah). It is in the Joseph story, of course, that the sibling rivalry theme reaches its culmination by being both acted out and reversed on a grand scale. In this account, moreover, a narrative representation of the unconscious appears for the first time, in Joseph's dreams and dream interpretation. Joseph, the dream interpreter, is also the first human being to recognize and verbalize the interdependence between past and future. Finally, the moral implications of this recognition are explicitly stated here (Gen. 45:5–8; see Alter 1981, 163 et passim), only to be further developed and orchestrated in the next book, Exodus. The journey from Cain to Joseph, and later to Moses, may therefore be seen as the earliest literary representation of a move from blind aggression to reasoned insight, from acting out to remembering and knowing.

But isn't this what the psychoanalytic process is all about? And wouldn't this insight lend a new meaning to the most prominent feature of biblical poetics, namely, narrative recurrence, known more popularly as repetition? Yes and no. Here we run into an intriguing paradox. For Freud (1920), the compulsion to repeat is associated with the death drive—the impulse to resist change, progress, and life. The analysand's unconscious repetitions, he argued (1914), have replaced memory; and it is precisely this vicious circle that the psychoanalytic process must disrupt, so that the subject can re-member his alienated experiences, thereby achieving a new integration of the self. In biblical narrative, on the other hand, it is through recall and recurrence that change is slowly brought about.

Yet notice the slight lexical difference I have introduced. "Repetition" is almost a misnomer when talking about biblical narrative. The emphasis in recent scholarship on biblical poetics is on "theme and variations." Whereas *verbatim* repetition, says Meir Sternberg (1985), marked the literary representation of the ancient prebiblical myths, repetition with a difference was the innovation and contribution of the Hebrew Bible (Alter 1981). It is for the sake of this poetic distinction that I have elsewhere proposed to substitute "narrative recurrence" for repetition (1989, 82). Yet by this reformulation I have gained something else—a common territory for biblical narrative and certain contemporary views of the psychoanalytic process.

Following Paul Ricoeur's (1970) phenomenological critique of psychoanalysis and his highlighting of both the verbal and narrative nature of clinical experience (1977a, 836–43), narrative psychology has been gaining ground, as in the theories of Roy Schafer, Merton Gill, and Donald Spence. In recent years, the emphasis on the function of metaphor (Ricoeur 1977b), multiple histories (Schafer 1979), and narrative truth (Spence 1982) in the psychoanalytic process has led to the highlighting of "narrative recursion."

"The original conflict or fantasy or early experience," says Spence, "is almost never literally repeated in the transference; rather, what we see is a series of variations on a single theme" (1987, 191). It is this polyphonic clinical recursion that "cuts down on the senseless repetition which would make the pattern seem mechanical and unnatural," thereby effecting the therapeutic transition from language to action (195).

The parameters of this action (e.g., change, growth, adaptation, sublimation) and the socioethical norms they imply are still being fiercely debated within the psychoanalytic community. And it is perhaps in this respect that the repetition in variation, or what I prefer to name the "spiral movement" (cyclical and linear at one and the same time) of biblical narrative, is most instructive. For, in contrast to Freudian thinking, in the Bible this movement toward change and sublimation is not inspired by another human being, paternal or otherwise. It is not the threat of *human authority* that gets internalized in the patriarchal stories, but rather the demand of *divine authority*. Nothing demonstrates this disparity better than the conflicting interpretations of the famous agon that secures Jacob's blessing (Gen. 32:25–33).

Freudians such as Rank (1912), Reik (1951), and Zeligs have had no problem identifying Jacob's nightly adversary with the figure of the father, locating here the resolution of the Oedipus complex. Elaborating on Rank's general statement that "brother and father already blend in the dream as a single person" (1912, 242), Zeligs claims that "the dream portrays with dramatic condensation how castration anxiety brings about the renunciation of instinctual wishes and the strengthening of the superego" (1974, 53), passing in silence over the fact that Jacob is now himself an aging *pater familias*.

The text itself, however, suggests an alternative possibility. Even as its plot dramatically prepares us for the brother, the enigmatic wording of the actual confrontation leaves the identity and nature of the adversary open to interpretation. Thus, the combat scene is preceded by a lengthy sequence (Gen. 32:4–24), marked by long, repetitive sentences (*a*typical for biblical style) devoted to Jacob's fears of Esau and to his various attempts to ward off any confrontation. In this sequence, Jacob repeats his brother's name *nine* times, as if hoping for some kind of verbal, incantational magic. By contrast, verse 25 abruptly states: "Jacob remained alone, and a man [*'ish*] wrestled with him until dawn." This stark stylistic transition from the verbosity of the "Esau repetition," paradoxically signaling the tactics of avoidance and denial, to the terseness and factual economy used in the depiction of inescapable reality, produces an uncanny effect. Yet, as far as the Hebrew text is concerned, this is not a dream state, as both Rank and Zeligs assume, nor is the *'ish* ("man") identifiable. On the contrary, his generic nonspecificity, reinforced by the notorious syntactic ambiguity of the dialogue between the combatants (Barthes 1975), enables a rereading that runs counter to the expectations aroused by the narrative itself. Thus it is neither the brother nor the father who is retrospectively read into the agon. Rather, both participants inscribe divine authority into the textually ambiguous space (Gen. 32:29–31).

In contrast to Freud, then, biblical narrative plays down the power of the human father, because it is not from him that the moral obligation to harness the instinctual drives (rather than "renounce" them, as Freud would have it) generally issues. This may sound paradoxical, since the

Hebrew Bible is perceived (by popular Christianity in particular) as the origin not only of monotheism in general ("the Father Religion," in Freud's [1939] formulation), but also of the specific image of the God of Vengeance, the obvious archetype of the castrating, paternal authority postulated by Freud. Setting aside the blatant partiality of this perception, let us ponder the meaning of the paradox for Freud's masterplot.

If, as I claim, the Hebrew Bible channels all its "paternal energy" (both harsh and benevolent, if we are to be true to the text in all its nuances) into the image of the heavenly father, it leaves little room for paternal authority within its human drama. In that sense, the Binding of Isaac may perhaps be emblematic, not only of the Hebrew Bible, but of Jewish culture at large.[5] What it dramatizes is not the Promethean defiance of authority (see chapter 2 below) glorified by the Romantics and popularized by Freud's positive Oedipus complex, but rather a chain of same-sex submissions and identifications, more in line with Freud's negative Oedipus complex.

The significance of this divergence cannot be overestimated. Clearly, there is a world of difference between these two aspects, not only in their inception (the negative Oedipus complex was not discovered until two decades after the positive; see Freud 1923), but also in their cultural appeal, evaluation, and popular dissemination. While professional clinicians insist on the ubiquity of the negative Oedipus complex, and recent scholarship finds it, ironically, in the material and behavior of Freud's own self-analysis around the turn of the century (and even in Sophocles' original *Oedipus*; Rudnytsky 1987, 253–74), the concept hardly exists in the popular imagination. For the average consumer of twentieth-century wisdom, there is only one "Oedipus"—the one competing with his father (figures), and not necessarily over the mother. A good example of this selectivity is Harold Bloom's literary appropriation of the positive Oedipus complex in *The Anxiety of Influence* (1973). This study perfectly illustrates how the vestiges of Romanticism continue to shape contemporary culture by absorbing from the new (in this case psychoanalysis) what is in line with its own premises and rejecting what is not. There is no doubt that the negative Oedipus complex, with its bisexual and homosexual implications, was a threatening discovery even for Freud, let alone his (and our) fellow citizens, particularly of the male persuasion. It was probably this threat that delayed his recognition of it, and it may have been one of the reasons for his reliance on Greek drama rather than on biblical narrative.

The irony of the last observation should not elude us. It was in Greek culture, of course, that male homosexuality was a societal norm, while biblical law forbade it outright (Lev. 18:22; 20:13). This is why biblical narrative cannot openly acknowledge its own psychological makeup. Rather, the latter is successfully disguised by the rampant use of intra-generational conflict. From this point of view, the emphasis on sibling rivalry helps to highlight the distinctiveness of biblical psychology, although psychoanalysis has usually refused to accept it. Freudians tend to conflate the oedipal and the sibling conflicts, seeing one as a displacement of the other. The impulses repressed in the relationship with the parents, says Rank, are developed among siblings "in a less impeded and more lasting manner" (1912, 363). My argument, on the other hand, is that the psychological economy of the sibling plot is different, and that this difference is of crucial importance, because it touches on the contemporary debate over sexual essentialism—a debate that to a great extent is still bogged down by pro-Freudian and anti-Freudian dichotomies (see particularly the French feminist school, Irigaray vs. Kristeva, for example; Fuss 1989). What I am suggesting, in short, is that biblical psychology, at least as far as the Jacob story is concerned, can offer a model that frees the family structure not only from rigid generational strife as postulated by Freud, but also from the no less rigid gender roles imposed on it by the oedipal masterplot and its insistence on essentialist sexual difference. To illustrate my point, let us go back to the opening of this essay—the psychological structure underlying the Isaac household.

Of all biblical families that of Isaac is the closest to the monogamous modern nuclear family. Isaac is the only patriarch not to take or be given a second wife, despite Rebecca's long infertility. But how are we to interpret this uniqueness? Is it another symptom of Isaac's ubiquitous passivity, his lifelong repetition of his traumatic binding? Or is some other force at work here, a new element only tersely and obliquely hinted at by the text?

What I am referring to is the notion of affective attachment, introduced for the first time with Isaac's love for Rebecca (Gen. 24:67). The only earlier mention of the verb "to love" is the notorious 'asher 'ahavta of chapter 22, where God tells Abraham to take "your son, your only son, the one you love" to Mount Moriah (Gen. 22:2). But embedded as this phrase is in a subordinate clause of a reported speech, it does not have the "objective," fact-establishing force of the narrator's discourse, as we hear it repeatedly in the Isaac-Rebecca-Jacob story (Gen. 24:67; 25:28; 27:14; 29:18,20,30,32). The first of these instances is of particular interest, as it appears in a wonderfully economic sequence, in which Isaac "brings Rebecca to his mother Sarah's tent," "takes her," she "becomes his wife," *vaye'ehaveha* (and "he loved her?" "fell in love?" "was enamored of her?"—the density of Hebrew semantics makes it difficult to determine), and—as if this were the hidden agenda of the whole series— "he was comforted for his mother" (another typically elliptic Hebrew phrase, apparently referring to Sarah's death, mentioned briefly and without emotion at the opening of the previous chapter [Gen. 23:1]).

One need not be an astute Freudian to read into this breathless chain, in its linear progression from external actions to interior states, a biblical representation of the psychoanalytic concept of transference love. This is neither love at first sight nor the grand passion that Jacob later experiences with Rachel. As the ordering of the verbs subtly encodes, this is a substitute love, replacing lack and grief with the comfort that grows out of shared proximity. But it is nonetheless the first time in Genesis that a male-female relationship is defined by its *affective* aspect rather than by its generative function (*vayeda'*, "and he knew") or the lack thereof.

That this redefinition is introduced through Isaac, the otherwise shadowy character, who, with ostensible naïveté, repeats his father's ruse with the same local gentile, Avimelech (Gen. 20 and 26), should come as no surprise. We may be witnessing here the beginning of a long Western tradition in which the world of action and the world of affect are polarized and understood only in their negation of each other.

What I would like to suggest, however, is that what is traditionally seen as Isaac's passivity, his merely walking in his father's footsteps, can be otherwise interpreted if we bracket our received, unquestioned valorization of activity in the public sphere. To do this permits us to notice the one conspicuous detail in which Isaac's entanglement with Avimelech diverges from that of his father. While in the case of Abraham, Avimelech is forewarned by God (Gen. 20:3) who alerts him (in a dream) that "the woman you have taken [Sarah] is husbanded," in the case of Isaac, Avimelech finds out for himself (Gen. 26:8) before any action was taken

(another turn in the spiral movement of the narrative, implying the substitution of human internalization for divine intervention). Moreover, the
long dialogue between Avimelech and God in chapter 20 is replaced here
by a terse observation. As Avimelech was watching through his window
he saw "Isaac playing/laughing [*Yitzhak metzahek*] with Rebecca his
wife." Again, the compactness of Hebrew syntax, accompanied by its
dense but elusive semantics, makes an accurate contemporary rendering
of this pun almost impossible. It is clear, however, that this Avimelech
takes his cue not from divine intervention, but from the observable fact
of Isaac's apparent "joy" or "fun" or "bliss," perhaps "*jouissance,*" or
however one wishes to render the playfulness of the verb *metzahek,* in
his relationship "with Rebecca his wife." This detail, with its hint of
mutuality ("with"), nicely dovetails with Isaac's initially avowed love for
Rebecca. As such, it adds a new dimension to the character trait implied
by his name (*Yitzhak*). Formerly the object of disbelieving laughter (Gen.
18:12–15) and possibly mockery (21:9), Isaac is now in the subject
position, the agent of another kind of laughter, that of sexual playfulness
and domestic bliss. We may surmise, then, that in the figure of Isaac a
different option is hesitantly sketched out, that of internalized action,
the sphere of the heart and the hearth.

If by now the reader is wondering why I have been avoiding the
simple code word generally associated with this sphere—the "feminine"—then I have just made my point. It is not the Bible's fault,
definitely not poor Isaac's, that our perception has been so thoroughly
clouded by two millennia of misreading, reinforced in this century by
Freudian gender essentialism. Biblical narrative, or rather its ideological
underpinnings, is not without faults, but this problematic dichotomy
is not among them. The popular identification of the male-female axis
with "active-passive" and similar hoary binarisms (reason-emotion;
culture-nature; light-darkness), which persists in our thinking to this
very day despite Freud's careful questioning of it, is hardly known to
the biblical narrator.

And I do not mean just the surface fact, well publicized by now,
that the women in Genesis (as in Judges), to the extent that they figure
in what is, after all, a male-oriented narrative, are, in a sense, "phallic
women"—if the term is used neutrally, without any judgmental con-
notations. They take an active part in the unfolding of the plot, exerting
authority in various ways, from the confrontational (Sarah) to the

devious (Rachel), and from the self-centered (Tamar) to the other-centered (Rebecca). In a way, these women illustrate the complementarity implied in the Garden of Eden story, where what Man (*Adam*) failed to find among the animals of the field (thereby necessitating the creation of Woman [Eve]) is denoted by the wonderfully oxymoronic expression *'ezer kenegdo* (Gen. 2:20). The traditional translation of this phrase, "helpmeet," sorely misses the balanced tension between the two sides of the coin. The latter is even missing in Phyllis Trible's well-intended feminist correction: "A companion corresponding to it" (1978, 89) hardly preserves the original's lexical as well as ideational compactness. Literally meaning "assistance adversarial to him/it," it is best rendered as "counterpart" or "counterbalance."[6] Indeed, this expression may be the earliest intimation of "different but equal," ideally giving the two genders free rein to complement each other in whatever way, unhampered by any normative expectations.

But the freedom does not stop here. Biblical narrative takes a further step toward subtly crossing the boundaries within the same gender, so that stereotypical definitions lose their meaning. We have already seen how Esau, the hairy, ostensibly virile man of the field, is cast in the (traditionally) female role of the "nourisher" vis-à-vis his father. Isaac's blindness, on the other hand, makes him lose what contemporary criticism considers the major "sense" operative in male sexuality—the scopic or the visual. Predictably, he has recourse to the "other" senses, those that make up female sexuality—touch and smell (Irigaray 1977).

When it comes to Jacob, the clues are more obvious but also more complex. Traditionally, Jacob's characterization with respect to Esau has been attributed to the polarization of culture and nature (Hendel 1989, 128 et passim). But rarely has it been observed that this dichotomy overlaps with another one—that of male and female. The tent is not only the abode of the civilized shepherd, it is also the inner space occupied by mothers and wives, as the text so often tells us (see the tent of Sarah/Rebecca above; and cf. Judges 5:24). Jacob, then, grows up in the realm of the feminine, exhibiting from birth female features. (Would we go too far to associate his "hairlessness/smoothness" with the "nakedness/craftiness" of Eve's serpent? Or in reading metaphorically his fearful "but I am smooth" [Gen. 27:11] as expressing the female "phallic lack" postulated by Lacan?) And, of course, he has his mother's undivided love. But what kind of love is this?

With this question, we are back to the sibling issue and its gender-related implications. On the surface, I said, the double birth made possible a fair division of parental love. But this division is not symmetrical, just as the twins are not identical. In a single verse, masterfully controlled, we are informed of both the similarity and the difference: "Isaac loved Esau because of the game he fed him, and Rebecca loved Jacob" (Gen. 25:28). Both parents love, but only one of them loves unconditionally, as the sudden break in the syntactic parallelism forcefully demonstrates. ("A mother's relation to a son," says Freud, "is altogether the most perfect, the most free from ambivalence of all human relationships" [1932, 133].) A contextual reading, however, may yield a different story. If Isaac loves Esau for his otherness, Rebecca loves Jacob for his sameness (he is a tent-dweller, as verse 27 informs us). In other words, difference and similarity are created here *outside* gender lines, perhaps in spite of them. Jacob, in short, fulfills the narrative function of a female.

One almost has the sense that beneath the sibling rivalry of the fraternal twins there lurks another ancient symbol—that of the opposite-sex twins, who complement rather than compete with each other (Glenn 1966; Glenn and Glenn 1968). "Unique among all androgynous symbols for its persistence through the ages is the 'identity' of opposite-sex twins," says Carolyn Heilbrun. "Complementary, they seem to encompass between them complete human possibility" (1973, 34). In the biblical words, "Male and female created he them."

Androgyny is also the cross-gender quality associated with Dionysus, the god who constantly changes masks and personalities so that "to comprehend him we must ourselves give up our controlled, socially desirable sexual limitations" (Rosenmeyer 1968, 154). Masquerade and trickery are the arts of Rebecca and Jacob. And Jacob is the one who will go on to experience a life of "complete human possibility"—of love and pain, of physical labor and wily survival, of escape and confrontation, of weakness and endurance. He is as close as the Hebrew tradition has ever come to a representation of androgyny, an androgyny that was made possible by a "pleasant but somewhat shiftless father" and a "doting, energetic and domineering mother."

These last characterizations come from Peter Gay's biography of Freud (1988, 11); one can only imagine how little Freud cared to be reminded of them.[7]

Notes

1. "It is only in a world freed from the organization of the *Freudian or biblical* nuclear family that a non-power-driven relationship between women and men is possible," says Carolyn Heilbrun in her afterword to the collection of essays *Daughters and Fathers* (1989, 418; italics added). Curiously, this collocation is never repeated in the afterword, and the "biblical family" is not mentioned again. Instead the afterword consists of a sustained feminist critique of the "oedipal family" and seeks to celebrate family structures that differ from this model. Ironically, a similar critique is implied by my analysis, except that I claim that the family organization of the Hebrew Bible may offer such non-oedipal dynamics. Structurally, the "weakness" of biblical fathers can be compared to the frequent "absence" of fathers in black families that serves as one of Heilbrun's alternatives (421). But to see these similarities one has to forego the blanket bias against the Hebrew Bible that unfortunately has characterized much of feminist criticism since the appearance of Elizabeth Cady Stanton's *Woman's Bible* (1895) a century ago.

2. "The fear of castration being thus excluded in the little girl, a powerful motive also drops out for the setting-up of the super-ego" (Freud 1924, 178).

3. I am indebted to Dr. Barbara Rosenfeld for calling my attention to these collections.

4. The most recent probing into this divergence is Yerushalmi's impassioned "Monologue with Freud": "Why it is that throughout your work you have concentrated so exclusively on patricide, why only the Oedipus complex and not a 'Cain complex,' has remained an enigma to me" (1991, 92). Although Yerushalmi's query derives from a different context, that of the historical rivalry between Christianity, "the younger son," and Judaism, "the older son," I hope the following argument may shed some light on the enigma he points out.

5. I elaborate on this point in my forthcoming essay, "The Positive or the Negative? A. B. Yehoshua between Freud and Jewish History."

6. I owe this suggestion to Prof. Steven Bowman, whose challenging arguments inspired some of the ideas elaborated here. See also Everett Fox's note to his translation of this phrase in his *In the Beginning*, New York: Schocken Books, 1983, p. 13.

7. I am delighted to find that Yerushalmi concurs (at least partially, since he focuses mainly on the father-son relationship) with my tacit assumption that this familial dynamic is typically Jewish: "In these aspects the relationship seems almost to follow an archetype of the relations between immigrant Jewish fathers and their talented sons in modern times. All such sons have been, in a sense, father-slayers. *But unlike the Primeval father of Freudian mythology,* these Jewish fathers have been more than willing victims, eager to be slain" (1991, 63; italics added). Although Yerushalmi's exhaustive argument has

convinced me about the Jewish identity of Freud's *father*, I see the problematics of the son's Jewishness somewhat differently. It seems to me that the recent preoccupation with Freud's identity is totally misplaced. The question should be not whether Freud was or was not a "godless Jew" (Gay 1987), nor whether he has or has not profited from the Kabbalistic or Talmudic techniques inherited from the Jewish tradition (Bakan 1958; Frieden 1990), but rather the "identity" of his teaching, of his basic understanding of human nature. It is in the choice of his models that his ambivalence is most palpable. For despite his early Jewish training and his emotional identification with Moses (and, by extension, with the lot of Jews in 1939), Freud constructed a mythology that was very alien to his personal experience, to biblical narrative, and to Jewish culture at large. Whether this was personally or politically motivated is hard to determine today (probably both). But the fact remains that one of the greatest Jewish contributions to this century not only bears a Greek name, but also runs counter to the grain of biblical narrative which had to a great extent determined Jewish psychology throughout the centuries.

References

Alter, R. 1981. *The Art of Biblical Narrative*. New York: Basic Books.
Bakan, D. 1958. *Freud and the Jewish Mystical Tradition*. Boston: Beacon.
———. 1966. *The Duality of Human Existence: An Essay on Psychology and Religion*. Chicago: Rand.
Barthes, R. 1975. The Struggle with the Angel. In *The Pleasure of the Text*, trans. R. Miller. New York: Hill and Wang, pp. 123–41.
Bloom, H. 1973. *The Anxiety of Influence*. New York: Oxford Univ. Press.
———. 1990. *The Book of J*. New York: Grove and Weidenfeld.
Feldman, Y. S. 1989. Recurrence and Sublimation: Toward a Psychoanalytic Approach to Biblical Narrative. In B. Olshen and Y. S. Feldman, eds., *Approaches to Teaching the Hebrew Bible as Literature*, New York: MLA Publications, pp. 78–82.
———. In press. The Positive or the Negative? A. B. Yehoshua between Freud and Jewish History. In *Critical Essays on Mr. Mani*, ed. N. Ben Dov. Hakibbutz Hame'uchad. 1993.
Freud, S. *The Interpretation of Dreams*. In *The Standard Edition of the Complete Psychological Works* (hereafter *S.E.*), ed. and trans. J. Strachey et al., 24 vols. London: Hogarth Press, 1953–74, vols. 4 and 5.
———. 1914. Remembering, Repeating and Working Through. *S.E.*, 12:145–56.
———. 1920. Beyond the Pleasure Principle. *S.E.*, 18:3–64.
———. 1923. The Ego and the Id. *S.E.*, 19:12–66.
———. 1924. The Dissolution of the Oedipus Complex. *S.E.*, 19:173–79.
———. 1932. Femininity. *S.E.*, 22:112–35.

————. 1939. *Moses and Monotheism. S.E.*, 23.

Frieden, K. 1990. *Freud's Dream of Interpretation.* Albany: State University of New York Press.

Fuss, D. 1989. *Essentially Speaking: Feminism, Nature and Difference.* New York: Routledge.

Gay, P. 1987. *A Godless Jew: Freud, Atheism, and the Making of Psychoanalysis.* New Haven: Yale Univ. Press.

————. 1988. *Freud: A Life for Our Time.* New York: Norton.

Gill, M. M. 1979. The Analysis of the Transference. *J. Am. Psychoanal. Assn.*, 27, supp.: 263–87.

Ginzberg, L. 1913. *The Legends of the Jews*, Vol. 1. Philadelphia: Jewish Publication Society.

Girard, R. 1972. *Violence and the Sacred*, trans. Patrick Gregory. Baltimore: Johns Hopkins Univ. Press, 1977.

————. 1982. *The Scapegoat*, trans. Yvonne Freccero. Baltimore: Johns Hopkins Univ. Press, 1986.

Glenn, J. 1966. Opposite-Sex Twins. *J. Am. Psychoanal. Assn.* 14: 736–59.

Glenn, J., and S. Glenn. 1968. The Psychology of Twins. In S. A. Karger, ed., *Supplement to Dynamics in Psychoanalysis.* Athens, Greece: no pub., pp. 1–12.

Heilbrun, C. 1973. *Toward a Recognition of Androgyny.* New York: Harper.

————. 1989. Afterword. In L. E. Boose and B. S. Flowers, eds., *Daughters and Fathers.* Baltimore: Johns Hopkins Univ. Press, pp. 418–23.

Hendel, R. S. 1989. *The Epic of the Patriarch: The Jacob Cycle and the Narrative Traditions of Canaan and Israel.* Atlanta: Scholars Press.

Irigaray, L. 1974. *Speculum of the Other Woman*, trans. G. C. Gill. Ithaca: Cornell Univ. Press, 1985.

————. 1977. *This Sex Which is Not One*, trans. C. Porter. Ithaca: Cornell Univ. Press, 1990.

Jones, E. 1961. *The Life and Work of Sigmund Freud*, ed. and abrg. L. Trilling and S. Marcus. New York: Basic Books.

Kristeva, J. 1986. Freud and Love: Treatment and Its Discontents. In *The Kristeva Reader*, ed. T. Moi. New York: Columbia Univ. Press, pp. 238–71.

Lacan, J. 1957–58. The Formation of the Unconscious. In *Feminine Sexuality*, ed. J. Mitchell and J. Rose. New York: Norton, 1982, pp. 37–39.

Psychoanalytic Inquiry. 1988. *Sibling Relationship.* Ed. E. Agger. 8:1–107.

The Psychoanalytic Study of the Child. 1983. *The Sibling Experience.* Ed. A. Solnit. 38:281–351.

Rank, Otto. 1912. *The Incest Theme in Literature and Legend*, trans. G. C. Richter. Baltimore: Johns Hopkins Univ. Press, 1992.

Reik, T. 1951. *Dogma and Compulsion: Psychoanalytic Studies of Religion and Myth.* New York: International Univ. Press.

Ricoeur, P. 1970. *Freud and Philosophy*, trans. D. Savage. New Haven: Yale Univ. Press.

————. 1977a. The Question of Proof in Freud's Psychoanalytic Writings. *J. Am. Psychoanal. Assn.*, 25:835–71.

————. 1977b. *The Rule of Metaphor*, trans. R. Czerny et al. Toronto: Univ. of Toronto Press.

Rosenmeyer, T. 1968. Tragedy and Religion: *The Bacchae*. In E. Segal, ed., *Euripides*. Englewood Cliffs: Prentice-Hall.

Rudnytsky, P. L. 1987. *Freud and Oedipus*. New York: Columbia Univ. Press.

Schafer, R. 1979. The Appreciative Analytic Attitude and the Construction of Multiple Histories. *Psychoanal. and Contemp. Thought*, 2:3–24.

————. 1983. Narration in the Psychoanalytic Dialogue. In *The Analytic Attitude*. New York: Basic Books, pp. 212–39.

Shengold, L. 1979. Freud and Joseph. In M. Kanzer and J. Glenn, eds., *Freud and His Self Analysis*. New York: Jason Aronson, pp. 67–86.

Shoham, G. S. 1976. The Isaac Syndrome. *Am. Imago*, 33:329–49.

Spence, D. P. 1982. *Narrative Truth and Historical Truth: Meaning and Interpretation in Psychoanalysis*. New York: Norton.

————. 1987. Narrative Recursion. In S. Rimon Kenan, ed., *Discourse in Psychoanalysis and Literature*. New York: Methuen, pp. 188–211.

Spiegel, S. 1950. *The Last Trial: On the Legends and Lore of the Command to Abraham to Offer Isaac as a Sacrifice, the Akeda*, trans. Judah Goldin. New York: Behrman.

Sternberg, M. 1985. *The Poetics of Biblical Narrative: Ideological Literature and the Drama of Reading*. Bloomington: Indiana Univ. Press.

Trible, P. 1978. *God and the Rhetoric of Sexuality*. Philadelphia: Fortress Press.

Wellisch, E. 1954. *Isaac and Oedipus: A Study of Biblical Psychology of the Sacrifice of Isaac*. London: Routledge.

Yerushalmi, Y. 1991. *Freud's Moses: Judaism Terminable and Interminable*. New Haven: Yale Univ. Press.

Zeligs, D. 1953. Two Episodes in the Life of Jacob. *Am. Imago*, 10:181–203.

————. 1955a. The Personality of Joseph. *Am. Imago*, 12:47–69.

————. 1955b. A Character Study of Samuel. *Am. Imago*, 12:355–86.

————. 1974. *Psychoanalysis and the Bible: A Study in Depth of Seven Leaders*. New York: Bloch.

TWO

Promethean Positions

Ellen Handler Spitz

Nothing that hurts shall come with a new face.
—Aeschylus, *Prometheus Bound*

Contemporary psychiatry tends to emphasize the biological determinants of mental states and of human behavior. Psychoanalysis, which in the United States has been and continues to be closely linked with psychiatry, has, especially recently, been tending also in that direction. Yet the traveling exhibition of Sigmund Freud's antiquities has reminded us that Freud, both a scrupulous scientist and a devoted clinician, also cherished an ongoing relationship with the ancient world (Gamwell and Wells 1989). A dedicated classicist, Freud took the arts and literature of the Graeco-Roman tradition as a prime source of knowledge about the human condition. Parenthetically, however, although it is not my topic here, it is important to note, as current books, articles, and symposia remind us, that Freud was also deeply and conflictually indebted to his *Judaic* heritage, an indebtedness documented through his antiquities collection and the contents of his library—a complex subject currently under rein-

Versions of this chapter were presented at the American Psychiatric Association annual meeting in New Orleans, May 1991, and at a symposium entitled "Archaeology and Psychoanalysis: The Freud Connection," sponsored by the Michigan Psychoanalytic Institute and Foundation, Ann Arbor, June 1991. I wish to thank Charles Segal for his generous reading of it in an earlier form.

vestigation (see Beller 1989; Gay 1978, 1987; Klein 1981; Yerushalmi 1991, among others).

Peering intently into the *classical* reservoir, Freud saw his own reflection most clearly in the figure of Oedipus. Fascinated with this image, he fashioned Sophocles' version into a cornerstone of psychoanalytic theory. In so doing, however, he deemphasized other myths and tragic tales that have had a comparably powerful impact on Western imagination. Among these are the legends of the house of Atreus, which include the characters of Agamemnon, Clytemnestra, Orestes, and Electra, and the figures of Teiresias, Dionysus, Phaedra, Medea, and Prometheus. In my catalogue essay for the antiquities exhibit, "Psychoanalysis and the Legacies of Antiquity," I considered possible restructurings of our understanding of mother-daughter relations based on an examination of the Demeter-Persephone myth, which is, however, a story not dramatized in any of the extant tragedies (Spitz 1989). In this chapter, I shall focus on the figure of Prometheus, particularly as figured in Freud's own scattered references to this character and his myth and in the play by Aeschylus that bears his name. There will be space to sketch only a few themes, but I should like to preface them by a general plea for closer relations between the mental health disciplines and the humanities.

Today, even the most thorough training in psychiatry, psychology, and psychoanalysis gives short shrift to the humanities. Yet, if a clinician's principal task is to listen attentively to the voice and words of another human being and endeavor to make sense of that person's private world of symbols, a world that resonates with culturally shared desires and meanings, then, surely, humanistic knowledge is of the utmost value. We in the West, even with our lately awakened sensitivies to multiculturalism, remain indebted in large part to language and symbol systems that hark back to deeply buried sources in Greek mythology, tragedy, and philosophy. Ingested, assimilated, rejected, reintrojected, and ingeniously combined with myriad other influences, these symbol systems continue to influence if not still actually to shape our cultural heritage. In an ongoing engagement with this legacy, we inhabit a kind of afterlife of the classical epoch. A backward glance, a fresh look at the originary texts themselves, cannot, therefore, fail to spark and stimulate us so that we may, after such glances, attend with more nuanced sensitivity to contemporary speech, behavior, and fantasy. At the very least, an engagement with antiquity, both its texts and its objects, reminds us that the endeavors of modern clinicians exist on a continuum that extends back in time to the dawn of Western civilization—thus offering historic ground for both pride and humility, not to mention, occasionally, despair.

Especially fecund are the Greek tragedies! For, like the modes in which we view our own lives, they too are dramas, narratives, spectacles. Tenaciously, they insist on the persistence of ambivalence in the most intimate of human affairs. Relentlessly, they track the roots and consequences of that ambivalence. Above all, they demonstrate the deeply human project of attempting to wrest meaning from the uncertainty, arbitrariness, and devastation of human life. To grapple on a daily basis with the entanglements of individuals and families is to recognize, in the tapestry of images evoked by these dramas, familiar brocades—both personal and professional. To revisit the ancient Greek tragedies is to hone and extend our attunement to fantasy. Turbulent wills of husbands, wives, siblings, lovers, and children clash in chilling strife in these paradigm dramas, grand passions are enacted onstage, and conflicts stripped of disguise.

The value, therefore, of restoring to psychiatry, psychoanalysis, and the mental health professions more generally an engagement with antiquity and with the humanities more broadly is, I would suggest, to enrich our interpretive repertoire by compelling confrontations with templates, backdrops, scrims, and stage sets against which contemporary psychic enactments continue to be played out in our lives and can be even more insightfully observed.

Freud, in some half dozen textual moments scattered throughout the *Standard Edition,* makes passing reference to the figure of Prometheus, although, unlike Oedipus, this enigmatic Titan always remained peripheral to his theorizing. I shall, in the first section of my essay, review some of Freud's allusions to the myth of Prometheus and offer glosses on them.

In a late essay entitled "The Acquisition and Control of Fire" (1932), Freud focuses on Prometheus in his role as fire-bringer. According to myth, and as recounted by the character of Prometheus himself in Aeschylus' tragedy, he, though himself a Titan, chose to align himself against his brethren by siding with the new, rebellious forces of Zeus in the latter's successful overthrow of Kronos, ruler of the Titans. This was, furthermore, a supplanting that replicated an earlier uprising by Kronos against his own father Uranos, whom he had castrated. Later, however, switching his allegiance yet again, Prometheus chooses this time to defy his former ally Zeus by stealing fire from the forge of Hephaestus. Bringing this fire down to earth, he bestows it on the human race and teaches men and women the arts of civilization, thereby empowering them to evade the destruction planned for them by Zeus. It is for this act of defiance, compassion, and cunning that Zeus punishes him—confining him in a spectacle of cruel bondage with complex figurative meanings in Aeschylus' play, *Prometheus Bound*.

In his 1932 paper, Freud develops a characteristically anatomical reading. Taking flames as symbolic of the alternately rising and collapsing phallus, he interprets the Promethean fire, by extension, as signifying the unquenchability of human sexual desire. Further, he analogizes the inability of the male organ to perform its procreative and urinary functions simultaneously to the incompatibility of fire and water, and the punishment of Prometheus to the stolen fire itself, namely, to the erotic desires that, although daily satisfied, nevertheless continually revive. This works cleverly since Prometheus is, according to myth, mutilated by an eagle who flies to him daily where he is chained to the rock and sates itself on his liver which is then regenerated each night. Thus, the tearing beak of the eagle conjoined with the attacked flesh that is continually being replaced serves as a variant on the motif of reiterated self-mutilation and self-consumption that the flames themselves also seem to suggest. Flames, furthermore, not incidentally, initiate mankind into civilization (Ehrenzweig 1967). Metaphorically, therefore, civilization itself can be seen as brought about by, and maintained at the cost of, continuous pain. On this reading, the myth serves Freud as illustrative of several psychic mechanisms that he has theorized, including symbolic representation and reversal into an opposite.

A propos, furthermore, of the parallelism between fire and sexuality that Freud employs in this paper, it is fascinating to note that the myth of Prometheus is one of irreversibility (Blumenberg 1979). Neither Prometheus himself, nor his antagonist Zeus, nor the human race on whom fire has been bestowed is allowed to return in the end to an original state. All are changed permanently. Once fire has been stolen from the gods and conferred upon mankind, it is henceforth no longer the exclusive prerogative of the inhabitants of Olympus. It works to render mortals resistant, forever, to divine control and anger. This is so because the ancient method of producing fire by friction (rotating stick, soft board, socket against which it rubs [Blumenberg 1979]) can be seen as representing symbolically carnal knowledge (genital sexuality) which, once known and experienced, cannot be retracted. Thus, Zeus is precluded from wreaking vengeance by reversing the Promethean theft: he cannot, once it has been given, repossess the fire.

This level of meaning, when *added* to the interpretation that Prometheus is, above all, a culture-hero who empowers mankind to discover by means of fire all the arts, crafts, and sciences, ties the myth to Freudian theory, specifically to the notion of *sublimation*, that is, to efforts to understand relations between erotic and intellectual, creative and social energies. For, just as the sexuality symbolized by fire becomes, once discovered and experienced, a permanent human possession, so likewise does culture—culture defined here as an unbounded set of irreversible transformations wrought by fire on nature (one thinks, for example, of "cooked from raw," as in the discourse of Lévi-Strauss). Thus, both the con- and di-vergence of these doubled strata of meaning—the *stolen* and *given* fire as representative of sexuality *and* of culture, interlocking elements in the Promethean myth—presage the problematics of Freud's own efforts to link these realms. As has been pointed out (Bersani 1986), Freud's theoretical moves on this project, particularly his fretted notion of sublimation, have ensnared him in webs of proliferating contradiction. Yet contradiction, albeit inimical to *theory*, is, arguably, crucial to the deep structures of *myth*. The fiery emblem of Prometheus, burning in its vermilion viscosity, signifying both human sexuality *and* culture, thus prefigures the steaming alloys concocted centuries later by Sigmund Freud.

My further gloss on this 1932 paper and its sexual focus invites consideration of the related myth of Pandora. Here Zeus attempts to revenge himself on Prometheus for the theft. He commands Hephaestus to form a beautiful and charming woman of clay as a lure. Wreathed with flowers, sumptuously dressed, and brought to life by Athena, this woman Pandora is taught all manner of guile and deceit by Hermes and then sent by Zeus cannily *not to Prometheus directly* but to his more gullible brother Epimetheus—who, despite fraternal warning, accepts the lovely creature.

Lavishly gifted by each of the Olympian gods (hence, her name, Pandora, "All-Gifts"), this woman, in turn, wrings a reversal. From the depths of her infamous jar, she bestows on mortals a miasma of plagues and evils. In so doing, she incarnates a kind of demonized sexuality. Her feminine presence in this quintessentially misogynistic tale thus serves as

agent for Zeus' counterattack, Zeus being, of course, ironically, an in-
veterate womanizer. And the great Promethean gift, the fire that symbolizes, as we have seen, both culture and erotism, is now tainted. Zeus,
by using Pandora to accomplish his deception, renders it forever ambiguous. After Pandora, after Prometheus, the male heterosexual object of
desire is, even in its protean embodiments and myriad cultural displace-
ments, eternally suspect, equivocal, dangerous...

In other texts ("Psychopathic Characters on the Stage" [1906] and
Totem and Taboo [1913]), Freud treats the story of Prometheus quite
differently. There, the Titan becomes, directly in the first text and implicitly in the second, a paradigm of the rebellious hero who transgresses
prescribed limits, who, in Freud's terms, stands in for the primal horde
in its uprising against the father and who at the same time plays the role
of sacrificial victim with whom that horde can identify and through whom
it can vicariously expiate its own guilt.

This thematic permits us to segue into the text of Aeschylus' play. In
an exquisite display of empathy in its closing moments, the female chorus,
daughters of Oceanus, who have wavered throughout, seeming to side
now with Prometheus, now against him, huddle at last around him and,
standing in close, recite the words, "We / will bear along with him what
we must bear" (lines 1067–68). As they surround him, he declaims his
final speech of defiance ("Now it is words no longer") before being dashed
by thunderbolts into the black recesses of Tartarus.

Thus Prometheus, prototypic insurrectionist, must endure long and
terrible punishment, must suffer, as it were, for mankind, for, specifically
in his case, the human beings he has assisted. What I find interesting to
note here as well is that, derived from those antique gods associated
archaically with potter's kiln and smithy's forge, Prometheus in fact
creates humankind doubly—both literally, out of clay, according to myth,
and, secondarily, by providing human beings with the means of, and
importantly, the motivation for, ongoing creativity. Parenthetically, Genesis also offers a double story of creation (for discussion in relation to
the arts, see Spitz 1991).

Freud's eyes, however, blinded by the towering figure of Sophocles'
Oedipus, were never able (as were Nietzsche's) to see this aspect: Prometheus as a figure for the creative artist, as a great genius of "stern
pride" for whom even eternal suffering is merely a slight price to pay.
In my view, this perspective matters deeply here and offers, for example,

a persuasive reading of the ferocity of Zeus toward his former ally: the brutal animosity as motivated by envy of the latter's creativity, envy of his initiative and artifice.

In the opening scene (to which we'll return later), Hephaestus, nailing Prometheus to the rock, claims a deep identification with him that encompasses craft as well as blood. In his second speech after the bondage has been completed, Prometheus cries out that he, a god who should be envied, is not: "Look, see with what chains / I am nailed on the craggy heights / of this gully to keep a watch / that *none should envy me*" (lines 141–44, my emphasis). Yet, it is precisely envy and, as Melanie Klein has so brilliantly described, the wish to spoil and destroy the other's creativity that, in part, can be seen as motivating punishment here—a punishment by enchainment that works precisely to prohibit further action. At the end of Aeschylus' tragedy, when Hermes is sent as messenger by Zeus to warn Prometheus of his dreadful fate—the fall into Tartarus—Prometheus says he is the enemy of all the gods (lines 975–76). Hermes then tellingly replies: "No one could bear you *in success*" (my italics).

My further reflections, which constitute the second half of this chapter, were augmented (and challenged) by the comments of psychiatry residents and psychology fellows at Cornell as well as psychoanalytic candidates at Columbia with whom I have read the play in my teaching. They take the form of questions on themes that cluster around a hint found in the title of Aeschylus' play. Parenthetically, *Prometheus Bound* was written, we believe, after the great Persian War battles at Marathon in 490, B.C., and Salamis in 480 B.C., in which its author proudly participated. As was customary, this tragedy belonged, apparently, to a trilogy, but its companion plays, putatively entitled *Prometheus Unbound* and *Prometheus the Firebringer,* are lost. To complicate uncertainty, not only are both the existence and order of those lost plays in dispute, but the very authorship of the present text has been called into question (Griffith 1977). Debates over these and other textual perimeters, conducted in the academy by classical scholars, deserve passing mention here because they remind us of the methodological snarls to which every discipline is subject. Here, however, I have relied exclusively on David Grene's 1942 translation as text, an idiosyncratic choice based on personal history: this was the version I first encountered as an undergraduate and that, as a first love, I have never been able subsequently to abandon.

Aeschylus' title hones in on the idea of probing a limit or *bound*ary. And indeed, this proves a motif that resonates throughout the drama, the opening scene of which takes place on a bare and desolate crag at what is described as the *edge*, the *rim* of the earth. The introductory lines read: "This is the world's limit that we have come to . . . an untrodden desolation."

Nailed, chained to a rock at the bidding of Zeus by his servants Might and Violence and the Olympian smith Hephaestus, Prometheus remains immobile throughout the drama, his actions limited to choices between *silence* and *speech*. He is visited in successive scenes by Oceanus (a fellow rebel Titan), by Io (another, but female, victim of Zeus), and finally by Hermes (the messenger sent by Zeus to warn Prometheus of his impending fate)—each of these a character who intensifies our participation in his plight and works to engage us with it both empathically and critically. Physically *in*ert but psychically *al*ert, metaphorically at the *limits* of his own endurance and understanding, Prometheus may suggest to us the figure of an analytic patient who, likewise in pain that often seems at least initially imposed from without, must submit, for the duration of each treatment session, to the suspension of action in order to probe psychic limits.

And the inhibition of action matters focally here to the range of perspective afforded to and by Prometheus, whose name, of course, means "Forethinker." What are the relations posed here between *stasis* and *foreknowledge*? Between *paralysis* and *prediction*? Between an inability to act effectively in the world, fantasies of omniscience (or omnipotence), and a clinging to pain (see the fine article on masochism by Novick and Novick 1991, that interrelates these themes)?

What would it do to us if we *were* actually able to foresee future events? Would it stop us dead in our tracks, immobilize us, *vide* Prometheus? Or do we already in a certain sense know what will happen (as Plato teaches, and as psychoanalysis hints via the repetition compulsion)? Is it that we know but mercifully and/or perilously forget? Aeschylus continuously invites us to probe the benefits and dangers of foreknowledge. Alone on his rock, Prometheus, speaking for the first time after his binding, cries out:

> Oh woe is me!
> I groan for the present sorrow,
> I groan for the sorrow to come, I groan

questioning when there shall come a time
when he [Zeus] shall ordain a limit to my sufferings.
What am I saying? I have known all before,
all that shall be ...
nothing that hurts shall come with a new face.

(Lines 95–102)

Can we hear in this lament the script-writing tendencies of the masochistic patient who establishes powerful prophecies of pain that are subsequently both enacted and, importantly, displayed, while the self is simultaneously experienced as victimized (Novick and Novick 1991)?.

Later, when the chorus of daughters of Oceanus appear onstage horrified at his sufferings, they ask Prometheus what he could possibly have done to so provoke the wrath of Zeus. The Titan answers that he has saved the human race from destruction and done so by giving them gifts. The first gift he mentions, however, is not fire. Rather, the gift to which Aeschylus accords priority here is, fascinatingly, "blind hopes," or, in other words, false foreknowledge. Prometheus responds to the chorus: "I placed in them blind hopes." To which the Oceanids approvingly rejoinder: "That was a great gift you gave to men" (lines 252–53).

Our text, then, implies that, for human beings to live at all, to care, to will their own (our own) continuing existence, all true knowledge of what is to come must be forbidden. We cannot be privy to the details of our own mortality. We must be defended from the knowledge of when and how our ends will come. To keep us from perishing, what we need are *false hopes,* defenses, illusions, fantasies, shades, or, as that great American heir to Aeschylus, Eugene O'Neill, put it piquantly in *The Iceman Cometh* (1939), "pipe dreams." Self-deception stays self-destruction. To contemplate human life in the rawness of its brevity and misery can only be fatal. Thus, even before Prometheus bestows the gift of fire, he equips men and women with blind hopes; without these, the text implies, even sexuality and culture must come to naught.

Prometheus himself, however, can, in fact, presage his own future as well as that of others. What are the consequences of *his* foreknowledge? And what role, the text invites us to ask, does *secrecy* play in the preservation of a threatened and tormented self? For, in addition to advance notice of his own suffering, Prometheus also bears a powerful secret: as Forethinker, he knows the details of the future demise of his tormentor

Zeus. Yet, despite the direst of threats, he refuses steadfastly to speak of them. Why? Are there, the play asks, secrets perhaps that may not be told without dismantling the scaffolding of the self?

How does retaining a secret affect the *limits* of suffering that can be imposed, and what are the results of pain? Can physical torture, in its visibility and onstage specularity, work as a figure for mental anguish? Prometheus is inactive, nailed to the rock, but his mind continues to wander and cannot be so pinioned. Or can it? For Prometheus refuses steadfastly throughout the play to alter his stance vis-à-vis Zeus and maintains, despite all threats, his rebelliousness. He never, one might argue, changes. Withstanding the trials forced upon him, he remains unwavering in his opposition. Does this intransigence betoken a heroic sense of principle that transcends bodily agony or an insane and irrational masochism that embraces pain, as Hermes accuses in the closing moments of the play? Or perhaps, does Aeschylus, consummate artist that he is, pin *us* down and force *us* to admit a certain inextricability of *morality* from *masochism?*

In any case, the stubbornness constitutes, for better or worse, a constant. It forces us to question the role of physical and mental pain in the acquisition of knowledge. Is there, in other words, a learning process figured in the protagonist as the scenes unfold, or is the portrayal one of the thoroughgoing stasis?

Take, for example, the poignant scene when Io appears. Io, a tragic and deranged girl who, having been raped by Zeus and transformed thereafter into a heifer, is portrayed as being stung continuously by a gadfly who pursues her. Forced to wander aimlessly over the earth, she exquisitely figures for our modern sensibility the endless effects of rape and sexual trauma on the mind and behavior of young girls, trauma in this case associated with indifference, rejection, and disguised incestuous longing on the part of her father.

Here is the tale Io tells Prometheus shortly after her appearance, dancing, onstage: "There were always / night visions that kept haunting me and coming / into my maiden chamber and exhorting / with winning words, 'O maiden . . . Zeus is stricken / with lust for you; he is afire to try / the bed of love with you: do not disdain him . . . ' With such dreams I was cruelly beset / night after night until I took the courage / to tell my father . . . [who] cast me out / of home and country. . . . He [her father] drove me out and shut his doors against me" (lines 645–71).

Confused, fragmented, in torment, Io thus lives out a hell that is gendered differently from the stasis meted out to Prometheus. Rather than being fettered, like the action-craving male, she, who yearns to rest, to nest, to settle down, to establish roots, home, stability, is cursed with ceaseless movement, eternal wandering. She is caught in the immediate present of her crazed condition. Prometheus, meanwhile, despite his bound limbs, can, by contrast, range mentally far into the future, can offer her a centering and a focus; can provide her, from his rock, with a temporal and spatial organization; can orient her; can give her the kind of directional knowledge he gave also, importantly, to mortals when he taught them to write and to calculate, thus to remember and to project into the future (lines 440–508). How yoked, we might ask, is forethought to stasis? Contemplation and reckoning to the inhibition of action?

What other limits are figured here? What, their dimensions and functions? And how can we judge between their positive and negative force? Prometheus and Zeus, for example, are, despite their manifestly tilted relation, actually, as we gradually learn, twinned. Each must subordinate himself to an overarching limit of necessity, fate. Neither is free. Nor, as we know, is any therapist free in his or her relation to a suffering patient. Power, knowledge, and the confines of the domain itself impose limits that may prove alternatively, even simultaneously, both fertile and reductive.

What does it mean that, from a position of bondage, Prometheus challenges the limits of Zeus's power and opposes the uttermost of his cunning and intellect to that of brute force? Is the Promethean stance itself sustained by implacable enmity? Despite all entreaties (on the part, for example, of his fellow Titan Oceanus who comes astride a hippocamp to persuade him opportunistically to capitulate to Zeus), and despite all threats (on the part of Hermes, that is, who comes with ominous warnings direct from Zeus), Prometheus, as we have seen, refuses to alter his heroic stubbornness, his intransigence, his embrace of pain. A propos of his obstinacy, Hermes says: "These are a madman's words, a madman's plan: / Is there a missing note in this mad harmony? / . . . a slack chord in his madness?" (lines 1053–55). Either way, intrepid or insane, the steadfastness of Prometheus constitutes a *limit* beyond which he does not, cannot, will not, go. He is, as Hermes puts it, "slave to the rock" (lines 968–69), and we grasp ever more fully the complexity and intimacy of this enslavement as the drama unfolds.

Perhaps the play suggests then that maintenance of unwavering opposition *must* be coerced by shackles; that heroism, like the ravenous eagle, feeds upon oppression, injustice, harsh reprisal; that necessity, law, kinship, and might impose differing and conflictual limits. Perhaps it hints that such limits only *seem* to be evaded by craft, wit, and intellect. Surely, as noted, it is partly envy of creativity, the mental prowess of Prometheus, that motivates Zeus; whereas Prometheus by contrast expresses open contempt for the brutishness of his enemy who, newly installed as ruler of the gods, exemplifies to our modern clinical consciousness the overzealousness of a primitive superego. In the words of Hephaestus, as he nails Prometheus to the rock, "for the mind of Zeus is hard to soften... / and every ruler is harsh whose rule is new" (lines 33–34).

What about boundaries in the triple registration of mankind as divine, human, and animal? Where does Prometheus stand (or fall) in this hierarchy? The contours blur. In the first scene, as he is fettered to the rock, the terms applied to him are appropriate for animals: Prometheus is bound with chains that normally connect a bridle bit with the guiding rein; he is thrown around and girt as if being saddled; he is harnessed, tethered, broken, as one does a horse. At the same time, he, having helped and identified with mankind, is, in another register, compelled to suffer the peculiar limits and restraints of the human condition. Meanwhile, also a god, a Titan, he is possessed of prodigious psychic strength and of the power of prophecy. Furthermore, as we have seen, he, in what reads as an instantiation of masochistic pathology *avant la lettre,* objectifies himself, not only by relating the advance narrative of his afflictions but by pointing to himself as a spectacle, an object of ridicule and scorn: "look, see with what chains / I am nailed on the craggy heights" (lines 140–41); "Now as I hang, the plaything of the winds, / my enemies can laugh at what I suffer" (lines 158–59).

Related then, to the overarching motif of limits are other threads, woven together and all developed ambiguously—each undecided and, perhaps, undecidable. Thematizing the representation of pleasurable pain for example, the text resonates with a finding reported in the Novick and

Novick article cited above: "These [masochistic patients] remained exclusively and anxiously tied to their *mothers,* with the feeling that safety and survival depended solely on their mothers" (1991, 315, my italics).

Both the first and last words spoken by Prometheus are addressed to his absent *mother.* Identifying her with all the elements of nature, he apostrophizes:

> Bright light, swift-winged winds, springs of the rivers, numberless
> laughter of the sea's waves, earth, *mother* of all, and the
> all-seeing circle of the sun: I call upon you to see what I,
>   a god, suffer
> at the hands of gods—

(lines 89–92, my italics)

And the play ends with his pleas and protest, again to her as witness:

> O holy *mother* mine,
> O sky that circling brings the light to all,
> you see me, how I suffer, how unjustly.

(lines 1090–92, my italics)

To feel the power, in conclusion, the psychological astuteness and authority of this play, let us turn back quickly and zoom in on its initial scene, a tour de force of dramatic conceptualization. Might and Violence have just dragged their victim onstage before us, and Hephaestus is being enjoined to perform the act of enchainment. Prometheus is silent throughout.

For the duration of the scene, Might and Hephaestus spar with each other, one inciting the reluctant other to perform his cruel task. Might speaks: "Hurry now. Throw the chains around him.... Put them on his hands: strong now with the hammer: strike. Nail him to the rock.... Hammer it more; put in the wedge; leave it loose nowhere. He's a cunning fellow at finding a way even out of hopeless difficulties.... Drive the obstinate jaw of the adamantine wedge right through his breast: drive it hard" (lines 52–65 *passim.*).

Protesting, Hephaestus identifies with his victim, for Prometheus is both his relation (they are descended from Uranos) and fellow artist: "I have not the heart to bind violently a God who is my kin here on this wintry cliff," he demurs. "Yet there is a constraint upon me to have the heart for just that, for it is a dangerous thing to treat [Zeus'] words lightly" (lines 14–15). Then later, he says about Prometheus: "Our kinship has a strange power" (line 39). So, in his speech, ties of blood are pitted against dictates of law, as they are in the *Oresteia,* and here, as there, the latter win out over the former.

Hephaestus, furthermore, expresses the quintessential ambivalence of every artist to his own art, his awareness of its capacity to harm as well as to heal. He curses his expertise: "O handicraft of mine—that I deeply hate!" (line 44). Fascinatingly, however, Might turns on him as he protests while hammering: *"You,"* he points out, *"can be softhearted. But do not blame my stubbornness and harshness of temper"* (lines 79–80, my italics). In other words, though apparently opposed, the two characters are in fact locked in deep psychological embrace. Their attitudes are mutually dependent just as, the play gradually reveals, Prometheus and Zeus form mirror images of one another. The characters of Might and Hephaestus instantiate opposite sides of one coin—identification with the aggressor (on the part of the one who is not the actual perpetrator) and identification with the victim (on the part of the one who performs the actual act). Only because Might eggs him on can Hephaestus indulge empathic feelings, whereas Hephaestus' softheartedness spurs Might to ever-escalating displays of verbal savagery. Thus, brilliantly, Aeschylus creates before us, his audience, a perverse and sadomasochistic scenario where forbidden cruelty, expressed by one character, is legitimized by repeated repudiation on the part of another. This stratagem opens an aesthetic distance, a space, wherein guiltless pleasure can be experienced and meditated upon by spectators.

And, crucially, during this entire opening scene, Aeschylus gives his hero no words. Prometheus remains utterly silent as he is riveted to the rock. What about this silence? Does it work to provide a rich and fertile field for projection? Focused on the conflict between Might and Hephaestus ("I am forced to do this; do not keep urging me." "Yes, I will urge you, and hound you on as well. . . . Hammer the piercing fetters with all your power" [lines 71–72, 74]), we hear not so much as a groan from Prometheus.

We do *see* him, however, onstage before our eyes. We may not avoid him. His forbearance (or rather, that of Aeschylus) compels *us* to round out and complete this scene of bondage. His silence implicates us. It compels us, as audience, to make the stage resound with echoes from our own inner lives, from our own memories, fantasies, and imagination.

Bound now myself by the constraints of the essay format, I must stop, having nevertheless tried in the foregoing to provide a glimpse of the psychological richness that abounds in just one ancient myth and text. Freud, mezmerized by the plight of Oedipus, left Prometheus to hang upon craggy heights, a plaything of the winds. We, however, may choose to gaze more keenly at him. For, in all the enigma of his existential pain, he presents us with an image that, in the closing years of the twentieth century, we cannot afford to ignore.

References

Aeschylus. 1942. *Prometheus Bound*, trans. D. Grene. In *Aeschylus II: The Complete Greek Tragedies*, ed. D. Grene and R. Lattimore. Chicago: Univ. of Chicago Press, 1956.

Beller, S. 1989. *Vienna and the Jews: A Cultural History*. Cambridge: Cambridge Univ. Press.

Bersani, L. 1986. *The Freudian Body*. New York: Columbia Univ. Press.

Blumenberg, H. 1979. *Work on Myth*, trans. R. M. Wallace. Cambridge, MA: MIT Press, 1985.

Ehrenzweig, A. 1967. *The Hidden Order of Art*. Berkeley: Univ. of California Press.

Freud, S. 1906. Psychopathic Characters on the Stage. *S.E.*, 7:305–10.

———. 1913. *Totem and Taboo*. *S.E.*, 13:1–161.

———. 1932. The Acquisition and Control of Fire. *S.E.*, 22:187–93.

Gamwell, L., and R. Wells, eds. 1989. *Sigmund Freud and Art: His Personal Collection of Antiquities*. New York: Abrams.

Gay, P. 1978. *Freud, Jews, and Other Germans*. Oxford: Oxford Univ. Press.

———. 1987. *A Godless Jew*. New Haven: Yale Univ. Press.

Griffith, M. 1977. *The Authenticity of "Prometheus Bound."* Cambridge: Cambridge Univ. Press.

Hogan, J. C. 1984. *A Commentary on the Complete Greek Tragedies: Aeschylus*. Chicago: Univ. of Chicago Press.

Klein, D. B. 1981. *Jewish Origins of the Psychoanalytic Movement*. Chicago: Univ. of Chicago Press.

Lévi-Strauss, C. 1973. *From Honey to Ashes. Introduction to a Science of Mythology*, Vol. 2., trans. J. Weightman and D. Weightman. New York: Harper and Row.

Nietzsche, F. 1872. *The Birth of Tragedy*, trans. W. Kaufmann. New York: Vintage, 1967.

Novick, J., and K. K. Novick 1991. Some Comments on Masochism and the Delusion of Omnipotence from a Developmental Perspective. *J. Am. Psycyoanal. Assn.*, 39:307–31.

Rose, H. J. 1959. *A Handbook of Greek Mythology*. New York: Dutton.

Spitz, E. Handler 1989. Psychoanalysis and the Legacies of Antiquity. In Gamwell and Wells 1989. pp. 153–71.
———. 1991. *Image and Insight*. New York: Columbia Univ. Press.
Yerushalmi, J. H. 1991. *Freud and Moses: Judaism Terminable and Interminable*. New Haven: Yale Univ. Press.

THREE

The *Oedipus Rex* and the Ancient Unconscious

Martha C. Nussbaum

I shall be discussing the practical nature of the ancient unconscious—
its preoccupation with questions of good and bad fortune, control and
lack of control, security and insecurity. I shall be arguing that these
questions are more central to its workings than questions of sexuality
narrowly construed, indeed, that sexual anxieties function as just one
species of practical anxiety about control and security. It therefore seems
appropriate to begin with a dream, to all appearances sexual, which
really has, according to the ancient interpretation, a nonsexual practical
significance for the fortunes of most of the contributors to this volume—
people, that is, who make a living giving lectures and exchanging arguments. In the first book of Artemidoros of Daldis' work on dream
interpretation (*Artemidori Daldiani onicocriticon libri V*), in a section—
to which I shall return—on dreams whose content is that which violates
convention in sexual matters, Artemidoros, a professional dream analyst
of the second century C.E.[1] interprets the dream that one is performing
oral sex on a stranger.[2]

In general, Artemidoros says, this dream is a bad one, indicative of
some bad fortune to come—this in keeping with the pervasive Greek
view that such intercourse is unclean and base (Winkler 1990, 37–38;
Henderson 1975, 22, 25, 183–86). But there is an exception. With his
characteristic pragmatism and flexibility, Artemidoros notes that the

dream is a happy one, indicative of future good fortune and security, "for those who earn their living by their mouths, I mean flutists, trumpet-players, rhetors, sophists, and whoever else is like them." The sexual act is cheerfully read as a metaphor for the successful practice of one's profession. Beyond the information it imparts, so interesting to the professional academic, this example begins, I hope, to give a sense of some profound differences between ancient Greek and Freudian attitudes toward what the unconscious mind contains and how to decipher its contents. These differences—and also their significance for the reading of Sophocles' *Oedipus Rex*—will be the subject of this essay.[3]

I have often felt discomfort when hearing discussion of the Freudian Oedipus complex in connection with Sophocles' play. For while it seems plain that both Freud's theory and Sophocles' play explore important aspects of human experience and evoke in their readers a valuable sort of reflection about experience, I have (along, I suspect, with many readers of the play) much difficulty finding the closer link that Freudian interpretations of the play wish us to discover. For it seems difficult to avoid the conclusion that the play itself is not very much concerned with sexual desire as such, or with deep-hidden sexual urges toward one's parent, combined with aggressive wishes toward one's parental rival. Its subject matter does very much appear to be that of reversal in fortune. So it has been understood since Aristotle's *Poetics,* where it provides the central illustration of the concept of *peripeteia*—and, it appears, with good reason. Incest seems to figure in the plot as that which, when discovered, causes Oedipus to plummet from the summit of good fortune to the very bottom. It is, of course, crucial to the plot that Oedipus is not experiencing desire toward the person whom he takes to be his mother, toward the woman who raised him as a mother, nor, indeed, toward any woman who nursed, held, or cared for him at any time. So far as the intentional content of his desire is concerned, Jocasta is simply a well-placed eligible stranger. It is also perfectly clear that his aggressive action against Laios is in and of itself culturally acceptable, a counterattack in self-defense.[4] Nor is there any sign that Oedipus has at any level hidden knowledge about the identity of the stranger he kills. How could he, when he would never have looked upon his face, even in infancy? Finally, the whole question of erotic desire does not appear to be salient in the play's treatment of the marriage to Jocasta. The marriage is a political one, and is never described as motivated by *erôs. Erôs* is mentioned frequently in

Sophocles—but not in this play. In short: the play *seems,* as Aristotle says, to be concerned with the vulnerability of even the best fortune to abrupt disaster. And it is crucial to its construction that the collocation of circumstances that strikes Oedipus down is not regarded, by him or by anyone else in the play, as the product of his sexual intentions, whether conscious or unconscious.

To say all this is to state the obvious. And yet we post-Freudians have learned to doubt the obvious. We have learned to look in the play for signs of the repressed desires, erotic and aggressive, that Freud made the subject matter of his theory of the Oedipus complex and his reading of the play. Peter Rudnytsky's book (1987) persuasively documents the history of Freud's reading, setting it against the background of nineteenth-century German views of tragedy. It would be instructive to couple this history with a history of the avoidance, in that same period of post-Kantian German thought, of the apparently unseemly conclusions of ancient tragedy about the vulnerability of human flourishing and even of virtuous action to changes in fortune.[5] But if we are to move from understanding how Freud's account of the play came about to assessing it as an account of the play that Sophocles wrote, we must ask whether, in fact, an ancient Greek audience would have made the connections a Freudian makes between the surface of the play and deeper questions of sexuality, or whether, on the other hand, my initial hunch about the gulf between the play's preoccupation with security and Freud's preoccupation with sexuality is correct. But in order to know this we need, in turn, to know a great deal more than Freudian interpreters characteristically tell us about *ancient* attitudes to the unconscious mind and its decipherment.

This is a vast task, but I intend at least to begin it here, arguing that in some salient and, I think, representative pieces of the evidence we find that the ancient Greeks, unlike orthodox Freudians, did not think that sexuality lies behind every other wish. Instead, they understood the mind's deepest and most anxious preoccupations to be preoccupations—frequently unconscious on account of their upsetting character—about control and lack of control, security and the absence of security. Thus it will turn out, I think, that the best reading of the tragedy does present material bearing an account of what the unconscious mind contains—but not in the way that the Freudian supposes.

Now of course if one believes that Freud's theory is correct, and

universally so, one will not be much deterred from the Freudian interpretation of Sophocles by the discovery that the Freudian interpretation
is culturally anachronistic. For it will seem plausible to suppose that
Sophocles' brilliance has put him in touch with truths that other members
of his culture were slow to discover. And, on the other side, I confess
that the explanatory power and the general human plausibility of ancient
protopsychoanalytic views is, for me, a part, at least, of the appeal of
reading the play in conjunction with these views, rather than with the
Freudian views. But if we leave to one side the question of psychoanalytic
truth, we can still see that setting the play in its cultural context promotes
a much more economical and unstrained reading of the text, one that
can recognize as salient what the text itself presents as salient, rather
than searching for signs of what it nowhere says or implies.

I shall devote most of the chapter to the examination of two very different ancient Greek accounts of the unconscious mind and its symbolic and
motivational activity. First I shall examine a portion of the dream book of
Artemidoros, which, though written in the second century C.E., gives us
the most extensive evidence we have about popular beliefs concerning
these matters and testifies, it is clear, to deep and persistent cultural beliefs
about the crucial importance of "external goods" in the structure of the
mental life. Artemidoros confines his account to the reading of dreams,
which is, of course, his trade; he has no theory comparable to Freud's concerning the motivational role of repressed unconscious desires in one's
waking life. I shall therefore turn next to the one ancient theory of the mind
known to me that does develop in some detail such a motivational account—namely, to the Epicurean theory of unconscious fears and longings, and their role in explaining behavior. I shall draw some tentative
conclusions about the common ground between these two views, and then
turn more briefly to the play, to see what light, if any, this background
might have shed on how we might approach it. Finally, I shall briefly and
tentatively suggest that there is a contemporary psychoanalytic approach
that comes closer than Freud's does to tapping the play's central preoccupations—namely, the "object relations" approach.

Artemidoros: Incest and Fortune

The dream book of Artemidoros of Daldis has recently been the subject
of some valuable analyses: by Michel Foucault in the third volume of

his *History of Sexuality* (1986)—more convincing, I think, than the second volume (1985) as a reconstruction of Greek popular thought[6]—and by John J. Winkler in his recent book *The Constraints of Desire: The Anthropology of Sex and Gender in Ancient Greece* (1990, 17–44, 210–16).[7] Winkler's analysis is, I think, more fine-tuned and generally more incisive than Foucault's, especially in its stress on the flexibility and individuality of Artemidoros' dream-readings. I have the highest respect for Winkler's work on the dream-material (see Nussbaum 1990a); what I say here does not go very far beyond what he has already done. But I wish to connect this material with some more general observations about ancient ideas of the mind, and other texts dealing with the mind, in order to prepare the way for a contrast with the Freudian view and for a confrontation with Sophocles. For this reason I shall be looking more closely than Winkler does at certain sections of the text—especially, at its account of bodily parts as dream-signifiers, and its account of dreams of incest with the mother.

First, some general observations. Artemidoros is important to anyone who wants a better understanding of ancient attitudes to dreaming and sex (and many other things besides) because, although he is himself an expert practitioner with a theory, the theory operates through a detailed understanding of popular cultural symbolism and deeply rooted cultural attitudes (Winkler 1990, 28ff). To find out what a dream signifies, Artemidoros needs to know the various symbolic associations of the parts of the dream-content. Usually he does this in general cultural terms, since he is writing a general handbook. But he makes it clear that the good interpreter must really always take into account the peculiarities of the dreamer's own history, his or her own personal variations on the cultural symbolism. In a nonjudgmental way he must seek to uncover the facts about the dreamer's own practices and associations, so that no relevant symbolic connection will have been overlooked. In my opening example, the interpreter needs to know the dreamer's profession—for this will inform him that the dream of giving sexual pleasure with one's mouth, which has dire associations for most people, has associations with profit and success for the dreamer, as member of one of the occupational groups named. Elsewhere he makes it clear that he also needs full information about the dreamer's sexual practices, if dreams with a sexual content are to be correctly understood. In two cases where males dreamed, one of performing cunnilingus on his wife, the other of being fellated by his,

Artemidoros at first expected something bad to happen. He was amazed when it did not, and this seemed to him most "unreasonable." But later the puzzle was solved. He discovered (he does not tell us how) that the two men in question actually had all along had a personal taste for oral-genital activity, a taste that they had not reported to Artemidoros, presumably because of the cultural stigma attached to it. "Both were in the habit of doing that, and not keeping their mouths clean. So it was plausible that nothing happened to them, since they simply saw what excited them" (4.59).[8] Thus, though many dreams refer to future events, their significance must be read—as in the case of Freudian interpretation—in terms of the dreamer's own personal history, wishes, and associations (Winkler 1990, 29).[9]

Artemidoros in general divides dreams into two types: *enhupnia* and *oneiroi*. *Enhupnia* are dreams that directly express a current physical or emotional state. For example, "a lover necessarily sees himself with his beloved in his dreams, and a frightened man sees what he is afraid of, the hungry man eats, the thirsty man drinks" (1.1) The significance of such dreams is simple and relatively superficial: they signify the dreamer's current state in a transparent way (Winkler 1990, 32). In general, the presence in a dream of such indications of strong current desires tends to disqualify the dream from having a more complex significance: "Having sex with a known and familiar woman [sc. in a dream] when one is feeling sexy and desires her in the dream predicts nothing, because of the overriding intensity of the desire" (1.78). And, as we have seen, the fact that the two clients turned out to be devotees of oral sex disqualified their dream from predictive significance, even though they were not necessarily in a state of sexual arousal at the time of their dreams.

On the other hand, when dreams do not derive from the dreamer's immediate state, they can have a far more profound meaning. The class of such dreams, *oneiroi*, are the subject matter of Artemidoros' trade—and, he makes clear, of many competing theories and practices of interpretation, prior to and contemporary with his. The interpreter approaches the dream as a complex whole—looking not just at one or two images, but at "the systematized totality of the dream images" (4.28).[10] And this whole is regarded as a kind of symbolic coded language in which the dreamer's soul speaks to itself about matters of the greatest importance. Much of the code, as I said, is common and cultural; that is why it is possible for Artemidoros to write a general manual of dream interpretation. But a most important part of it is personal, as we have seen. To give another example of this, this time from a clear member of the class of *oneiroi,* a dream of beating one's mother, which would usually have been ill-omened, is auspicious for a particular potter, who came into a profit afterwards—the interpretation being that he beat clay (mother earth) for a living, and that the dream used a coded personal language to point to the profitable exercise of his profession (4.2). The art of the interpreter consists in unraveling such complex codes.

If one now asks about the place of the sexual in all this, three dramatic differences between the Freudian theory and the ancient theory will immediately emerge. The first and clearest difference is that for Artemidoros all dreams, sexual dreams included, signify future contingent events, usually events of the near future, whereas for Freudian analysis their significance is usually to be read in terms of the remote past, which is seen as having decisively formed the personality. This is a profound difference; but one should not, I think, overemphasize it, taking it to imply that the Artemidoran theory is magical and of no psychological interest. For Artemidoros as for Freud (as Freud himself saw) dreams are ways the soul has of talking to itself about deep and important things, usually by speaking in a condensed and displaced associative language. If Artemidoros believes the soul can have access to the near future, his dream contents still reveal, no less than Freud's, patterns of significance within the dreamer, and connections so deep that they are not always understood by the dreamer, perhaps because they lie too deep to be confronted in waking life without anxiety. *Oneiroi,* Artemidoros insists, "are the work of the soul and do not come from anything outside" (4.59). In the case of both theorists, then, dream-interpretation is the decoding of people's cryptic and hidden messages to themselves.

Second, again a rather obvious point, one is struck, in studying the sections on dreams of the sexual, by the complete absence of any belief in infantile, or even childhood, sexuality. In Book I, Artemidoros arranges the dream-contents according to the time of life depicted in the content, from birth to death. Dreams of intercourse come right in the middle, after dreams connected with being an ephebe, going to the gymnasium, winning athletic contests, and going to the baths—in other words, as phenomena connected with adult mid-life.[11] Artemidoros is not alone in this, clearly. In all the competing ancient philosophical theories about the natural and first desires of the infant, sexual desire is not advanced as a candidate by anyone.[12] Epicureans ascribe to the infant a basic desire for freedom from pain and disturbance. Stoics defend, instead, the desire for self-preservation. Aristotelians back, in addition or instead, a desire for cognitive mastery. So far as I am aware, no theorist even mentions sex in connection with the infant, and I think ancient readers would have found this idea absurd. (Longus' *Daphnis and Chloe* gives one representative example of the fact that sexual desire was taken to awaken at puberty for both males and females, therefore earlier for females than for males.) The radical and unconventional nature of the Freudian view is easy to overlook, since by now the view so infuses our popular culture. (One dramatic reminder of its radical and sudden nature can be found in Rousseau's *Emile,* the greatest account of the development of desire and emotion in the child in the centuries immediately before Freud. For there it is taken for granted—very much as in the ancient world—that sexual desire will awaken in the male at age sixteen. Much is made of this fact in accounting for the [late] genesis of other-regarding emotions like pity, and the related ethical dispositions.)

The fact that Freud's ideas on this subject are completely absent from the ancient Greek world is not a trivial one for my project. For if we are to manage to ascribe to Oedipus *any* formation of sexual desire in connection with his parents seen as such, we will obviously have to push this desire back into very early infancy, before his exposure. Whether we are even entitled to do this is, of course, unclear, since the play does not tell us whether this baby ever looked on its mother's face, or was held in her arms. Jocasta gave the baby to the herdsman in person, so much is clear; but presumably she did so soon after the birth, without nursing the child, and we have no reason even to suppose that she would have held the baby herself. Certainly the play gives us no reason to suppose the baby ever set eyes on Laios, even in the most early and attenuated sense, a fact which the remoteness of ancient Greek fatherhood (especially upper-class fatherhood) would in any case render most unlikely. Even if it is marginally possible that this infant had some vestigial awareness of its parents, the complete silence of the play about such matters—although nursing and holding might very easily have been mentioned—together with its emphasis on the fact that Oedipus' only real nurse was Cithairon, should make us wary of reading into the text any interest in infantile patterns of desire. The cultural evidence that such desire was not recognized by the Greeks in general should make us far more wary still.

But the most striking aspect of Artemidoros' view about sexual dreaming, for the post-Freudian reader, is the type of significance he attaches to the sexual in the interpretation of the soul's deliverances. The post-Freudian interpreter is inclined to seek for a sexual meaning beneath apparently nonsexual dream-contents. The deepest point at which one can arrive, in unraveling the mind's symbolic language, is a point at which one arrives at some sexual wish. Artemidoros moves, on the whole, in just the opposite direction. For him, even dreams that have an overtly sexual content are, like all other dreams, read off as having a significance for the rise and fall of the dreamer's fortunes, his or her command or lack of command over important items such as money, status, friendships, and the other important things in life.[13] In fact, if one reads the text in connection with the history of philosophical ethics, one notices a striking coincidence between the list of important signifieds to which Artemidoros' account recurs again and again, and the lists of "external goods" or "goods of fortune" that figure in Aristotelian and other accounts of *eudaimonia* (see Nussbaum 1986a, chs. 11–12). The items in question include: wealth, health, reputation and status, family and children, friendships, political roles—in short, all the things generally thought pertinent to *eudaimonia* (whether as instrumental means or as constituent parts)[14] that are not securely and stably possessed or controlled. Their importance in life is therefore a source of much anxiety to most ordinary Greeks, an anxiety that motivates a variety of reconstructive philosophical projects aimed at greater self-sufficiency.[15] Dreams, for Artemidoros, and sexual dreams among them, signify the dreamer's (future) command or lack of command over these significant external goods.

Sex can sometimes figure on the other side of an interpretation, as something signified by a dream content. For sex figures in various ways among the external goods, being an element in marriage, a necessary condition for childbearing, an aspect of one's status and self-assertion as a citizen,[16] and (in the case of unlawful sexual activity) the source of a diminution of status or citizenship. But it is in this connection with external goods that dreams are read, on the relatively rare occasions when they are, as being *about* sex. Much more frequently, one discovers an apparently sexual dream being read as "really" about external goods such as standing and reputation (see also Winkler 1990, 34–35).

A corollary of this emphasis on external goods and the dreamer's position in the world is that the interpreter must carefully scrutinize the specific details of the apparently sexual dream, taking note of the type of sexual activity performed, and above all of the positions of the actors. For the very same activity that might be auspicious if one is oneself penetrating another will be extremely inauspicious if one is on the receiving end. There is no clearer example of this—and of my general point about the nonsexual significance of the sexual—than in Artemidoros' matter-of-fact discussion of dreams of bestiality. Whatever the animal species in question is, says Artemidoros, if one dreams that one is mounting the animal, then one "will receive a benefit from an animal of that particular species, whatever it is." But if one dreams that one is being mounted by an animal, one "will have some violent and awful experience. Many, after these dreams, have died" (1.80).

The claim that sexual dreams are "really" about command over external goods can be illustrated from any number of passages in Artemidoros' account—and not least from its overall construction. For sexual dreams occupy only a brief three chapters, slipped in between dreams of being given a crown and dreams of being asleep. But for our comparative purposes it will be useful to focus on two portions of Artemidoros' analysis: the account of the manifold significance of the penis, and the account (within the three-chapter section on intercourse) of dreams of incest with the mother. Artemidoros discusses the penis as a signifying dream-content in the course of discussing, each in turn, the parts of the body. It is important to note that it is not more significant than many other parts. It is analyzed after the liver and before the testicles (which are said to signify pretty much the same thing as the penis). Although it takes up a fair amount of space in the discussion (27 lines of text, slightly more than the 18 allotted to the chest, the 20 to the legs, and the 25 to hands, just under the 28 given to feet and the 29 to the tongue, but far less than the 79 allotted to hair and baldness, the 84 to teeth and the loss of teeth)—it is not, as these numbers show, singled out as having any very special significance, or as a central focus of anxiety. The poignant anxieties surrounding baldness and the loss of teeth seem clearly to be far more pressing items in the soul's internal discourse.[17] In fact, the penis takes up as much space as it does only because there are so many slang terms for it, giving rise to a variety of verbal associations. Here is

Artemidoros' report on the associations connected with the penis in general, which are to be of use to the interpreter in approaching concrete cases:

The penis is like a man's parents since it contains the generative code (*spermatikos logos*), but also like his children since it is their cause. It is like his wife and girlfriend since it is useful for sex. It is like his brothers and all blood relations since the meaning of the entire household depends on the penis. It signifies strength and the body's manhood, since it actually causes these: for this reason some people call it their "manhood" (*andreia*). It resembles reason and education since, like reason (*logos*), it is the most generative thing of all. . . . It further suggests surplus and possession since it sometimes opens out and sometimes is relaxed and it can produce and eject. It is like hidden plans since both plans and the penis are called *mêdea;* and it is analogous to poverty, slavery, and imprisonment since it is called "necessity" and is a symbol of constraint. It is like the respect of being held in honor, since it is called "reverence" (*aidôs*) and "respect." (1.45, see Winkler 1990, 42)

The selection of which association to follow up will depend, here as elsewhere, on the totality of the dream content and on the role of these associations in the dreamer's particular history. But this catalogue should suffice to show that Greek beliefs do not understand the penis as signifying itself—at least, not very often. More often, its presence in a dream points elsewhere, to the network of external and public relations that constitute the focus of a male citizen's anxieties. Freud expressed the view that the excessive preoccupation with money and success that he encountered in America showed that Americans were overly given to sublimation, and indeed had become, as a result, sexual nonentities.[18] What is for him sublimation is for an ancient Greek the core and deepest point of desire and anxiety.

The account of mother-son incest occurs as part of the analysis of dreams of sexual intercourse, which itself falls into three sections: dreams about intercourse "according to convention," about intercourse "contrary to convention," and about intercourse "contrary to nature" (see Winkler 1990, 33–41). In the first category are dreams of all kinds of nonincestuous and nonoral intercourse, both active and passive, with partners of either gender (the one exception being "a woman penetrating a woman," which, as we shall see, falls in the third category). Although the goodness or badness of the events predicted by the dream is often connected with the generally approved or nonapproved nature of its content—thus the dream of penetrating someone is usually, though not always, more auspicious than the dream of being penetrated—the whole group is called "according to convention," regardless of the genders and positions of the actors. "Against convention" are two sorts of dream contents: dreams of incest, and dreams of oral sex. "Against nature" are contents that simply seem to Artemidoros too weird to have any ordinary social signification at all, things that are just off the ordinary map—having sex with a god, having sex with an animal, having sex with oneself (this not in the sense of masturbation, but in the sense of self-penetration and self-fellatio); and, finally, "a woman penetrating a woman."[19] It is important to note that the dream of something "against nature" need not be ill-omened; everything depends on the further analysis of the content, the postures of the actors, etc. (Thus, as we have seen, it can be very good to dream of mounting an animal.)

Artemidoros' account of mother-son incest is longer than any other discussion in the incest section—on account of the fact, he says, that "the analysis of the mother is intricate and elaborate, and susceptible of many discriminations. It has eluded many dream analysts" (1.79). Here is the main part of Artemidoros' account—the ancient analogue, or disanalogue, of Freud's oedipal wishing:

The intercourse in itself is not sufficient to show the intended significance of the dream, but the postures and positions of the bodies, being different, make the outcome different. First we should speak of frontal penetration with a living mother—for it also makes a difference in the meaning whether she is alive or dead (in the dream). So if one penetrates his own mother frontally—which some say is according to nature—and she is alive, if his father is in good health, he will have a falling out with him, because of the element of jealousy which would occur no matter who was involved. If his father happens to be sick, he will die, for the man who has the dream will assume authority over his mother as both son and husband. It is a good dream for all craftsmen and laborers, for it is usual to refer to one's craft as "mother," and what else could sexual intimacy with one's craft signify except having no leisure and being productive from it? It is good too for all office-holders and politicians, for the mother signifies the fatherland. So just as he who has sex according to the conventions of Aphrodite controls the entire body of the woman who is obedient and willing, so too the dreamer will have authority over all the business of the city.

And he who is on bad terms with his mother will resume friendly relations with her, because of the intercourse, for it is called "friendship" (*philotês*). And often this dream has brought together to the same place those who were dwelling apart and has made them be together (*suneinai*). Therefore it brings the traveler too back to his native land, provided his mother happens to be living in the fatherland; otherwise, wherever the mother is living, that is where the dream is telling the traveler to proceed.

And if a poor man who lacks the essentials has a rich mother he will receive what he wants from her, or else he will inherit it from her when she dies not long after, and thus he will take pleasure in his mother. Many too have undertaken to care and provide for their mothers, who in turn take pleasure in their sons.

The dream sets right the sick man, signifying that he will return to the natural state, for the common mother of all is nature, and we say that healthy people are in a natural state and sick people are not. Apollodoros of Telmessos, a learned man, also remarks on this. The significance is not the same for sick people if the mother (in the dream) is dead, for the dreamer will die very shortly. For the constitution of the dream woman dissolves into the matter of which it is composed and constituted and most of it being earth-like reverts to its proper material. And "mother" is no less a name for the earth. What else could having sex with a dead mother signify for the sick man but having sex with the earth?

For one who is involved in a suit over land or who wants to buy some land or who desires to farm, it is good to have sex with a dead mother. Some say that it is bad for the farmer alone, saying that he will scatter his seeds on dead land, that is, he will have no yield. But in my opinion this is not at all correct, unless however one repents of the intercourse or feels upset.

Further, he who is in a dispute over his mother's property will win his case after this dream, rejoicing not in his mother's body but in her property.

If one sees this dream in one's native country he will leave the country, for it is not possible after so great an error (*hamartêma*) to remain at the maternal hearths. If he is upset or repents the intercourse he will be exiled from the fatherland, otherwise he will leave voluntarily.

To penetrate one's mother from the rear is not good. For either the mother herself will turn her back on the dreamer or his fatherland or his craft or whatever might be his immediate business. It is also bad if both are standing upright during intercourse, for people adopt such a posture through lack of a bed or blankets. Therefore it signifies pressures and desperate straits. To have sex with one's mother on her knees is bad: it signifies a great lack because of the mother's immobility.

If the mother is on top and "riding cavalry," some say this means death for the dreamer, since the mother is like earth, earth being the nurturer and pro-genetrix of all, and it lies on top of corpses and not on top of the living. But I have observed that sick men who have this dream always die, but the healthy men live out the remainder of their lives in great ease and just as they choose—a correct and logical outcome, for in the other positions the hard work and heavy breathing are for the most part the male's share and the female role is relatively effortless; but in this posture it is just the opposite—the man takes pleasure without laboring. But it also allows him who is not in the light to be hidden from his neighbors, because most of the telltale heavy breathing is absent. (1.79)

There follows a brief digression on the naturalness of the frontal position; and then, in a transition to the following section on oral sex, Artemidoros analyzes the dream of oral sex with one's mother. To that dream we shall turn later; first, however, some comments on the material just cited.

The strikingly non-Freudian nature of the analysis is evident; but a few concrete observations will help to pin it down. First, there is nothing special about mother-son incest in Artemidoros' account of the soul's inner language. It is just one more signifier, and it is not singled out as playing an especially fundamental role. It is ranked along with other cases of incest, and all incest along with oral sex; and, as we have already said, the entire account of sexual dreaming is a very brief portion of the longer analysis.

Second, the dream of mother-son incest, like other sexual dreams, is significant, not in terms of underlying sexual wishes, but in terms of things like getting control over an estate, having authority in the city, getting on well with one's family and friends, getting or losing one's health, and so forth. The mother's body frequently signifies country or property. Even when, in the opening paragraph, a dispute with one's father is mentioned as one possible significance of such a dream, it is made just one possibility among many, and is not basic to what follows in any sense. Furthermore, the father's jealousy is just ordinary sexual jealousy, "the element of jealousy which would occur no matter who was involved." The dream signifies a rupture in one's fortunes, since good relations with one's family are conventionally taken to be a central part of one's fortunes. But neither its specifically sexual significance nor the identity of the parties is dwelt upon. And we must take note of the fact that very many of the dreams in this section are auspicious—again impossible if they were read as in every case denoting a hostile wish.

Third, the significance of these dreams is to be understood not by focusing exclusively on the fact of incest—to which, of course, the Freudian account single-mindedly directs us—but rather in terms of the specific sexual positions and activities employed. Artemidoros is very insistent about this. Thus, to penetrate one's mother from the front is usually good, to penetrate her from behind usually bad. Standing intercourse, in characteristic fashion, is immediately taken to have an economic significance, in terms of the lack of bedclothes and furniture. The position with the mother on top—in Artemidoros' novel interpretation, of whose cleverness he is evidently proud—is auspicious (for a healthy man) because it is associated with ease and an absence of heavy breathing.

Fourth and finally, there is not the slightest hint here that the dream should be connected to any deep and extended narrative pattern of sexual wishing going far back into one's childhood and repressed in adulthood. Such dreams are read matter-of-factly, like others, in terms of the dreamer's current profession, fortune, and so forth; the mother's significance in the dream frequently comes from his current professional activities. And far from expressing disturbing repressed sexual material, the dream's sexual content is not taken to be especially disturbing. Consider the case of the farmer, whose dream of incest with the *corpse* of his mother is auspicious, "unless one repents of the intercourse or feels upset"—apparently not the usual case! We might add that the range and variety of dreams of this type that were reported to Artemidoros may itself give evidence of an absence of repression of such ideas in Greek culture. For many contemporary people who read this section, what seems oddest is that all these dreams should have occurred at all, in this undisguised form. To the Greeks it seems, apparently, perfectly normal and natural, just as natural as the fact that one's especially deep anxieties about money, health, and citizenship should assume, in a dream, a disguised form. In short, if anything is, here, so disturbing that it invites repression, it is the soul's anxiety about external goods.[20]

Now we must turn to one further dream in the sequence, "the most awful (*deinotaton*) dream of all," says our author. For this dream might seem initially to cast doubt on some of our claims—although more closely inspected, I believe, it supports them. This dream, as I have said, forms the transition between the section on incest dreams and the section on dreams of oral sex. Its analysis goes as follows:

The most awful dream of all, I have observed, is to be fellated by one's mother. For it signifies the death of children and loss of property and serious illness for the dreamer. I know someone who had this dream and lost his penis; it makes sense that he should be punished in the part of his body which erred. (1.79)

A Freudian interpreter might suppose that Artemidoros here at last betrays the Freudian nature of his, and his patients' concerns. For the "most awful dream," after all, is a dream of intercourse with the mother. And having the dream is linked to the idea of a merited sexual punishment for a transgression that is, apparently, specifically sexual. Sexual error signifies a sexual loss. Don't we have here, after all, the proof that the deepest and most fearful things in the ancient unconscious are, after all, sexual things, and that a repressed thought of incest is, after all, connected in this culture with a fear of the loss of virility?

Things are not so simple. First of all, there is an obvious and striking departure from Freudian concerns in the fact that the dream is terrible not on account of its incestuous content—many incest-dreams, we recall, are auspicious—but on account of the mode of copulation. Here, as elsewhere in the discussion, Artemidoros expresses his culture's view that to perform oral sex is unclean and base; to be made to perform it on someone else is a humiliation. The discussion that ensues makes it plain that the uncleanness of the performer's mouth is thought to make it impossible to share kisses or food with this person any more. (In general, any dream of oral sex with a known person signifies a separation from that person.) Thus the dream of the fellating mother is understood as a dream of the humiliation of the mother by the son, a humiliation that is bound to destroy the household. It is for this reason, and not on account of its specifically incestuous content, that it is so inauspicious. And the son's error, for which he is punished, is not to engage in intercourse with his mother; it is to cause his mother to perform an unclean act after which the household can never be the same. Well might such a dream signify "the death of children and loss of property and serious illness."

Second, what the dream does in fact signify is, as we just said, "the death of children and loss of property and serious illness." The man who loses his penis is just one case of "serious illness," a case picked out by Artemidoros because of its ironically apposite nature. But, as elsewhere, the "real" significance of the dream is in the dreamer's relation to "external goods." And the punishment of the dreamer is the loss, not only of a bodily part, but of the chance to have, in the future, a family of his own. Because he did something destructive and antifamily, he loses the chance to have a family, and to enjoy the position of status and control signified by the penis.

In short: the dream of incest is, at bottom, a code, through which the soul speaks to itself about what it most deeply hopes and fears. Not sex, but control over external goods, are the content of those most basic hopes and fears.

Epicurus and Lucretius: Unconscious Fears and Waking Actions

With Epicurus we return to the fourth—third centuries B.C.E.—although most of the material I shall discuss is actually preserved only in Lucretius'

De rerum natura of the first century B.C.E. It is not clear which elements in Lucretius' account of unconscious fear can be traced back to the thought of Epicurus, but for now I shall proceed as if there is a single coherent shared view here.[21] It will become evident, I think, that, whatever the date of this view's origin, it reflects many of the cultural preoccupations that still animate Artemidoros' account somewhat later; and it seems possible to treat it as a source—however theoretically distinctive—for many similar points about what the mind represses and how it speaks to itself.

The Epicurean view of the unconscious differs from Artemidoros' view in two crucial ways. First, it abjures the popular connection between the life of the sleeping or otherwise unconscious mind and future events. Dreams and other voices in the breast have significance as the record of habits and practices, as the signs of a bodily condition, or as the rehearsal of pervasive anxieties. These categories are connected in that the pervasive anxieties of the soul frequently record the habits of a religious society. Anxieties are not innate, but learned, and habits of discourse and thought form patterns of fear and longing. This focus on the present and the past of the soul might seem to make Epicurus' view incomparable with that of Artemidoros; for he might seem to be denying the existence of what Artemidoros calls *oneiroi*, and giving us an account merely of *enhupnia* and related phenomena, all of which Artemidoros found rather uninteresting. But a closer look shows, I think, that things are not this simple. For Epicurus' theory, like Artemidoros', concerns itself with a secret language of the soul, a complex internalized symbolism in which the mind discourses to itself about what profoundly matters to it. Epicurus, like Artemidoros, is not concerned merely with transient states of little depth. And, like Artemidoros, he is interested in that which is still at work powerfully within—so, once again, he is not focusing, any more than Artemidoros, on obvious repetitions of the day's activities and wishes.

The first major difference, then, is less major than it at first appears. The second is more substantial. This is that Epicurus uses his account of unconscious wishing and fearing to explain behavior in waking life. The Epicurean unconscious is active in sleep, but not in sleep alone. As people live their daily lives, the theory claims, they are influenced in a variety of ways by wishes of which they are not aware. These wishes can be brought to light by philosophical examination—and when they are, they will turn out to have broad explanatory significance. This extension of the unconscious' explanatory role, together with the complex Epicurean account of how such desires are properly unearthed and confronted, gives Epicurus a claim to be called the primary ancient forerunner of modern psychoanalysis. But his account, as we shall see, is most unpsychoanalytic in its concrete content.[22]

According to Epicurus, then, the mind speaks to itself about what it most deeply wants and fears. And its deepest wants and fears concern its own finitude. The longing for immortality and the fear of death are at the heart of its discourse to itself (Nussbaum 1990d). This fear or longing is, as we shall shortly see, in the first place a response to the human child's perception of itself as powerless in a situation of great danger, as it emerges naked, hungry, needy, into the world. As the infant becomes increasingly aware, on the one hand, of its great weakness, and, on the other hand, of the delight of living, it develops, progressively, a desire to secure itself in life by protecting its fragile boundaries. This idea is pursued through various stratagems of aggression and self-fortification, described by Lucretius in convincing detail. Money-making, for example, is an attempt to fortify oneself against death, since poverty feels like a condition very vulnerable to death (Nussbaum 1990d). Warlike aggression is, once again, an attempt to make oneself invulnerable (Nussbaum 1990d, 1990b). The pursuit of honor and fame is a pursuit of one's own deathlessness, through securing power over one's society (Nussbaum 1990b). And finally, erotic love is, among its other features, a stratagem to solidify and secure oneself, by achieving a fusion with a person who is seen as an embodied divinity (Nussbaum 1989, 1990b). All of these stratagems are nourished by religious cult, which holds out the idea of an afterlife, further feeding both desire and fear. But in their basic form, such anxieties seem to belong to the condition of human life itself.

Lucretius makes it clear that most of the time people are unaware of the fears that are motivating their behavior. The "true voices" are buried "deep in the breast," beneath a "mask" of confidence (Nussbaum 1990d). They say that they do not fear death—and yet their behavior betrays them. "Thus each person flees himself" (Lucretius III.1068)—and is aware, at most, of a sensation of great weight in the region of the breast. In moments of abrupt confrontation with the facts of one's condition, however, rationalization becomes no longer possible, and the true voices emerge. It is this possibility of a confrontation which brings confirmation

of the fear from the patient herself that gives the hypothesis of unconscious fear—otherwise supported primarily through the linking of behavior patterns—such conviction and power (Nussbaum 1990d).

A central task of the Epicurean philosophical community is to diagnose
and then to cure such anxieties, and the "boundless" longing that is
linked with them. There is evidence that the community encouraged
pupils to divulge their hidden thoughts and feelings to the teacher, in
order to receive his philosophical criticism and therapy (Nussbaum
1986b, and 1994, ch. 4). The importance of this sort of "frank speech"
is repeatedly stressed as an essential tool of therapy; and one's friends
participate in the process, helping the teacher to know as much as possible
about the structure of the pupil's illness. We know little about how the
Epicurean teacher went about bringing repressed unconscious fears to
the surface—but the many analogies between philosophical teaching and
medical diagnosis show that they were well aware of this as a problem
and investigated the resources of personal narrative with this in mind
(Nussbaum 1986b, 1994, ch. 4). Meanwhile, the school placed great
emphasis on memorization and repetition, in order to drive the healthful
teachings of Epicurus deep down into the soul, to a level at which they
may even, as Lucretius reports, fill one's dreams (Nussbaum 1986b,
1989). Memory and repetition are the student's ways of taking Epicurus
into her unconscious, so that his teaching will "become powerful" (*Letter
to Herodotus* 85) in her inner world, and can help her in her confrontation
with error, even when she is not consciously focusing on the problem.
Like Menoeceus, she "will never be disturbed either awake or asleep"
(*Letter to Menoeceus* 132)—for the wise person, and that person alone,
"will be the same when asleep" (Diogenes Laertius X 120), undisturbed
by any flood of pent-up anxieties, such as those that occur in most people's
lives. Memory makes philosophical discourse active and effective in the
pupil's soul.

It should by now be apparent that, despite the differences in temporal
orientation and normative structure, the Epicurean view has much in
common with the popular beliefs summarized by Artemidoros. This
should be no surprise, since Epicurus' therapeutic target is just such
popular beliefs, and their deleterious effect on the mental life. What
Artemidoros takes for granted and makes the subject of his trade, Epicurus wishes to cure by philosophical therapy. But the content is very
much the same. In both cases, the human mind is seen as structured

around a very general set of anxieties about one's limited control over one's worldly position. These anxieties are seen as to some extent very hard to avoid; for even Lucretius stresses that every living thing longs for the continuation of its life, and consequently shrinks from death (Nussbaum 1990d). But they are powerfully fed by cultural teaching in which great importance is attached to "external goods" that the pupil does not control. The mind obsessively broods about command over these goods; and it cooks up elaborate symbols to meditate about its future with respect to them (in the case of Artemidoros), or its present emotional states that relate it toward an uncertain future (in the case of Epicurus). For Epicurus, the mind goes still further, moving the agent to undertake projects of self-fortification in waking life, projects of whose real significance the agent is unaware, and which will not really achieve the deep goal for which the agent pursues them.

For Epicureans, as for Artemidoros, sex is just one element in this pursuit of control. Epicurus has little to say about sex in the surviving texts; but he clearly does not think of it as a very deep or central force in human life. The desire for sexual gratification is classified as a desire that is "natural but nonnecessary": i.e., one that is not merely the product of false social teaching, but one whose gratification is inessential to the good human life (Nussbaum 1989). In a famously odd passage, he ranks sexual enjoyments along with other indulgences in unnecessary luxury items:

The truly pleasant life is not produced by an unbroken succession of drinking bouts and revels; not by the enjoyment of boys and women and fish and the other things that a luxurious table presents. It is produced by sober reasoning that seeks out the causes of all pursuit and avoidance and drives out the beliefs that are responsible for our greatest disturbances. (*Letter to Menoeceus* 132, see Nussbaum 1990c)

This passage presents Epicurus' view, not the popular views he criticizes. But still, it is evidence for his belief that in no person does sexual desire go, so to speak, to the very core of the personality. People may think sexual desire to be deeper than it is, just as they allegedly think the need for fish and meat to be deeper than it is. But, like other desires for luxuries, sexual desire is the sort of desire that can in fact be therapeutically removed, without injuring the personality in the process. Even culture, which ranks it too high, does not make it so central to the pupil's life that she will be injured by getting rid of it.

Thus even from the point of view of the cultural material that is internalized and buried in the average person's unconscious mind, sex apparently does not play a central role. Lucretius' famous critique of erotic love does show in detail how socially learned constructs of *erôs* influence both waking and sleeping life. But he does not seem, any more than Epicurus, to think of sex as offering a clue to the essence of the personality. He shows that the construction of love out of natural bodily desire is just a peculiar chapter in the soul's quest for transcendence of its mortal limits. For the wish of erotic desire, as I have said, is to achieve fusion with a partner who is seen as a goddess (Nussbaum 1989a, 1990c). The poet shows that this wish is the vehicle of a more general wish to transcend one's own finite mortal condition; its only remedy is to learn to "yield to human life," *humanis concedere rebus* (Lucretius V.1172). Erotic desire is a form of the basic desire to transcend one's limits and insecurities, achieving control and stability (Nussbaum 1990b).

Lucretius speaks of the family and its desires. But, once again, the treatment focuses on security rather than on sexuality. First of all, the relation between mother and child gets no special treatment in the poem. Both parents are believed to be intensely concerned about the survival and safety of their offspring; and the "softening" that comes about when they begin thinking of how to protect their vulnerable children is a major ingredient, the poem shows, in the development of morality and society (Nussbaum 1990b). But when the life of the infant itself is described, it is not the mother, but rather the nurse—as one might expect in this society, at least in the social classes who would be Lucretius' primary readers—who plays the central role. And in this relationship too, the issue is need and security, not sexuality. The infant, helpless and weeping from the disturbances of birth,

like a sailor cast forth from the fierce waves, lies naked on the ground, without speech, in need of every sort of life-sustaining help, when first nature casts it forth with birth contractions from its mother's womb into the shores of light. And it fills the whole place with mournful weeping, as is right for someone to whom such troubles remain in life. (5.222–27)

The "gentle nurse" now calms the child with rattles and baby talk, ministering to its lack of self-sufficiency; and the poet bleakly remarks that the rougher, better equipped wild beasts have no need of such soothing amusements (229–30). The drama of infancy is a drama of vulnerability and protection. The infant's desire is for freedom from pain and disturbance. The world it encounters is a world that contains countless sources of pain and disturbance. Its central perception of itself is therefore as a being very weak and very helpless. And its relation to the adults around it focuses on its passionate desire to secure to itself what nature on the whole withholds: comfort, clothing, food, protection.

I believe that the Epicurean account of the predicament of the infant, and of the fruits of this predicament in later anxieties, provides a comprehensive explanatory underpinning for the popular beliefs about "external goods" that Artemidoros records.[23] It also provides what Artemidoros, given his practical professional goals, does not try to provide, an account of the early origins of later deep anxieties. The Epicurean analysis of the anxieties of most human beings, and of their roots in infancy, really does, it appears, get at what people were really most deeply and often unconsciously worrying about. This should not surprise us, since Epicurus insists that therapy cannot proceed without correct diagnosis; and Epicurus' greatness as a psychoanalyst has been remarked before. But if we put the theory together with the rich and concrete record of ordinary belief in Artemidoros, we have at least the basic outlines of a non-Freudian theory of infancy, and of later unconscious anxieties, fears, and hopes. This theory focuses on the human being's lack of natural security and on its consequently urgent needs for various external goods. Relations to parents and other close adults are understood as mediated by this general need. Adults are providers of what is needed, bulwarks against danger, sources of support.[24] In another connection Lucretius remarks that when protection fails on account or some act or nonact of another, the natural consequence will be anger and aggressive behavior. Although he does not apply this observation to the case of the infant, it would not be hard to do so.[25] Thus we would also have the basis for a complex and interesting account of aggressive wishes toward parents and other caretakers, when pain and disturbance are not warded off. But this aggression would have little to do with specifically sexual longing and jealousy, everything to do with the desire for security and control.[26] It would be a fascinating task to work out further the details of such a theory.[27]

Oedipus and His Fortune

But now instead, all too briefly, I want to make some suggestions about ways in which this set of concerns might illuminate our approach to the

Oedipus Rex. I have spoken elsewhere (Nussbaum 1986a, 1992) of the central role of tragedy in providing Greek citizens with a map of human possibilities, showing, as Aristotle says, "things such as might happen" (*Poetics* 9) in a human life. I have also said that tragedies frequently seem to do this by exploring extreme cases, nightmares, so to speak of the human attempt to live well in an insecure world (Nussbaum 1986a, ch. 13). I would now like to suggest that we might fruitfully approach the *Oedipus* as, so to speak, a dream issuing from the unconscious of its citizen watchers, but an unconscious of the ancient, rather than the Freudian, kind. What I mean is that if we ask ourselves how an ancient audience might actually see in the play a kind of possibility for themselves, connecting themselves to the characters through the emotions of pity and fear, which (as Aristotle persuasively says) require, both of them, the belief that one's own possibilities are the same as those of the protagonists—if one asks this question, one is bound to focus, not on the literal events of the play, but on what one might call their Artemidoran symbolism. In the world whose preoccupations I have tried to depict, an average member of the audience is very unlikely to believe it a salient possibility for himself that he would actually do what Oedipus does here, killing his father and marrying his mother. For one thing, the net of circumstances that brought this about in Oedipus' life is too strange and complex to be very likely to be replicated. But if, on the other hand, we see the literal events as representing, as in an Artemidoran dream, possibilities for the rise and fall of human fortunes, we can far more easily see what a citizen would find terrifying here. If someone who enjoys the extreme of control, prosperity, and in general good fortune can be so brought low by events and circumstances beyond his control, then no human life seems safe from this possibility. For most lives start out more vulnerable and less prosperous than his was. Such was, in fact, the understanding of the play put forward as the obvious one by a very perceptive ancient critic, namely, the Stoic philosopher Epictetus. Tragedies in general, he wrote, show "what happens when chance events befall fools"—by "fools" meaning human beings who attach value to items beyond their control (Nussbaum 1992, 1993). And seeing the fall of Oedipus should, he argues, remind us just how uncontrolled items like power, wealth, and family connections really are, giving us a motivation to sever our concern from such things and to adopt the austere values of Stoicism.

If one turns to the play with these ideas in mind, one is struck by the fact that while, on the one hand, *erôs* seems to be absent from it, *tuchê* is omnipresent.[28] Oedipus is introduced as *kratiston,* most powerful (40); and yet the city itself has been afflicted by forces beyond its control, so that the citizens can already be addressed as "pitiable children," *paides oiktroi.* At line 145, beginning on his fateful search for the causes of the pollution, Oedipus announces, "We shall either emerge fortunate (*eutucheis*), with the god's help, or as fallen (*peptôkotes*)." Immediately the Chorus, entering, begins to speak of its anxious fear and tension (151ff.). And of course, from the first, Oedipus is present to the audience (through his name alone) as a cripple, someone cast out naked into the world and maimed by its dangers, a Lucretian, rather than a Freudian, infant.

The detailed working-out of this reading must wait for another time. Its direction and outlines should already be clear. But I can end this adumbration of such a reading by mentioning that, whether the final lines are genuine or not, they suit admirably the focus of the play as a whole, and of this account: for they portray Oedipus as, on the one hand, successful and "most powerful," on the other, as one who "came into such a great tidal wave of misfortune." And their famous moral is the moral of so much of the ancient Greek ethical tradition, insofar as it does not reject the importance traditionally attached to external goods: "Call no mortal prosperous ... before he passes the end of his life having suffered nothing terrible" (1529–30).

What relationship might such a reading of the play—and, in general, such an account of the stresses of infancy and of unconscious fears, longings, and aggressions—have to psychoanalysis? I have spent most of this chapter showing how much ancient "psychoanalysis"—for I think we may call it that—diverges from a single-minded and possibly reductive concern with sexuality that we find in some parts of the Freudian tradition. Indeed, it seems to show the Freudian emphasis on sexuality as time-bound, the local feature of a society unusually anxious about this particular aspect of human life, and therefore in need of repression on that topic.

But there are other psychoanalytic approaches that seem far more in tune with the emphases and concerns of ancient psychology.[29] I plan in future work to compare the ideas I have just investigated with some of Melanie Klein's ideas about infancy and the genesis of fear and aggression—and with other related work in the object relations school. For while the Kleinian theory is still in some respects Freudian, her account of infancy endows it with complex relationships to objects, seen as providers or hinderers of support.[30] And usually the issue of the infant's great neediness and its inevitable pain and frustration is stressed in her writings far more than that of sexual desire *per se*. Her infant's relation to the breast that either feeds or fails to feed it could usefully be compared, I believe, to the Lucretian account of the genesis of aggressive wishes, particularly if we expand his account as I have suggested. And since the Kleinian picture of the infant's life endows it, early on, with the possibility of complex emotions such as fear, anger, and envy, once again this seems to invite comparison with the Epicurean account of similar material, and of its eventual repression. Even though Klein does pay homage to Freud concerning the primacy of sexual desire, it seems plain that most of the time her concern is with a broad range of needs and longings, most of them connected around the issue of self-sufficiency and incompleteness. Pursuing the comparison would be of interest, if only for comparison's sake.

But my real interest in it is a deeper one. For I believe that the ancient views I have discussed are profound and highly plausible in a way that goes beyond strict cultural boundaries; and yet, equally clearly, that they are culture-bound in certain ways, and lack, in some areas, a richness of development that would be required if they were ever to become powerful and plausible for a contemporary understanding. It might emerge, however, that the confrontation between these views and the modern views of thinkers such as Klein, Fairbairn, and Winnicott, and of both with the best of recent cognitively oriented work in experimental psychology, for example the work of Lazarus (1991) and Seligman (1975), might generate a philosophical theory of the human longing for control and self-sufficiency that would preserve the best features of both sources, and link them in a new account of fear, aggression, pity, and love.[31]

Notes

1. For an excellent study of Artemidoros, to which I shall refer frequently in what follows, see Winkler (1990).
2. It is clear that both the dreamer and the dreamer's sexual partner may be

either male or female: in this case as in many others, that does not affect the dream's significance. Here as elsewhere, the Greek uses but a single word for what we distinguish as fellatio and cunnilingus: *arrhêtopoiêsai*, "do the unmentionable." The operative distinction in Artemidoros' account is between its active and passive voices, as the dreamer either performs such activity or has it performed upon him/her.

3. This chapter was originally written for a conference on Sophocles' play and modern psychoanalysis; in this version I have chosen to retain the focus on this particular tragedy on account of the great influence of Freud's reading, although numerous texts could have done as well for my purposes.

4. It is paradigmatic of the type of action Aristotle calls involuntary out of excusable ignorance—*Nicomachean Ethics*, III.1. I discuss this case, with other references, in Nussbaum 1986a, ch. 9 and interlude 2. See also Sophocles' *Oedipus at Colonus*, where Oedipus describes his acts as involuntary: lines 270–74, 5211–49, 960–87, and cf. 1565.

5. On the issue in tragedy, see Nussbaum (1986a); and on the German critics, especially ch. 13.

6. I reviewed Volume 2 critically in Nussbaum (1985); the relevant point to emphasize here is that, by concentrating on philosophical writers such as Plato and Xenophon, and neglecting other more popular sources, such as the orators and Aristophanes, Foucault could only reach partial conclusions.

7. See also Price (1986).

8. For 1.78–80, I follow Winkler's translation (1990, 210–16); elsewhere the translations are my own where Winkler does not translate the passage, his when he does. This case is discussed (though not translated in full) in Winkler (1990, 29).

9. Freud is mistaken about this aspect of Artemidoros' theory, charging him with reading dreams according to a fixed universal key; see Winkler (1990, 29–30), referring to *Interpretation of Dreams* (Freud 1900, 98–99).

10. This shows the unfairness of Freud's critique of Artemidoros for neglecting interconnections among dream images.

11. Here we find confirmation of the cultural view in accordance with which the young males who are the objects of (older) male desire—the *erômenoi*—are not thought to feel sexual desire themselves (or at least, this is the cultural norm—Dover 1978; Halperin 1990). This is why sexual dreams belong to a later time of life. Of course a young person might still use sexual imagery to signify some underlying anxiety; but I think that it is Artemidoros' point that the signifiers have to be familiar from experience, in order to establish their connections with the deeper signified.

12. On the study of children and their inclinations in ancient thought, see Brunschwig (1986). On the appeal to the nature of the child as part of Epicurean ethical argument, see Nussbaum (1994, chs. 4,12) and the earlier version of the argument in Nussbaum (1986b).

13. See also Winkler (1990, 26–27, 33ff.).

68   Martha C. Nussbaum

14. Friendships are, for Aristotle, constituents of *eudaimonia*, not just external instruments. Money, property, etc. are instrumentally valuable. Virtuous action, the primary constituent(s) of *eudaimonia*, is not called an "external good," since it is caused by virtuous traits of character, which are within the agent's own control. Strictly speaking, however, it can be impeded by fortune—by the absence of some of the usual "external goods."

15. Central in such projects is usually the claim that virtue is sufficient for *eudaimonia*—this idea is defended, it seems, by Socrates, Plato, and the Greek and Roman Stoics.

16. On this see "The Democratic Body," in Halperin (1990). On sex as an aspect of the public sphere, see also Winkler (1990, 27).

17. Of course, strictly speaking, anxiety is what is signified by a dream, not the signifier in a dream. But Artemidoros seems to suggest that experiences that are themselves sources of anxiety (baldness for example) will naturally serve a signifiers for other deeper fears.

18. See Abelove (1993) for references to Freud's correspondence on this point.

19. Penetration is the fundamental sex act for the Greeks—see Winkler (1990, passim); Halperin (1990). So fundamental is it that a sex act between two women can only be imagined as (per impossibile) a form of penetration; and it is for this reason that the act seems to require an alteration in the laws of nature.

20. It is noteworthy here that Artemidoros does not dwell often on the anti-conventional or illicit status of incestuous intercourse, which might have been a way of linking incest with external fortunes without focusing centrally on its sexual wish-content. This, I think, is the direction Plato takes in the passage on dreaming in *Republic* IX, where he speaks of the incest dream as something that appetite will contrive, unfettered by reason: in other words, unfettered by reason, appetite is altogether lawless.

21. For further discussion of this point, see Nussbaum (1990), and Nussbaum (1994, ch. 4).

22. Fuller development of the account presented here is found in Nussbaum (1989, 1990d, 1990b, 1990c, and 1994, chs. 4–7). (Ch. 5 is a later version of 1989a, ch. 6 of 1990d, ch. 7 of 1990b.) All of these articles contain full references to the relevant ancient texts, and to the secondary literature.

23. We arrive here at a complex issue in Epicurus' thought. For to the extent that he presents the concern for externals as motivated by an appropriate and more or less inevitable concern for one's own safety, he would appear to endorse these concerns, or at least some of them, as rational. On the other hand, he is determined to reject most of the concerns society actually has for these goods—including all anxious concern about death—as irrational. The difficulties this creates for his project are analyzed in Nussbaum (1990d, 1990b).

24. Compare the view of animals and infants in Lazarus (1991) and the related observations in Bowlby (1982, 1973, 1980).

25. See especially Bowlby (1973), Klein (1984, 1985). On Lucretius, see Nussbaum (1990b).
26. On the enormous importance of control for the emotional life of both animals and humans, see the remarkable analysis in Seligman (1975).
27. This is what I am trying to do in *Need and Recognition: A Theory of the Emotions*, The Gifford Lectures for 1993.
28. *Tuchê* designates those aspects of life that human beings do not control: it means "luck" in that sense, not in the sense of "randomness."
29. Indeed, cognitive psychology is now to a great extent converging with psychoanalysis on this point—see Lazarus (1991); Seligman (1975); Oatley (1992).
30. Klein (1984, 1985), Fairbairn (1952). The same is true of the theory of emotion now most favored in cognitive psychology: see Lazarus (1991); Ortony, Clore, and Collins (1988); Oatley (1992).
31. This chapter was originally presented at Cornell University at a conference on the *Oedipus Rex* and modern psychoanalysis. I wish to thank Phillip Mitsis for the invitation, and for helpful comments. I am also grateful to Myles Burnyeat and Peter Rudnytsky for their suggestions.

Bibliography

Abelove, H. (1993). "Freud, Male Homosexuality, and the Americans," in *The Lesbian and Gay Studies Center Reader*, ed. H. Abelove, M. A. Barale, D. M. Halperin. New York: Routledge, 381-93.
Artemidoros. 1963. *Artemidori Daldiani Onirocriticon Libri V*, ed. R. A. Pack. Leipzig: Teubner.
Bowlby, J. 1973. *Separation: Anxiety and Anger*. New York: Basic Books.
———. 1980. *Loss: Sadness and Depression*. New York: Basic Books.
———. 1982. *Attachment*, 2d ed. New York: Basic Books.
Brunschwig, J. 1986. The Cradle Argument in Epicureanism and Stoicism. In *The Norms of Nature*, ed. M. Schofield and G. Striker. Cambridge: Cambridge Univ. Press, 113–44.
Diogenes Laertius. *Lives of the Philosophers*, ed. and trans. R. D. Hicks, Vol. 2. Loeb Classical Library. Cambridge, MA: Harvard Univ. Press, 1979.
Dover, K. J. 1978. *Greek Homosexuality*. Cambridge, MA: Harvard Univ. Press.
Fairbairn, W.R.D. 1952. *Psychoanalytic Studies of the Personality*. London: Tavistock.
Foucault, M. 1985. *The Use of Pleasure (The History of Sexuality*, Vol. 2), trans. R. Hurley. New York: Pantheon.
———. 1986. *The Care of the Self (The History of Sexuality*, Vol. 3), trans. R. Hurley, New York: Pantheon.
Freud, S. 1990. *The Interpretation of Dreams*. In *The Standard Edition of the*

70   Martha C. Nussbaum

Complete Psychological Works, ed. and trans. J. Strachey et al., 24 vols. London: Hogarth Press, 1953–74, Vols. 4 and 5.

Halperin, D. 1990. *One Hundred Years of Homosexuality and Other Essays on Greek Love*. New York: Routledge.

Henderson, J.J. 1975. *The Maculate Muse: Obscene Language in Attic Comedy*. New Haven: Yale Univ. Press.

Klein, M. 1984. *Envy and Gratitude and Other Works, 1946–1963*. London: Hogarth.

———. 1985. *Love, Guilt, and Reparation and Other Works, 1921–1945*. London: Hogarth.

Lazarus, R. 1991. *Emotion and Adaptation*. New York: Oxford Univ. Press.

Nussbaum, M. 1985. Review of Foucault. *New York Times Book Review*, November 10.

———. 1986a. *The Fragility of Goodness: Luck and Ethics in Greek Tragedy and Philosophy*. Cambridge: Cambridge Univ. Press.

———. 1986b. Therapeutic Arguments: Epicurus and Aristotle. *The Norms of Nature*, ed. M. Schofield and G. Striker. Cambridge: Cambridge Univ. Press, 31–74.

———. 1989. Beyond Obsession and Disgust: Lucretius' Genealogy of Love. *Apeiron* 22:1–59.

———. 1990a. Review of Halperin 1990 and Winkler 1990. *Times Literary Supplement*, June.

———. 1990b. "By Words, Not Arms": Lucretius on Anger and Aggression. In *The Poetics of Therapy*, ed. M. Nussbaum, *Apeiron* 23:41–90.

———. 1990c. Therapeutic Arguments and Structures of Desire. *Differences* 2: 46–66. (Volume on *Society and Sexuality in Ancient Greece and Rome*, ed. D. Konstan and M. Nussbaum.)

———. 1990d. Mortal Immortals: Lucretius on Death and the Voice of Nature. *Philosophy and Phenomenological Research* 50:303–51.

———. 1992. Tragedy and Self-Sufficiency: Plato and Aristotle on Fear and Pity. Long version in *Oxford Studies in Ancient Philosophy* 10. Short version in *Essays on Aristotle's Poetics*, ed. A. Rorty. Princeton: Princeton Univ. Press, pp 261–90.

———. 1993. Poetry and the Passions: Two Stoic Views. In *Passions & Perceptions*, ed. J. Brunschwig and M. Nussbaum. Cambridge: Cambridge Univ. Press.

———. 1994. *The Therapy of Desire: Theory and Practice in Hellenistic Ethics*. Princeton: Princeton Univ. Press.

Oatley, K. 1992. *Best Laid Schemes: The Psychology of Emotions*. Cambridge: Cambridge Univ. Press.

Ortony, A., Clore, G.L., and Collins, A. 1988. *The Cognitive Structure of Emotions*. Cambridge: Cambridge Univ. Press.

Price, S. 1986. The Future of Dreams: From Freud to Artemidorus," *Past and*

Present, 113:3–37. Rpt. in Halperin, D., Winkler, J., and Zeitlin, F., eds., *Before Sexuality: The Construction of Erotic Experience in the Ancient Greek World*. Princeton: Princeton Univ. Press, 1989.

Rudnytsky, P. 1987. *Freud and Oedipus*. New York: Columbia Univ. Press.

Seligman, M.E.P. 1975. *Helplessness: On Depression, Development, and Death*. New York: Freeman.

Winkler, J.J. 1990. *The Constraints of Desire: The Anthropology of Sex and Gender in Ancient Greece*. New York: Routledge.

FOUR

Sophocles' *Oedipus Tyrannus:* Freud, Language, and the Unconscious

Charles Segal

Freudian interpretations of the *Oedipus Tyrannus* tend to concentrate on the *contents* of the unconscious as acted out in the dramatic events, and these contents make up the core plot of the "Oedipus complex." The play grips us, Freud argued, because it enacts the (male) viewer's most buried fears and desires, namely the wish to kill the father and possess the mother. Equally important, however, and in some ways more suggestive for literary study, are Freud's remarks on the *process* of discovering unconscious knowledge: "The action of the play consists in nothing other than the process of revealing, with cunning delays and ever-mounting excitement—a process that can be likened to the work of a psychoanalysis—that Oedipus himself is the murderer of Laius, but further that he is the son of the murdered man and of Jocasta" (Freud 1900, 261–62).

It remains Freud's achievement to have extrapolated from the *Oedipus* a model of reading in terms of a hidden *other* side of reality, a side that begins to surface through the cracks in the rational, logical structure of our words and our lives. It is this radical otherness for which the Freudian unconscious stands and to which it points. Sophocles' play, as Freud remarked, is analogous to the work of psychoanalysis in the sense that both Sophocles and Freud explore mental and linguistic behaviors in which actions and/or desires repressed into the darkness of the unknowable and unspeakable are forced into conscious speech and, in the case of the *Tyrannus,* into clear, theatrical vision.[1]

The play exploits the special power of drama by playing the visual enactment of events before our eyes off against the unknown, demonic events in the background: the plague, the Sphinx, the various oracles, the exposure of a child, the killing of a father. It gradually works back to this world of a hidden, terrible past and uncovers it. The climax of the action in the present is also an act of uncovering, namely the revelation of Jocasta's suicide and of Oedipus' discovery of her body. These scenes are not shown on stage; but they are narrated in such a way that we become conscious of penetrating into a closed, inner space, a terrible interior chamber whose doors we force in, with Oedipus, to reveal the awful sight (lines 1251–85). After this narration we see doors really opening—this time the doors of the scene-building representing the palace gate—to show Oedipus to us, now blinded, on the stage (lines 1296–97).[2] The Messenger begins his narrative by emphasizing his partial knowledge of what happened: "Of the things that were done, the most painful are absent, for vision was not present. But, as much as lies in my memory, you shall learn the sufferings of the unhappy woman" (lines 1237–40). He ends by announcing the throwing open of the gates "to show to all the Thebans" the land's pollution (lines 1287–88). His last words call attention to the "spectacle" thus revealed: "These fastenings of the gates are opening; soon you will see a sight such that even the one who loathes it will take pity" (lines 1294–96). And the chorus responds with words that underline the impact of this vision: "O suffering most terrible for men *to see*" (line 1298).

This scene is both the climax of the play and a microcosm of its action, which consists in moving from the unseen to the seen, from the hidden to the revealed. In that pattern it uses the resources of the theater to the fullest effect. For the same reason, it is the quintessential play for psychoanalysis, for it reveals the hidden, repressed realm of the irrational beneath the surface of rational consciousness.

The famous "tragic ironies" of the play are so powerful because they are doubled by the theatrical situation: in a manner analogous to Poe's much discussed "Purloined Letter," what is in plain sight of the audience is hidden from the participants. The play's central trope for this irony is of course the interchange between blind and sighted. But Sophocles' special genius lay in enormously enhancing this visual effect by making language itself the field that most fully enacts the play between the hidden and the obvious. Oedipus' words seem to speak a truth that he himself cannot (consciously) utter, as if his language were somehow out of his control: it wants to speak a truth that he does not fully know. He sets his investigation under way, in fact, with a glaring "misstatement" when, by a kind of Freudian slip of the tongue, he insists on the singular "robber" after Creon has emphatically reported the sole survivor's report that the assailants were plural, acting "not with *single* force but with a *multitude* of hands" (lines 120–25).[3]

The scene between Oedipus and Teiresias puts on the stage the paradoxical contrast between the king's eyes that do not "see" and the blind prophet's that do. But the paradoxes of blind vision are doubled by paradoxes of deaf hearing. Oedipus cannot "understand" the truth spoken in Teiresias' unambiguous words, even after his own anger has spurred the prophet to tear away the veil of silence that he had hoped to throw over the truth (lines 332–58). Oedipus' insistent anger even pushes Teiresias to leave his enigmatic language of revelation (lines 350–53) for the most open, blatant accusation possible: "I declare you to be the killer of that man whose murderer you are seeking" (line 362). True vision belongs to the blind man, but Oedipus is, as he says of Teiresias, as "blind in his ears as in his eyes and mind" (line 370f.).

These paradoxes of synesthesia in a scene with a blind but inwardly seeing prophet entwine the hiddenness of truth with the fallacy of sense and speech. The parachresis calls attention to the fact that Sophocles has staged the parallelism between "blind" language and blinded vision. Synesthesia has probably never been used with such telling effect (Segal 1977). Its overdetermination of false sensory perception and verbal error sets off the special nature of a knowledge that can be spoken only through the distorting mechanisms of language, the processes of condensation, displacement, splitting, doubling, that Freud began to study intensively in his *Interpretation of Dreams*. (1900)[4]

Truth, *alêtheia*, is a major issue in the play, and we shall return to it in more detail later. Focusing on the casting of statement of "truth" into distorted linguistic forms enables us to appreciate a number of specific features of the text that otherwise escape observation. At issue here is the recognition that poetic language "means" by indirect suggestion and paradox as well as (or in deliberate contradiction with) one-to-one correspondence. A Freudian approach demands an even more radical view of language: words may mean the opposite of what they say, or their "meaning" may lie in what they do not say.

In an acute and influential critique of the Freudian approach, Jean-Pierre Vernant has objected that Oedipus has no "Oedipus complex" because any "oedipal" feelings would be directed toward Merope, whom he believes to be his mother, not toward Jocasta, who has no maternal associations for him (Vernant 1972, 107–9). For Sophocles' play, however, Oedipus' relation to Jocasta and Merope, and to Laius and Polybus as well, also belongs to the linguistic processes by which the unconscious is displaced into language.[5] Merope and Polybus, the people whom he assumes to be his real mother and father, are parental figures whom the language of Oedipus constructs in ways that are both illuminating for and illuminated by Freud's theories of repression, language, and the unconscious. The scenes involving Merope and Polybus are crucial for Oedipus' construction of his past and so of his identity through the language of narration; and we shall begin with these and then move both forward and back to other parts of the play.

It is important to observe, first of all, that only new data from the external world can push Oedipus outside the closed circle of his own attempts to learn about his past and his guilt. This happens with the arrival of the Corinthian Messenger who brings the news of King Polybus' death. Left to themselves, he and Jocasta remain trapped in deductions, conjectures, partial memories, and incomplete knowledge. This condition itself resembles a state of neurotic anxiety, and we see Oedipus' keen investigative mind increasingly paralyzed by this anxiety as he tries to recall and put together the fragments of his buried past.

In the previous scene Jocasta and Oedipus shared their recollections of the past. Jocasta told of Laius' oracle, their child, and his exposure; Oedipus told of the events of his youth at Corinth, climaxing in his killing an old man at the crossroads between Delphi and Thebes (lines 707–858). They exit with the repeated determination to question the Old Herdsman, the sole survivor of the attack on Laius (lines 859–62). The chorus of Theban citizens then sings its ode on the "high-footed laws" of Olympus and the dangers of an abrupt fall that awaits the tyrant who is lifted too high in pride and violence. They are troubled by the problem of reconciling their continuing belief in Oedipus' innocence with their belief in the oracles and in a moral divine order generally (line 910).

At the end of their song, Jocasta returns to the stage bearing propitiatory offerings to Apollo. She is deeply disturbed by Oedipus' anxieties. His swings of emotion seem to deprive him of a clear, rational course of action: "For Oedipus lifts his spirit too high in pains of every kind; nor, like a man in full use of his mind (*ennous*), does he make inference about the new things by means of the things of old, but is at the mercy of whoever says anything if he speaks of fears" (lines 914–17). At this emotional crisis, the Corinthian Messenger enters—instead of the Old Herdsman whom Oedipus and Jocasta are awaiting—and offers totally unexpected but eagerly welcomed relief, the news of King Polybus' death (lines 924–44). Jocasta immediately summons Oedipus, to share the good news of the present as they previously shared the anxiety-provoking memories of the past (lines 945ff.). Oedipus has a moment of euphoric exultation (lines 964–72); but at Jocasta's "I told you so," he speaks again of "fear" (*phobos*, line 974) and relapses into anxiety (*oknein*, line 976) about the other part of his oracle, incest with his mother: "And how must I not fear my mother's bed?" (line 976). Jocasta replies by taking up his word "fear" (*phobos*, line 977) and tries to dispel it by urging the inconclusiveness of oracles. Human life is so uncertain, and there is no clear foreknowledge of events. So the best thing, she advises, is to "live randomly" (lines 977–79).

The context of dismissing the veracity or prognostic power of oracles is the setting for Jocasta's famous speech about the incestuous dreams in which "many men have slept with their mothers" (lines 981–83). These dreams, she argues, are not to be taken seriously, and so she counsels, "He to whom these things are as nothing bears life most easily" (line 983). Although she dismisses the oracle with the generalizing, euphemistic expression "sleep with one's mother," her previous line referred more specifically to "marriage with one's mother," *ta mêtros nympheumata* (line 980). Here she replicates, in reverse order, Oedipus' first account of his oracle in the previous scene. There, in reporting "the fearful and miserable things" predicted by Apollo (line 790), he first referred to the incest in explicitly sexual terms, "mingling [in intercourse] with my mother" (*mêtri meichthênai*, line 791) and producing offspring, "a race unendurable for men to see" (see Hay 1978, 70). A little later, however, he describes this union as "being yoked in marriage with my mother" (*gamois mêtros zygênai*, lines 825–26), softening the horror with the general term "marriage" and the conventional metaphor of "yoking."

The arrival of the Corinthian Messenger, though intended to bring comfort, plunges Oedipus back into his dreaded past and its fears. It is not entirely surprising, then, that Jocasta's words do not allay Oedipus' anxieties; and he repeats that powerful "fear" (*oknein*, line 986; cf. line 976) about the mother who is still alive.[6] The two then have this brief exchange:

Jocasta: And yet the father's tomb is a great joy [literally, "eye," *ophthalmos*].
Oedipus: Great, I agree; but there is fear of the [mother] who is alive. (Lines 987–88)

As we move close to the revealing of unconscious fears, and fears of the unconscious, which Jocasta's mention of incestuous dreams has already called into play, the dialogue takes on an eerie, phantasmagoric quality. Here the son rejoices in the "tomb of the father" and is afraid of the "living mother." In pronouncing and sharing with Jocasta his ophthalmic joy in his father's death, he is acting out, unknowingly and in language, the oracle, that is, the "fate" that defines his life, or the structure of the unconscious that Freud defined as the Oedipus complex.

When these fears, so deeply embedded in Oedipus' past, are evoked, they have to be displaced initially into the neutral terms or the generalized, conventional metaphors of social institutions, like the "marriage" and "yoking" in lines 825–26 (quoted above). As the Messenger's news seems to remove the oracle's prediction of patricide, the horror in the words that Oedipus had used—"murder of my father who begot me" (line 793), "kill my father Polybus" (lines 826–27)—fades and softens into the general term "tomb" or "burial" (*taphoi*, line 896). This toning down of the aggressive violence of the patricide to an endurable alternative that brings psychological relief is already at work in the Messenger's way of describing Polybus' death: "He exists no longer but perished" (line 956); "he departed in death" (line 959). "The poor man perished by illness" is Oedipus' conjecture in reply (line 962). Only Jocasta, specifically evoking the oracle and the past in her first impulse of joy and relief, used the active verb "kill" (*ktanoi*) and associated it with Oedipus' physical reaction of "trembling" in a fear that she regards as long past and in fact about to become obsolete: "O you oracles of the gods, where are you? Oedipus fled *long ago trembling* lest he *kill* this man. But now this man *has perished from chance*, not from Oedipus" (lines 946–49). Her very movement from "kill" (*ktanoi*) to "perish" (*ololen*), from the transitive to the intransitive verb, enacts in language the denial of the truth of the violence that Oedipus is "fated" to commit and has already committed.

The rest of the scene, calling up those past fears and probing them, gradually removes the veils of euphemism, the linguistic devices that have shielded Oedipus from (unconscious) knowledge. As the truth of the oracles emerges into the light, it defeats the linguistic strategies that Oedipus and Jocasta have both used to block or soften it. The repressed sexual and aggressive reality of the "fated" acts begins to reemerge from behind the words *marriage* and *tomb,* just as the truth of incest and patricide emerges from behind the names "Merope" and "Polybus."

The Messenger, responding to the atmosphere of fear, asks, "For the sake of what woman are you so afraid?" (line 989). The question seems innocent and reasonable, but the Messenger's word for "woman" here, *gynê,* also means "wife," Oedipus' form of address to Jocasta shortly before (lines 950, 964), We the audience, of course, know the truth hidden from him that his words are saying, namely that this "living mother" (line 988) is the "woman/wife" who now stands beside him on the stage. The vague fear of a future incest will soon become the absolute terror of the incest that he has already committed.

It is at this point that Oedipus, for the second and last time in the play, names his two supposed parents, Polybus and Merope:

Messenger: For the sake of what woman/wife are you so afraid?
Oedipus: Merope, old man, with whom Polybus dwells. (Lines 989–90)

And immediately after, he repeats his oracle of the patricide and incest, now for the third time (lines 994–98). The sense of horror becomes more insistent as we hear the words "fear" (*phobos*) or "terrible" (*deinon*) again and again in this scene. They will be repeated often in what follows.[7]

The element of "fear" here is a sign of what Freud, in a famous essay, referred to as "the uncanny": "an uncanny experience occurs either when infantile complexes that have been repressed are once more revived by some impression, or when the primitive beliefs that have been surmounted seem once more to be confirmed" (1919, 249). The literary effect of "the uncanny" here takes the form of the simplest words becoming vehicles of the "fearful" or "the terrible" (*phobos, deinon*) that surfaces from repressed knowledge, from the unspeakable. What could be more ordinary than giving the name of one's father and mother? This is how Oedipus began the story of his life in the previous scene with Jocasta:

"My father is Polybus the Corinthian, my mother Merope of Doris" (lines 774–75). Yet this most natural and most assured of all his statements is the one most fraught with horror. That horror begins to emerge as the vague "Merope," named only here and in line 775, becomes an object of the "fear" that dominates the scene. When he pronounces the name now, it is amid a cluster of words for "fear" (lines 987, 989, 991, 992) and in the context of what is "speakable" or "knowable" (line 993).

By invoking Merope so vividly in the Messenger scene, Sophocles introduces a contrast between three mother figures: the woman Oedipus assumes to be his "real" mother (Merope); the unknown mother of his fears, with whom he is fated to commit incest; and Jocasta. The audience, knowing the truth, watches this relation destabilize before its eyes as the feared mother of the incestuous relation turns into Jocasta (lines 964–1025). Hence the special power of this scene derives from the rapid succession of the following motifs: Jocasta's famous lines about men sleeping with their mothers in dreams (see Freud 1900, 264); Oedipus' satisfaction at his father's death; his recounting of his version of the oracle of the incest and patricide that he received at Delphi long ago; and the Messenger's revelation which now opens up the gap between the supposedly known "parents" in Corinth and the unknown, dreaded parents somewhere else. This mention of Merope (line 990) introduces a powerful play of difference and sameness between Merope, the mother still unknown to Oedipus himself, and of course Jocasta. When the Messenger mentions an unknown set of parents, he converts the scene of initial relief into a nightmare-world of anxiety (*phobos*) in which the oracle must once more be allowed its voice as a possibly true statement of Oedipus' condition.

The "truth" that language conveys now shifts from the "sayable" and "knowable" (line 993) to the unspeakable. In Freudian terms, the contents of the unconscious, which are contained in the oracle, can no longer be suppressed but are breaking forth into the light. "I shall *speak forth the truth* to you, O wife," Oedipus says to Jocasta as he begins the fateful account of the triple road in line 800, shortly after his announcement of his "parents" names (lines 774–75). "If I do not *speak the truth*, I deserve death," the Corinthian Messenger says in lines 943–44, as he swears the veracity of Polybus' death. The two affirmations point to two different versions of the "truth" about the death of the father. The difference that keeps them apart is the substitution of Polybus for Laius. "To speak the truth," *alêthê legein,* occurs in only one other place in the play, again in the mouth of a supposed stranger and again at the verge of a terrifying revelation about fathers and sons, namely the Old Herdsman's reluctant confirmation of the Messenger's story about Oedipus' birth: "You *speak truth,* although from a long time past" (line 1141). Before line 800— that is, before the point at which Oedipus begins to unveil the violent events of his past—all the statements about "truth" are confined to Teiresias, introduced as "the man who alone has truth as inborn nature" (line 298f.).[8] To Oedipus, however, "truth" comes only through struggle and with painful reluctance, and what he has "from inborn nature" is deeply concealed. The word for "truth" was often understood etymologically in early Greece as a negation of "forgetting," *a-lêthê,* and we may wonder whether this meaning is also present in our play, so intent on verbal ambiguity.[9]

This "un-forgetting" of "truth" is all the greater because it contrasts with the gentler, more loving surface of conscious (but erroneous) relationships. When Oedipus enters to hear the Corinthian Messenger's news, he first addresses Jocasta in the most affectionate terms: "O dearest person of my wife, Jocasta" (line 950). Literally, this verse reads, "O dearest head of my wife, Jocasta." The effect of the Greek poetic idiom, so stilted in English, is difficult to convey (see Carne-Ross 1990, 113– 14); but the affection and hopefulness in this address will be dashed to the ground at the report of Jocasta's suicide, which uses the same honorific metaphor: "The divine head of Jocasta has died" (line 1235). The poetic phrase "divine head" recalls the language of Homer and gives the queen the dignity of an epic heroine (in the *Iliad,* for example, Helen is "divine among women"). As the full truth emerges here, however, Jocasta is the most wretched and polluted of women.

After addressing Jocasta in line 950, Oedipus asks about the manner of Polybus' death and expresses pity for the death of an old man:

Messenger: A small blow puts to sleep bodies that are old.
Oedipus: Poor man, he died by illness, as seems likely. (Lines 961–62)

Oedipus then exults that he has escaped his terrible oracle (lines 964– 69), but he checks this happy mood with the more somber reflection that perhaps Polybus "wasted away with longing for me, and in this way would be dead from me" (line 969f.).

Oedipus here offers an alternative story of the death of a father and of the relation between a father and a son. Instead of the murderous blow of the club at the crossroads, this father dies by the metaphorical "small blow" of illness in old age. Instead of a father who fears and hates the son who may kill him, this father is killed by love and longing for a son who is away. Indeed, Oedipus' phrase, "longing for me," may echo a famous scene of tender affection between parent and child in Homer, the meeting between Odysseus and his mother Anticleia in the Underworld. Here she tells him how she died out of "longing" for him (*Od.* 11.202). But over against this relation of love and longing and the gentle, guiltless death of a father stands the nightmarish "truth" of Oedipus' relation with his unknown, absent, father—the "truth" (line 800) that he had described to Jocasta in the previous scene as a brutal, anonymous meeting. Oedipus can envisage in consciousness and in spoken language a metaphorical "small blow" of illness against an aged, beloved father (lines 961–62, 968–70); but hidden in the background is the violent, murderous blow against a powerful father, full of vigor and authority, who struck him first.[10] In like manner, the horrific, nightmare relation with the unknown mother stands behind the relation with the known, named mother in Corinth.

When we approach the oracle now in its dramatic and linguistic context, we appreciate anew Freud's insight: the oracle proclaims as fact the repressed incestuous and patricidal desires of the unconscious. In a famous passage of the *Interpretation of Dreams* Freud described the oracle as "the fate of all of us," namely "to direct our first sexual impulse towards our mother and our first hatred and our first murderous wish against our father" (1900, 262).

The specific names of "Merope" and "Polybus" as Oedipus's parents at Corinth (lines 990, 774–75) stand between him and the generic "mother" and "father" against whom he is to commit the crimes predicted by the oracle at Delphi (lines 821–33). On each of the two occasions of naming his parents, in fact, he repeats this oracle about his "mother and father" immediately afterwards. He now defends himself against his terrible, unacknowledged knowledge, as he has defended himself against the inexorable "fate" hanging over him, by interposing the name of Polybus and the story of Polybus' peaceful death from a "small blow" as the screen between the Oedipus who is a just and respected king at Thebes and the murderous, criminal Oedipus, or, as we would say today, the self-image that Oedipus has buried in his past, in his unconscious. This is the impetuous young Oedipus who traveled, temporarily nameless, in the triangular no-man's-land between Corinth, Delphi, and Thebes, killed his father, and married his mother.

The manner in which this oracle emerges into narrative consciousness also requires closer observation than it often receives, for it too participates in this paradoxical knowledge and ignorance through which the "uncanny" emerges from apparently matter-of-fact language.[11] What is "uncanny" here is precisely the way in which this matter-of-fact clarity becomes transparent to feared and horrible acts.

According to Oedipus' account of his visit to Delphi—his first statement about his oracle in the play (lines 788–93)—Apollo gave no direct answer to Oedipus' question about his parents but only a negative response, which Oedipus reports as follows: "He sent me forth unhonored," i.e., without the honor of a reply, *atimon exepempsen* (line 789). By uttering these words, Oedipus places in his own mouth that gesture of being "sent forth" or "expelled without honor" that has marked his life from his first days (cf. lines 717–19) and that he will be compelled to repeat again and again (cf. lines 387, 399, 657, 1081, 1340–46, 1381–83, 1411–13, 1451–54). The disjunction between his question, *Who are my parents?* and the god's answer, *You must commit incest and patricide,* contains one of the play's profoundest explorations of tragic knowledge. The self that Oedipus is driven to discover is hidden in the riddle of Apollo's prophecy.

In the next stage of his life's journey, this riddle will be encoded into another enigmatic discourse, the riddle of the Sphinx. The oracle and the riddle are symmetrical and analogous, and Teiresias plays on the interchangeability of the two terms (cf. lines 439, 393; Segal 1981, 238–40). There is also an inverted symmetry (a structural chiasmus) between these two trials of Oedipus' youth, the consultation of the oracle and the meeting with the Sphinx. Both result in an "enigmatic" pronouncement. At Delphi Oedipus questions, and the divine power (Apollo) answers; at Thebes the divine power (the Sphinx) poses the question, and Oedipus answers. But in both cases, as also in the scene with Teiresias, the common term is Oedipus' ignorance of who he is and where he is, both literally and in a Freudian sense.

Delphi is the point of transition between these two stages of Oedipus' life: a childhood and adolescence buried in ignorance, and a manhood marked by gradual discovery. We view the scene of his consulting the oracle retrospectively through the eyes of the young and confused wanderer. He comes to Delphi helpless and in need, and he leaves the oracular shrine not only ignorant but in greater distress than when he came. In his meeting with the Sphinx, he demonstrates his strength and uses his special intelligence. Oedipus himself, however, says almost nothing about the Sphinx, except that he defeated it by his wits. Indeed, Sophocles' play, unlike the modern versions of Cocteau, Hofmannsthal, or Pasolini, for example, omits any detailed account of this mythical episode, for its focus is on the tragic quality of the human reality, not the fabulous element in itself. When Oedipus, frightened by Jocasta's story of Laius' death, tells about his journey from Corinth to Thebes, he makes no mention of meeting the Sphinx on the way. His silence about this major victory now, in contrast to his pride in this exploit when he confronted Teiresias, marks the anxiety that has come to overshadow his view of his past. Now, at this critical point in the action, he gives a highly detailed account of the fatal encounter with his *human* adversary at the crossroads (line 798ff.). Sophocles thus keeps the human events in the foreground and shifts the fabulous elements to the remote background. But he also keeps his emphasis on the point where ignorance rather than intelligence in action proves to be the decisive factor for the meaning of this event in the protagonist's life.

This symmetry between ignorance and knowledge darkly in the background of this section of the play dominates Oedipus' life as Sophocles (re)constructs it before our eyes. That symmetry is already active in the Teiresias scene in the present, which both parallels and continues Oedipus' consultation of Apollo at Delphi in the past. Both scenes are characterized by the misunderstanding of revealed truth and the disjunction between the question and the answer. In the Teiresias scene the question is, *Who killed Laius?* and the answer, or one answer, is a statement about *Oedipus' origins* (cf. lines 413ff., 436f.). At Delphi those elements appeared in the reverse order: Oedipus asked about *his origins* and immediately after *kills Laius*.

When Oedipus asked Apollo if Polybus and Merope were his parents, Apollo gave no reply. Yet despite the uncertainty, Oedipus still believes in his putative Corinthian origins enough to "measure the Corinthian land henceforth by the stars" (line 794f.) and rush to "these places" (i.e., the crossroads near Delphi) where the old king will meet his death (line 798f.). Sophocles does not tell us what Oedipus' conscious motives may be; but, thanks to the very abruptness and illogicality of the oracular response, the scene does follow the Freudian model of the unconscious, and specifically in the area of the Oedipus complex, that is, concern with desire for the mother and hostility to the father. The man who asks about his hidden origins receives from a mysterious divine voice the reply that he is doomed to have union with his mother and kill his father (lines 790–93). He at once denies that knowledge by headlong flight from it, only to fulfill it without consciously knowing that he is doing so.[12]

The first mention of the oracle in the house of Laius is Jocasta's story of her child that would cause its father's death (lines 711–14). When Oedipus hears this, he responds not to the coincidence (partial, to be sure) of Jocasta's oracle with his own, but to her mention of the triple road (line 730). He focuses on a tiny fragment of her narrative and misses the total pattern. When he narrates his own oracle, as he does twice in the ensuing dialogue (lines 788–93, 821–29), he connects it with Jocasta's account only in so far as his identity as Laius' killer will cause his expulsion from Thebes and thus bring about his homelessness, for he cannot return to Corinth lest he fulfill his oracle *in the future*. He is utterly blind to the possibility that he has already fulfilled the oracle *in the past*, even though he now possesses two reasons to think that he may have done so, namely Jocasta's story about the exposure of her child and his own knowledge that he killed an older and important man at the crossroads where Laius also was killed (line 716ff.).

Recognizing that he may be Laius' killer and thus may have cursed himself in his imprecations upon the murderer, Oedipus is aware of the additional pollution of having begotten children on the wife of the man whom he has slain: "But the bed of the dead man in my hands I pollute— the hands through which he perished. Am I not then evil? Am I not wholly impure?" (lines 821–23). This literal translation conveys the surface meaning of his words. The verb "pollute" here is so placed that it can refer both to "hands" and to "bed," that is, to the pollution of sexuality and of bloodshed.[13] The words thus intimate a close "oedipal" connection between the bed and the murder. It is the struggle for the bed of wife/mother that links the father and son in this murderous contest. And this is, of course, the knowledge that Oedipus cannot allow to surface, even though it is contained in words of whose full meaning he is unaware.

Early in the play, when Oedipus thought that he was defending Laius in seeking his murderer, he spoke of "possessing his bed and his wife who bore him seed in common with me" and of their thus having "children in common" (lines 260–61). There, in his ignorance, this "common seeding," bed, and children formed part of a bond with the past of Thebes that he, as the usurper, wishes to assert and defend. But now that sharing of Laius' bed adds to the horror of his pollution. As we know, however, that pollution is far more terrible still, for he shares Laius' bed and children not just as the successor to his throne, but as his son. Thus the terms "common children" and "of common seeding" have a horrible secondary meaning of which Oedipus will soon become aware.[14]

After the reference to the pollution of Laius' bed in lines 821–23, Oedipus goes on in the next lines to describe the oracle for the second time: "Am I not impure in every way, if I must go into exile and in exile may not see my people nor tread upon my fatherland, or else in marriage must be yoked with my mother and kill my father, Polybus who nurtured and begot me" (lines 823–27). When Oedipus matches his life-story to Jocasta's, the pollution that he consciously contemplates is not incest or patricide, but having killed Thebes' king and married his wife, thereby also having in a sense polluted his marriage-bed and his children with the blood of his murder. This is a serious pollution, but it is far from the horror of the truth.

Although Oedipus reverses the order of "begot" and "raised" in speaking of his supposed father ("Polybus who raised me up and begot me," line 827), the name "Polybus" in place of the name of his real father still protects him from the truth. Yet the reference to the bed in the lines just before (821–23) sensitizes us to the sexual meaning of the deadly conflict between Laius and Oedipus and points to the repressed content of that knowledge which Oedipus logically should know but psychologically cannot know at this moment. The reversal of the "natural" order in Oedipus' reference to Polybus here as the one who "nurtured and begot" him also gives a hint of the hidden truth: Polybus is his father through the secondary act of "nurture," not the biological fact of "begetting." The Corinthian messenger, however, breaks through these defenses against the truth by removing the buffer between the names of his supposed parents (Merope, Polybus) and the parent figures he has violated.

We have already noted how the naming of Merope in line 990 begins to destabilize the division between the safe and the feared mother. A similar process occurs with the name of Polybus. Jocasta's summary of the Messenger's news is ambiguous. When she says that the Messenger has come "to announce that your father Polybus is no longer [alive]" (lines 955–56), Greek syntax allows her words also to mean, "to announce that Polybus is no longer your father." The Messenger responds by emphasizing the clarity of his announcement and the certainty of Oedipus' "knowing": "If I must first *announce this clearly, know well* that he is departed in death" (line 958f.). But nothing could be further from "clarity" and "knowledge" in this section of the play; and in fact the Messenger's supposedly "clear" account of the "small blow" that puts to sleep an aged body has an even more horrible ambiguity, for it can refer metaphorically to the old age that killed his supposed father and literally to the blow of Oedipus' club that killed his real father at the crossroads (see Ahl 1991, 164–65).

As Oedipus is separated from his alleged Corinthian parents at the news of Polybus' death, he also draws closer to the Messenger, whose special tie to him gradually emerges in the course of their dialogue (line 1018ff.). The Messenger initially addressed those onstage as "strangers" (*xenoi*, line 924); and he is so addressed in turn by the chorus, by Jocasta, and by Oedipus (*xene*, lines 927, 931, 957). But with his mention of Merope and Polybus in 990, Oedipus calls him "old man" (*geraie*, line 990), changes back to "stranger" in line 992, and then calls him "old man" again after Oedipus reveals his oracle (*geron*, line 1001). The Messenger for the first time addresses Oedipus as "lord" (*anax*, line 1002) but then, surprisingly, calls him "child" (*ô pai*) as he reveals to him that he does not know the truth of his parentage. "Old man" is Oedipus' return address in the following line (*ô geraie*, line 1009), which soon after becomes the somewhat more dignified word for old, *presbys*, "elder" (line 1013). When the Messenger tells his story about having found the infant Oedipus on Cithaeron, he addresses the king with an even stronger term of generational difference and affection, "child" (*teknon*, line 1030).

As the scene goes on, then, the terms of address subtly enact the changing relationship between the two men, shifting from "stranger" to "child" and "old man." These vocatives recreate in language their old, forgotten relation as "child" and "elder" that the dialogue gradually brings to light. The term "old man" that Oedipus addresses to this foster-father figure, moreover, also evokes the anonymous "old man" whom he struck and killed as a "stranger" at the crossroads (lines 805, 807, 813).[15] Once more a "truth" about a murderous relation to a father is overlaid and concealed, momentarily, by a gentler relation. This shifts again to a harsher relation as Oedipus is once more about to do violence to an old man, giving this address to the Old Herdsman as he is about to have him tortured (line 1147).[16]

The shifting terms of address between Oedipus and the Corinthian Messenger—"stranger/old man" and "stranger/child"—are all the more striking because one of the crucial matters in Oedipus' investigation is "naming a child": "For what reason did [Polybus] give me the name of child?" he asks as his nonrelation to Polybus comes to light (line 1021). Instead of Laius calling him "son," the man who saved him from Laius, a temporary surrogate-father and giver of life, calls him "child." In like manner, Oedipus at one point calls this man "elder," *presbys* (line 1023), the term given to "the elder Polybus" at the beginning of the scene (*presbys Polybos,* line 941).[17]

In the climactic moment of Jocasta's horrified recognition at the end of the scene, the problem of address becomes extreme. Oedipus entered with a full verse of affectionate address to Jocasta as his dearest wife (line 950); but at the end she cannot call him either "husband" or "child," only "unfortunate," *dystenos,* "the only thing I have to call you, and nothing else ever again" (lines 1071–72). The effect repeats in microcosm the play's larger movement wherein Oedipus, in the opening scene, had introduced himself as "called famous by *all*" (*pasi,* line 8), but, as Jocasta's final address shows, he had in fact no name in the most intimate relations of his life. That name of Oedipus is itself the token of his deprivation of house, life, and name by his parents, a mark of their attempt to negate his existence in the world. Instead of being "called famous *to all*" in the illusion of false names, he is "shown *to all* the Thebans" as the incestuous and parricidal pollution (line 1288f.), the bearer of "the names *of all* the sufferings that exist" (line 1284f.).[18]

Oedipus puts out the eyes that failed to "see" this "truth" in order to see what was before hidden in his unconscious. Sophocles, we must emphasize, would hardly think of the issues in these terms; they are possibilities inherent in the images and symbols that he has himself taken over and reinterpreted from the past and especially from Aeschylus. Freud, one could say, is only another stage in the life of the myth: he continues the process of interpreting its meaning by translating its symbols into an area and a set of terms compatible with, though different from, those that Sophocles has used. Where Sophocles implies divine powers, Freud implies the processes of the unconscious; and Freud is explicit about this translation, as is clear from the way in which he speaks of "fate" in the play.

Some Conclusions

One may object that the *Oedipus Tyrannus*, written at the height of the Sophistic Enlightenment, is much more about conscious than unconscious knowledge. Seen in its historical context, the play may certainly be read as a critique of man's confidence in understanding and controlling his world through his ever-increasing power in the physical, biological, and medical sciences, and in the "human sciences" of language, politics, history, and so on.

This historical reading of the problem of knowledge in the play, brilliantly set forth by Bernard Knox (1957) a generation ago, remains valid, but does not invalidate a psychological reading. It is possible to argue that Oedipus' passion for conscious, factual knowledge, his determination to discover his past, is at least as strong as his blindness to the clues in his path.[19] But this fact only brings out the radical otherness of the kind of "knowledge" that he does not have and, for much of the play, refuses to have, a repressed knowledge to which the organs of consciousness—the "ears, eyes and mind" of line 371—are indeed "blind" and to which the blind eyes of Teiresias, more accustomed to the darkness, are open.

A Freudian analysis, to be sure, uses an interpretive system extraneous to Sophocles and his time; but then virtually all interpretive systems applied to Greek tragedy, from Aristotle's *Poetics* on, are extraneous to the original author and audience and might well baffle them. The fact that psychoanalysis is part of our horizon of expectations but not part of Sophocles' or his public's horizon does not automatically disqualify it. At this point, it is customary to invoke the hermeneutic awareness of how works of art change their significance as they are received at different periods of history or viewed in different intellectual and aesthetic contexts. But with regard to Freudian interpretation and the Freudian unconscious specifically, Walter Benjamin, in a famous essay, has said the essential:

Fifty years ago, a slip of the tongue passed more or less unnoticed. Only exceptionally may such a slip have revealed dimensions of depth in a conversation which had seemed to be taking its course on the surface. Since the *Psychopathology of Everyday Life* things have changed. This book isolated and made analyzable things which had heretofore floated along unnoticed in the broad stream of perception. (1969, 235)

And of course the fact that phenomena like "Freudian slips" were unnoticed and unnamed does not mean that they did not exist.

Even though a narrowly Freudian approach will not give us the totality, or perhaps even scratch the surface, of our play's meaning, we should not turn away from the areas of meaning that it does illuminate in a way that no other method can. Thus, *pace* Vernant's cautionary remarks (1972, 110–11), we should not entirely dismiss Jocasta's dream-statement about the desire of men to sleep with their mothers or the oneiric status assigned to this vision. It is several degrees removed from the immediate, dramatic reality of the events on the stage, but it is also only a level or two behind the mysterious oracles or the shadowy, elusive events of Oedipus' past. The fiction of the play enables Sophocles to keep such events in the dreamworld of hypothesis and imagination; unlike Freud, he does not suggest that such actions are mental events in actual individuals. As Jean Starobinski has observed, for Freud "a tendency rediscovered in the history of childhood... is made explicit and universal through the Oedipus myth, whereas the Sophoclean tragedy takes on the guise of a dream and is seen as the realized desire of a subjectivity identical with humanity itself" (1989, 166).

The "oedipal" actions and desires within Sophocles' play contribute to creating a world of emotional phenomena, what we may call its "imaginary," its image-directed evocation of areas of conscious and unconscious or subconscious thought processes that we can reach only by intuition and leaps of the imagination. There is enough in the play to warrant the existence of such an "imaginary," and Freud intuitively grasped it. We need not try to psychoanalyze Oedipus as if he were a real person, but we can scrutinize the patterns of language in the oneiric realm of those dangerous desires and aggressions that make up the substance of the play; and here, as I have tried to show, Freud's insights are indeed fruitful.

My second point has to do with the fact that the *Oedipus* works so powerfully upon us because it combines the visual enactment of gripping events, of a life story, with a deep and subtle probing of the paradoxes of a language that both conceals and reveals. A textually oriented and linguistically sophisticated Freudian approach to literature, such as that adumbrated by Shoshana Felman, goes beyond the uncoding of symbols in a one-to-one equation with male or female genitalia (like Oedipus' staff/scepter or the triple road, respectively) and enables us to view reading itself as an interactive relation between the unconscious of the text and the unconscious of the reader so that we can recognize our cooperation and involvement with the text in the creation of meaning (1977, 197ff.). Freud offers no magic key, but his approach is itself a method of interpretive unveiling that answers to the way in which texts lure us into their secrets and into the process of uncovering their secrets.[20]

The dramatized actions of the *Oedipus* are a search for knowledge, but they equally constitute a series of refusals to tell, the resistance to conscious knowledge acted out by Teiresias, Jocasta, and the Old Herdsman. Each of these characters reveals what he or she knows only reluctantly, and indeed in the last case only under the threat of torture. The play enacts a sequence in which the audience is led to identify either with the one who knows or the one who refuses to know. We shift between the two positions, becoming both insiders and outsiders, analysands and analysts, in turn (see Felman 1977, 196–203; Wright 1984, 129–31). This unstable situation of our identification builds up that tension that all interpreters have admired in the play.

Applied in such a way, Freud can provide a way of recognizing how we construct meaning in the projection of our unconscious into those models of knowing implied in the texts. He offers a way of superimposing "the model of the functioning of the psychic apparatus on the functioning of the text" (Wright 1984, 121–24). The process of reading or seeing thus becomes analogous to that of the Freudian transference, the process by which the patient in psychoanalysis relives crippling emotional conflicts by acting them out unconsciously in his or her relation with the analyst. In the experience of the drama, we identify our deep conflicts or repressed wishes with the actors in the work. This analogy, however, also makes us aware of the precariousness of interpretation, since every act of interpretation also includes some element of repression.[21]

Applying Freud's theories to the literary experience also holds the danger of fetishizing the process of reading, as it were, by turning emotional life into pure textuality.[22] This essay has attempted to study how the paradoxical workings of language may illuminate the representation of the unconscious, at least in literary art; but the unconscious should not necessarily be reduced only to a feature of language, as if it were just an epiphenomenon of the signifying process of linguistic signs. Such an approach belongs to what we may now (and increasingly) recognize as the poststructural fallacy, reducing what can appear only through language to a solely linguistic existence. It thereby risks forgetting the emotional reality of personal conflicts, the struggles between desire and reality, the paralysis brought by neurotic anxiety and guilt, and all the other forms of mental suffering that Freud's therapeutic method sought to heal or alleviate.

Notes

1. All translations from Sophocles are by the author. For the importance of unconscious knowledge generally in the *Oedipus Tyrannus*, see Rudnytsky (1987, 269–72).
2. For a detailed discussion of this scene, see Segal (1986, 97–99); also Segal (1993, ch. 11).
3. For the issue of the one and many and its implications, see Segal (1981, 214–16). The problems of this passage and the question of whether or not the Herdsman/Escort has lied in his report continues to be much discussed, most recently by Ahl (1991), who has attempted to revive the thesis of Goodhart (1978) that Oedipus in fact did not commit the patricide. However plausible the thesis may look, however, it remains unconvincing both in terms of the dramatic conventions that Sophocles uses and in terms of the nature of the tragic effect of the play. It does not, for instance, take account of the issue of incest, and we would have to assume, for example, that Jocasta's suicide is a mere side effect of Oedipus' false self-conviction. Nor does this approach give sufficient weight to the oracles in the background and the role of the gods, issues whose importance has again been argued, in a balanced and convincing way, by Burkert (1991, 15–18, 22–27). For a systematic examination and cogent refutation of Goodhart, see Rudnytsky (1987, 350–57).
4. The refocusing of the work of the unconscious on the processes of language is implicit in Freud. See, for example, his famous essays, "The Antithetical Sense of Primal Words" (1910) and "Negation" (1925), and the analysis of language practiced in *Psychopathology of Everyday Life* (1901) and *Jokes and Their Relation to the Unconscious* (1905); but it is especially developed in the work of Jacques Lacan (1968, 1977).
5. Vernant's criticism is directed, quite rightly, against some exaggerations and distortions by D. Anzieu (*Les Temps Modernes* 245 [October 1966]: 675–715) rather than by Freud, for example Anzieu's notion that in fleeing Corinth

Oedipus is "unconsciously obeying his desire for incest and parricide," as if he somehow suspected even then that Polybus and Merope were not his true parents (Vernant 1972, 103–4), or the idea of Creon's incestuous attachment to his sister Jocasta (109). I would certainly endorse Vernant's methodological emphasis, to which I owe much, on tracing "this complex interplay of conflicts, reversals, ambiguities... as they are conveyed through a series of tragic discrepancies or tensions" (91).

6. In both of Jocasta's allusions to incest here, moreover, the "poetic" or generalizing plural (*nympheumata*, line 980; *polloi brotôn*, line 981) is accompanied by the singular word for "mother," which contributes to keeping the situation personal, despite her attempt to widen and depersonalize the frame of reference. This individualized reference may in part account for the ineffectiveness of her attempt at reassurance.

7. Cf. Oedipus' "terrible and unfortunate," when he first reported the oracle in line 790; "terrible insult" in line 1035; "terrible," repeated three times at the shouts and sights of Jocasta's suicide and Oedipus' discovery in lines 1260–67; "terrible, most terrible," when Oedipus is shown to the city in line 1297f.).

8. In addition to line 298f., Teiresias speaks of "truth" (*alêtheia, alêthes*) in lines 349f., 355f., 368f. In the only other reference to "truth" in the play, line 501, the chorus is also speaking of Teiresias and is puzzled in their "judgment" or "decision" about his accusations of Oedipus (*krisis alêthês*).

9. For suggestive interpretations of this etymological meaning of *a-lêtheia*, see Heidegger (1947, esp. 11ff.); Detienne (1967, 23ff.).

10. Ahl (1991, 165) seems to me to give insufficient emphasis to the gentler side of Oedipus' response to the news of Polybus' death in lines 961–72: "Not a word of grief escapes him when he hears of Polybus' death, only a sense of triumph over the oracle and a curious realization that Polybus might have died of grief and longing for him." This view entirely neglects *ho tlêmôn* in line 962, "poor man," and refuses to acknowledge the sympathetic identification with Polybus in the "longing," *pothos*, which must be trivialized as "curious."

11. In his critique of the excesses of Anzieu, Vernant (1972, 106–7) finds conscious and "more truly psychological reasons" for Oedipus' behavior, namely his excessive self-confidence, pride, and fear of being discovered a "supposititious" child of Merope (i.e., of servile birth) rather than in any pattern of unconscious motivation. But the power of Sophocles' play lies precisely in the plausibility of this conscious motivation alongside the unconscious. The repressed wishes of the unconscious are always capable of being rationalized and thereby hidden. What the play does is to enact the processes by which these rationalizing defenses are forced to give way to the unspeakable "truth." Vernant is right to point out that Sophocles nowhere shows Oedipus as one who desires the incest and the patricide; but the heart of Freud's

approach lies in his reading of the oracle as a voice both external and internal to Oedipus, that is, as the repressed contents of his unconscious. As Vernant himself acknowledges, he carries within himself the hidden shadow of the tyrant who does in fact both wish and perform such acts: "Oedipus is unaware of the part of himself that is a shadow that he carries within him as the sinister reflection of his glory" (106).

12. The plot here is guided by motives other than conscious logic, for, as many critics have pointed out, Oedipus came to Delphi out of uncertainty about the identity of his father and so still did not know where to flee to escape committing patricide. Ahl, for example, notes the contradiction in Oedipus' response but offers no interpretation: "Instead of realizing that to avoid killing his father he must first know who his father is, he responds as if Polybus were in fact his father and Merope his mother— although it was uncertainty on this point that first sent him to Delphi" (1991, 145).

13. The antecedent of the relative clause, "through which he perished," is "hands." But it is equally possible to understand *lechê*, "bed," as the antecedent of *hônper*, "which," with the sense, "I pollute in my hands the dead man's *bed, through which he perished.*"

14. The phrase in line 260, "a wife of common seeding," *gynaika homosporon*, thus reveals its double meaning as both "the wife who bore seed to him in common with me" and "the wife of seed in common," in the sense of incestuous union with and bearing children to her own son.

15. *Presbys*, "old man," is used of Laius in lines 805 and 807, of Polybus in line 941 (by Jocasta), of the Corinthian Messenger in lines 1013 and 1121, and of the Old Herdsman in line 1147. Oedipus also addresses the chorus collectively as "Elders," *presbeis*, for the only time in the play at the arrival of the Old Herdsman in line 1147.

16. As a slave, the Old Herdsman would be subject to interrogation by torture, and this would be regular procedure under Athenian law.

17. Note too the subtle shift in the meaning of Oedipus' relation to "the inhabitants of the country," *hoi epichôrioi*, in lines 939 and 1046. Instead of being the ruler of these inhabitants (the Corinthians in 939), Oedipus moves to an ambiguous and uncertain relation with them (the Thebans) in line 1046.

18. On the issue of naming in the play, see Segal (1981, 211–12, 242–43).

19. See, e.g., Ricoeur (1970, 516ff.); Poole (1987, 90).

20. See Wright: "The lure of all texts lies in a revelation, of things veiled coming to be unveiled, of characters who face shock at this unveiling" (1984, 121).

21. See Rudnytsky: "No work of analysis is ever complete, because repression continues to manifest itself in the process of interpretation" (1987, 51).

22. For a good statement about the limitations of this "textualization" of experience, see Rudnytsky (1987, 333f).

94   Charles Segal

References

Ahl, F. 1991. *Sophocles' Oedipus: Evidence and Self-Conviction.* Ithaca: Cornell Univ. Press.
Benjamin, W. 1969. The Work of Art in the Age of Mechanical Reproduction. In *Illuminations,* ed. H. Arendt, trans. H. Zohn. New York: Schocken Books, pp. 217–51.
Burkert, W. 1991. Oedipus, Oracles, and Meaning: From Sophocles to Umberto Eco. *The Samuel James Stubbs Lecture.* University College, University of Toronto.
Carne-Ross, D. S. 1990. Jocasta's Divine Head: English with a Foreign Accent. *Arion,* 3d series, 1.1:106–41.
Detienne, M. 1967. *Les maîtres de vérité en Grèce ancienne.* Paris: Maspero.
Felman, S. 1977. Turning the Screw of Interpretation. In *Literature and Psychoanalysis. The Question of Reading: Otherwise,* ed. S. Felman. *Yale French Studies* 55/56:94–207.
Freud, S. 1990. *The Interpretation of Dreams.* In *The Standard Edition of the Complete Psychological Works of Sigmund Freud,* ed, and trans. J. Strachey et al., 24 vols. London: Hogarth Press 1953–74 vols. 4 and 5.
———. 1919. The "Uncanny." *S. E.* 17:219–56.
Goodhart, S. 1978. *Leistas Ephaske:* Oedipus and Laius' Many Murderers. *Diacritics* 8.1:55–71.
Hay, J. 1978. *Lame Knowledge and the Homosporic Womb.* Washington, DC: Univ. Press of America.
Heidegger, M. 1947. *Platons Lehre von der Wahrheit.* Berne: Francke, pp. 5–52.
Knox, B. M. W. 1957. *Oedipus at Thebes.* New Haven: Yale Univ. Press.
Lacan, J. 1968. *Speech and Language in Psychoanalysis,* trans. A. Wilden. Baltimore: Johns Hopkins Univ. Press.
———. 1977. *Ecrits: A Selection,* trans. A. Sheridan. New York: Norton.
Poole, A. 1987. *Tragedy: Shakespeare and the Greek Example.* Oxford: Blackwell.
Ricoeur, P. 1970. *Freud and Philosophy,* trans. D. Savage. New Haven: Yale Univ. Press.
Rudnytsky, P. L. 1987. *Freud and Oedipus.* New York: Columbia Univ. Press.
Segal, C. 1977. Synaesthesia in Sophocles. *Illinois Classical Studies,* 2:86–96.
———. 1981. *Tragedy and Civilization: An Interpretation of Sophocles.* Cambridge, MA: Harvard Univ. Press.
———. 1986. *Interpreting Greek Tragedy: Myth, Poetry, Text.* Ithaca: Cornell Univ. Press.
———. 1993. *Sophocles' Oedipus Tyrannus: Tragic Heroism and the Limits of Knowledge.* Twayne Masterworks Series. New York: Macmillan.

Starobinski, J. 1989. Hamlet and Oedipus. In *The Living Eye,* trans. Arthur Goldhammer. Cambridge, MA: Harvard Univ. Press, pp. 148–70.

Vernant, J.-P. 1972. Oedipus without the Complex. In Vernant and P. Vidal-Naquet, *Myth and Tragedy in Ancient Greece,* trans. J. Lloyd. New York: Zone Books, 1988, pp. 85–111.

Wright, E. 1984. *Psychoanalytic Criticism: Theory in Practice.* London and New York: Methuen.

The Oedipus Myth: An Attempt at Interpretation of Its Symbolic Systems

Vassilka Nikolova

This chapter is inspired by Aristotle's idea that thinking and knowledge are the driving forces in human life. In what follows, I shall try to reveal that these forces are also to be found at the semantic base of the well-known myth of Oedipus, the tyrant of Thebes.

In 1897, when Freud first glimpsed the Oedipus complex in a letter to Fliess, he revived this ancient myth on the ground of medicine and psychology. In his writings on creativity (1908, 1910a, 1910b), Freud pointed out the connection between literature and health and between popular myths and unconscious motives. The genius of Aristotle anticipated this important aspect of Freud's discovery of the unconscious, for he was the first to note the relationship between literature and myths and between art and health.

In the *Poetics* (1449 b), Aristotle proposed that the effect of art on the beholder is analogous to a purge which he called *catharsis* and, what is more, he concluded that the soul of drama is not *ethos* (character) but *mythos* (plot). Usually, when speaking about these problems, scholars do not consider the chain "myth-art-catharsis-health" and they try to explain Aristotle mainly on a philosophical level, entirely disregarding the fact that he was first of all a physician who viewed man from a medical point of view and who based his theory on psychology and its healing practices. Aristotle's scientific approach to the problems of man and the universe prescribed the achievement of *eudaimonia* (happiness) through catharsis as the sole and most efficacious cure for all diseases (*Nich. Eth.,* 1.4). Support for this medical interpretation is to be found in the works of many ancient authors who discuss the *Poetics:* Diogenes Laertius (7.1.63), Clement of Alexandria (*Strom.,* 2.16), Cicero (*Tusc. Disp.,* 4.8), and Seneca (*De Clem.,* 2.5).

Integrating ideology with social organization, myth is always used ad hoc to fulfill concrete cultural functions. In accordance with their psychological disposition, the ancient Greeks both lived and created within myths, and their thinking is thus generated from components which act as a composite whole but do not otherwise interact. This mosaic quality of myths is well suggested by Freud's idea that "all genuinely creative writings are the product of more than a single motive and more than a single impulse in the poet's mind and are open to more than a single interpretation" (1900, 266).

In the myth of Oedipus we find combinations of elements from different myths comprising the "Theban cycle," especially from the lost poems *Thebaid* and *Oedipodeia,* references to which are found in many ancient authors. There are three main components of the Attic myth used by Sophocles for his tragedy, even though the versions of the myth over the course of the development of Greek culture are innumerable.

The first and oldest component of the myth is the story of the Sphinx, a central figure in the Boeotian mythological system. The earliest versions present her as one of the "storm demons," symbolizing disaster and plague, and name her a "sacred disease." The same appellation is used later on in medicine for epilepsy, and the association of this disease with the Sphinx is rooted in the symbolic explanation given by the dream books of antiquity (Artem. *Oneiroc.,* 2.12).

The second component is the story of the exposed child, both an agent and victim of fate, symbolizing the sun-hero (Achilles, Perseus, Romulus and Remus, etc.). This child is usually endowed with sacred feet, a characteristic element in the mythological thinking of ancient peoples, whose ceremonies frequently prescribed ritual crawling and maiming. In order to justify such rites, the myth depicted a hero whose feet were pierced by nails, and hence he was given the name Oedipus. The most common linguistic explanation for the name, supported by Sophocles in *Oedipus*

Rex (lines 1169–73), is that it comes from the words *oidao* (to swell) and *pous* (foot) and hence means primarily "a man with swollen feet." The combination of these two basic elements from the myths of the Sphinx and Oedipus was at first understood as a symbolic representation of the purely physical conflicts between the sun and storm clouds. But changes in the social conditions brought about a change in the interpretation, so that gradually the story developed and became enriched into a myth tracing the daily or yearly career of the sun, which was believed to kill his father (the night) and marry his mother (the dawn). The psychological motive for such an interpretation is connected with the awe of primitive people at unknown and inexplicable natural phenomena.

This is how the main constituents of the well-known story were formed. There was only one thing missing—a rationale for the incestuous union which sets the plot in motion. For that purpose the popular idea of riddles was used, which gave the third component of the structure of the myth. In fact, the riddle combines elements from two Boeotian folktales: (1) the story of a king who offers his daughter's hand to the man who would kill the monster torturing his kingdom; and (2) the tale of a Theban queen who sets her suitors three riddles (the last one of which in later versions is "the riddle of the Sphinx"). In this plot, the essential feature to be noted is that marriage and the throne come to the hero as a prize for his wisdom.

These were the sources out of which the famous myth of Oedipus was created. Sophocles himself called the story "a paradigm of a common law" (line 1193) and this may be the best explanation for its popularity throughout the ages. Yet it should be remembered that Freud (1916–17, 158–65) compared myths to the secular dreams of youthful humanity and that Marx (1971, 133) in the *German Ideology* considered Greek antiquity to be the childhood of human society. These remarks make it obvious why the Oedipus myth should appeal to the human race at different stages of its development: it is a dream from the childhood of mankind that touches the psychic experience of all people. But, as Marx has reminded us in the *Communist Manifesto*, man's consciousness changes with every stage in the material and social conditions of life (1971, 123ff). Consequently, the reading of texts varies with each new historical situation, and myths, like all forms of imaginative expression, always admit of validly fresh exegesis on the part of the interpreter.

Convinced that the Oedipus myth distills the essence of ancient culture,

I shall try to interpret its symbolic system on a semantic basis, relying mainly on works by classical authors. Wherever possible, however, I also range beyond ancient sources for, if the symbols are consistent with the later development of European culture, the analogies follow of their own accord. But I shall not dwell too long on the psychoanalytic interpretations of these symbols, since they are well known to the modern public.

Myth and Religion in Primitive Society

It was a common belief in primitive societies that life began from an incestuous copulation between brother and sister, which was forbidden to humans but considered highly sacred in the sphere of mythology. This is why the presence of Oedipus and the Sphinx in the same myth must be interpreted as a symbolic expression of that idea. Indeed, several of the earliest versions (Pausan., 9.26.2–4; schol. Eurip. *Phoen.*, line 26) represent the Sphinx as Laius' daughter, and hence as a sister to Oedipus. Furthermore, the meeting between Oedipus and the Sphinx and his victory over her, enacted in the myth by his unraveling of the riddle, symbolizes sexual intercourse between man and woman in general.

The theme of incest appears throughout the world in cosmogonic tales depicting a primordial pair of brother (sun, sky) and sister (earth) as progenitors of the human race. For example, Plutarch (356 b–358 e) preserves one of the best Egyptian stories concerning the ritual marriage of Isis to her brother Osiris. Later, the Roman writer Julius Firmicus Maternus (4th c. A.D.) affirmed that the same subject is to be found in the eastern religions of Mesopotamia and Babylon. According to the texts of Plutarch and Maternus, the Egyptians equated Isis with the earth, and linked her sexual union with her brother-husband Osiris to the idea of copulation with Mother Earth, which was unconsciously represented by symbols of ploughing and planting.

I shall not pursue the analogy between agriculture and incest revealed throughout the world both in the universal symbols of vegetation and fertility cults and in linguistic usage. More interesting for our purposes is the further association that can be made with the help of this Egyptian myth: Oedipus and the Sphinx, being a primordial pair of brother and sister, are to be seen as primal father and mother as well. (To Freud's reminder that "the mother-goddess in general preceded the father-gods" [1913, 149], we may add sister-goddesses as well.) There is no doubt that the Sphinx can be interpreted as Mother Earth. Some of the early versions (Eurip. *Phoen.*, line 1041; Apollod. 3.5.8) present her as autochthonous, a typical expression of this ancient belief. The gradual metamorphosis of the Sphinx from an embodiment of hostile natural forces and diseases into one of earth and Mother Nature is confirmed by the evidence of extant statues and vase paintings, where her demonic features give way to human and feminine ones.

As Freud pointed out, figures of this kind are the religious equivalent of the "phallic mother" symbolized in cults by objects such as a totem (1910a, 94). Pausanias (1.24.5) is the first to name the Sphinx an *eidolon* (idol). C. R. Badcock writes: "Hence she becomes the phallic mother and therefore she is the Magna Mater...the goddess of many names, the queen of heaven, the parent of nature. In her many guises the goddess represents all the aspects which a mother shows to her child. She is... an intercessor with the father-god, embodiment of beauty, origin of all things" (1980, 91). In addition to the evidence from visual art that supports this idea, it finds strong corroboration in ancient scientific thought.

Myth as Primitive Science

With the rise of philosophy and the beginnings of science, religion declined and an attempt at a rational explanation of things developed. So, upon the preexisting myth of the Sphinx, individual thinkers imposed their philosophical ideas. The primal mother of the religious cults became Mother Nature and was revealed by the first scientists to be a union of *stoicheia* or primordial elements. In Latin, the word *mater* is undoubtedly at the base of the word *materia,* which is the synonym for the Aristotelian *hyle* (essence). Mythology gave way to the concepts of natural philosophy, and the image of the Sphinx was explained by the Ionic philosophers, building on their forerunners, as a symbolic presentation of the elements comprising the macrocosm and the micrososm.

The structural elements which form the body of the Sphinx—woman's face and breasts, lion's body, eagle's wings, and the tail of a serpent— were now construed as an allegory of earth, fire, air, and water, which mingle into one another and thereby create a harmonious structure (Cl. Alex. *Strom.*, 5.8.48). This is why in the new epoch this demonic creature from the archaic period came to be known as the "harmony of nature" and the "essence of the universe," names which reveal the rationalization of the myth and express the tendency in Greek society to see natural causes as underlying divine phenomena. (In the fifth century B.C., Hippocrates [*De morbo sacro*, 1–2] contended that the "sacred disease" of epilepsy had a natural cause, Heraclitus seems to have been a skeptic, perhaps even an atheist, and Protagoras was persecuted for atheism.) Ultimately, Greek religion declined to the point where living men could be "deified" and where only the mysteries and the cult of Asclepios at Epidaurus remained. This advance in rationality at the hands of the Greeks may remind us of Badcock's words concerning "the great progress which a child makes in his intellectual apprehension of the world after the resolution of the Oedipus conflict" (1980, 97). Certainly, in no other period in the history of thought do we find the same childlike mixture of naïveté and lucidity of insight as in the early stages of Greek philosophy, which is notable especially for its sense of wonder at the world.

Myth as Psychology of Culture

The same period witnessed not only the rise of science in ancient Greece but also the golden age of its art. The turning back from myth to reality may be seen not only in philosophy and science but also in the artistic transformations wrought by Greek drama. Through the theater the Greeks tried to solve their problems—sex, will to power, parental authority—and thus to articulate what words alone failed to express. But, in order for something to be understood rationally, it must have a sense— some coherent semantic basis, a matrix of meaning inherent in language and in the symbolic systems of life itself.

I would like now to consider the incest that propels the plot in *Oedipus Rex*. In fact, because of the symbolism which puts it at the center of a whole system, incest contains the psychological explanation of the ancient Greek *Weltanschauung*. On the one hand, the incest is symbolically represented by the meeting between Oedipus and the Sphinx and by his solving of the riddle; on the other, it is shown literally by Oedipus' marriage to Jocasta. This method of representation, in which two parts of a theme repeat or complement each other in different terms, is basic to myth.

One key to understanding the Oedipus myth is provided by what Nietzsche called the "will to power." Here, it is important to recall the folk version in which the marriage to the queen comes as a prize for wisdom and brings with it glory and power. The point is that the early versions do not contain any idea of guilt, and even the later accounts introduce the deed of patricide with the sole purpose of laying the ground-work for the incest to come, and not to reproach Oedipus. Among many examples, I may adduce those of Homer (*Od.*, 11.273–74) and the late versions of the paradoxographers Socrates of Argos (schol. Eurip. *Phoen.*, line 45), Palaephatos (*De Incred.*, 4), and Mallalas (*Bonn.*, 49), all of which leave unmentioned the theme of patricide. The argument is further supported by the later symbolic system of alchemy in the Middle Ages, which entirely omits the image of the father. After all, Oedipus can be imagined without guilt or without patricide, but without incest the myth is impossible.

The cultural and psychological ground for the priority of incest is readily provided by the most popular symbolic system of antiquity—dream-interpretation. According to the allegorical language of dreams then employed, incestuous marriage with one's mother had the meaning of winning the power to rule. In his *Oneirocritica* (1.79, 91–92), Artem-idoros Daldamus (4th c. A.D.) wrote that the dream of sexual intercourse with one's mother was a good sign for any politician or tyrant, because the mother symbolizes the country, that is, Mother Earth. Such a con-strual of the incestuous relationship may easily be grasped. Man takes possession of his country as of a woman who surrenders to him and by that act he is transformed from a citizen-son to a master-husband. (There is nothing odd about this because Artemidorus' explanation has merely preserved a tradition having its source in what Freud terms "some pri-maeval dream-material" [1900, 263].) In fact, Oedipus is identified as a tyrant in the title of Sophocles' tragedy, and Jocasta, as an offspring of the earth-born Thebans, is an obvious symbol of Mother Earth. This part of the myth reveals a new dimension of the ideas already disclosed through the image of the Sphinx.

People have had oedipal dreams since the earliest period of their self-consciousness. In Sophocles' words, "many a man hath seen himself in dreams / his mother's mate" (lines 1120–21). Giving a modern twist to the traditional idea of the role of analogy in myths and dreams, Freud cited these lines to uphold his thesis that imaginative works cope with libido by means of symbolism (1900, 264).

There are further examples from ancient literature that reinforce the political emphasis given by Artemidorus. According to Herodotus

(6.107), in 490 B.C. the tyrant Hippias had an incestuous dream, which he interpreted in the same way. Suetonius (*Caes.*, 7.2) attributed a similar dream and its interpretation to Julius Caesar: "he had a dream in which he saw himself copulating with his own mother, but the interpreters excited his hopes much more, saying that the dream promised him power ... because the mother he had seen under himself was nothing but earth regarded as a parent of all living things." The dream of Julius Caesar is found also in Plutarch, Dio Cassius, Zonnaras, and other ancient and Byzantine authors. It is noteworthy that in his youth Caesar wrote a tragedy titled *Oedipus*, the mention of which was forbidden by Augustus. Both the instances of Hippias and Caesar are cited by Freud in *The Interpretation of Dreams* (1900, 398).

Verbal analogies of this kind are characteristic not only of the dream-interpreters but are also to be found in Plato, a glorious interpreter of the symbols in the Greek cultural tradition. In the *Republic* (571 d), he writes that the life of a tyrant is like a dream in which nothing could hamper a man from copulating with his own mother. There could be no clearer expression of the belief that to be one's mother's husband means to be a tyrant. As Nilson says: "In spite of their detestation of tyrants, the Greeks could not help admiring them as the equals of the gods, who could likewise permit themselves to do whatever they pleased" (quoted in Badcock, [1980, 66]). Incest is thus an immemorial representation at once of extraordinary power and of sacred or forbidden knowledge.

Now I shall consider the interpretations that link the Sphinx with knowledge and wisdom, as these are decisive for understanding all the other symbols. From the earliest periods, the Sphinx was regarded as the embodiment of the unknown, an enigma, a poser of riddles, and hence also as the personification of wisdom. This is why some later accounts made Apollo send her to the people and why she became the wise, mysterious, and musical messenger of divine justice. The tragic poets used to call her Virgo or "the wise virgin" (Pind. frg. 177; Soph. *OT*, line 393; Eurip. *Phoen.*, lines 48, 1049, 1353). This name immediately suggests an association to the goddess Athena, the virgin patroness of knowledge, intellect, and wisdom. Some of the oldest statues of the Sphinx, moreover, depict her with a helmet—the attribute of Athena—which confirms Athena to be her later counterpart in the guise of a goddess.

On the other hand, the Greek *Weltanschauung* considered the Sphinx as a parallel to Cassandra and the Sybil, and her riddle was related to a series of oracular sayings and proverbs with quite unintelligible meanings. Apollodorus (3.5.8.) affirmed that the Sphinx had learned her riddle from the Muses, and so also did Sophocles and Euripides. This led to the creation of a new analogy. For the authors of later periods the Sphinx became a Muse. An especially good review of this transformation is given by Roscher (1909–15, 1298–1407), who supports his statements with pictures from ancient vases, in which the image of the Sphinx is humanly animated, revealing strongly an inner dimension of enigmatic and intelligent suggestion. Most of these pictures depict the Sphinx in front of Oedipus, who is sitting deep in thought resting his head on his hand (the analogy to Rodin's statue is striking). The conclusion follows that these two images, which I have treated as sister and brother or primal mother and father, are ultimately two sides of *homo sapiens:* the enigma and its apocalypse, the secret and its undoing, the eternal woman and the eternal man. Finally, the Sphinx is a symbol of woman's ambiguity, which Freud held to be a dark continent for psychology, setting to man the "riddle" of the nature of femininity: "Nor will you have escaped worrying over this problem, those of you who are men; to those of you who are women, this will not apply—you are yourself the problem" (1933, 154–55).

As early as the fourth century B.C., Xanthos (Cl. Alex. *Strom.,* 3.515) mentioned in his *Magica* the custom of the Persian Magi of copulating with their own mothers and sisters, observing that to be born of such a marriage was a precondition that enabled the Magus to penetrate into the supreme secrets. (The word "Magus" is used for those same sorcerers whom Cicero [*De div.,* 1.23] termed the "kin of sages and mentors.") This is how incest attained the character of a sacred rite—impious but at the same time revelatory—as the only possible way by which humans could find out divine secrets. The idea is suggested also by the linguistic data, as both Aristotle and Freud (1910b) noted, in the phenomenon of so-called "primal words," such as the Latin *sacer,* which means both "sacred" and "accursed." The antithetical sense of the primal words in ancient languages enabled Freud, by analogy, to explain the coincidence of opposites in dreams.

In addition, the psychology of archaic society closely associated magic with handicraft—both called *techne* in Greek—for each trade is a specific form of skill performed by initiated men. It is interesting to note that in some of the oldest versions of the myth, Oedipus is equated with Hephaistus, the divine patron of craftsmen. In the *Oneirocritica* of Artemidoros we read that "the incestuous dream is good for any craftsman, since the craft is usually called 'mother'" (1.79). This association has penetrated deeply into the European tradition, as the persistence of Alma Mater as the most popular appellation for universities attests. During the Middle Ages the idea of the magus-craftsman—the son of his trade who unites with his mother—became a central theme for alchemy and included incest as a structuring principle. Rabinovitch (1985, 6) quotes Jung, who defines alchemy as a "symbolic creation of the collective unconscious rooted in the cultural and biological determinants existing from immemorial times." Myth, in turn, is always magical, and alchemy combines myth, natural philosophy, visual art, and mysticism.

At the basis of alchemical practice is to be found the Aristotelian doctrine of the four elements (*stoicheia*) as well as Plato's theory of the demiurge in the *Timaeus*. But alchemy—the late bloom of Christian gnostic consciousness—adopted these classical sources at second hand and in a dogmatic way. Thus were the cosmogonic principles of Greek philosophy, symbolized by the body of the Sphinx, transformed into alchemical principles whose unification was interpreted as a metaphor for the relation of macrocosm (the universe) to microcosm (the human body), while the combination of these same principles—represented by incest—was considered to be an allegory of alchemical processes. As Jung shows, the alchemists were seeking more or less consciously for a substance that would heal the disharmony both of the world and of the human soul (1959, 354).

Evidence concerning the goal of the alchemists' quest is to be found in the manifold texts dealing with the art of obtaining such a cure-all substance. In the thirteenth century, the famous Salernian physician Arnold of Villanova wrote: "Take the mother [matter] and put her in bed with her sons [the elements], so that she will give birth to a son-sun [gold]" (Höfer 1842, 411). An eighteenth-century text still describes the preparation of a medicine as a symbolic incest between two brothers and their sister (quite similar to the myth of Isis), but with the new social conditions it was interpreted as a symbolic childbirth and a symbolic incest giving birth and life by means of death (Rabinovitch 1985, 245).

These texts recall the symbolic copulation of Oedipus with Jocasta or the Sphinx, who, as I have argued, are two expressions of one essence, one polysemous image of the mother. This idea is further supported by several considerations. First, there is the original folktale of the queen and her riddle. In the Oedipus myth, the functions of the queen are divided between the Sphinx, who sets the riddle, and Jocasta, who obtains her husband as a result of its solution. A modern folk version of the myth actually depicts Jocasta and the Sphinx as one person (Robert 1915, 1:44–45). Then there are the linguistic data from the ancient versions, which reveal the symbolic correspondences of the myth with the cultural and psychological perceptions of the time. Lexically, the Greek verb *gignosko* means both "to know" and "to come in connection with somebody, to copulate." Therefore, "to find an answer to the riddle" equals "to copulate with the woman who asks the riddle." (This is why the ancient folk versions present the guessing of the riddle as a condition for and analogous to the night of love.) There is also the verb *oida*, meaning "to gain knowledge," which is frequently used in the sense of "to be intimately aware of a woman." We find it used thus by Menander (frg. 372), Plutarch (*Alex.*, 21; *Galba*, 9), Callimachus (*Epigr.*, 58.3), and even in the Septuagint (*Gen.*, 4:1).

It is thus clear that the *Weltanschauung* of the ancient Greeks imputed to verbs of knowledge a sense of erotic possession and penetration into the most sacred human secrets. This linguistic material enables us to find a meaning encoded in the name of Oedipus beyond the previously mentioned interpretation of a "man with swollen feet." For, in addition to *oidao* (to swell), in the name of Oedipus is also to be found the verb *oida*, the connection of which to knowledge is hinted at by Aristotle in the *Poetics* (1452 a) when he writes that "recognition, as is shown by the word, means to bear in mind as a result of experience." Such a definition coincides with the image of the thinker seen on Greek vases, as well as with the interpretation of the Sphinx as a symbol of wisdom. What is more, there is abundant evidence from folklore to suggest that the riddle has to be interpreted as a popular version of the famous inscription on the temple at Delphi—*gnothi seauton* ("know thyself")—which marks the beginning of philosophical and medico-scientific interests in Greece.

The act of incest is therefore symbolically associated with extraordinary power and extraordinary knowledge, and makes these interchangeable with each other. Knowledge *is* power. The same nexus also underlies the concept of technology—a special kind of knowledge that enables man to master the secrets of the universe, but leaves him unaware of his inner self. At the close of antiquity, these three lusts of incest, power, and knowledge—symbolically represented in the legend by the crossroads where Oedipus kills his father—were given by St. Augustine (*De civ.*, 14.15) the famous names of *libido carnalis, libido dominandi,* and *curiositas.*

The association of knowledge with power and with man's aspiration to a divine level of existence is fundamental to the psychology of people in the ancient world. For, as a violation of human taboos, incest is also a violation of the boundaries between human and divine realms—that is, an act of self-divination. This is why Oedipus assumes the prerogatives of divinity and puts himself in the position of the primal father in relation to the citizens of Thebes. Yet the arrogance of seeking to rival the Creator also causes man to be smitten by blindness, for blindness symbolizes the turning inward of vision. Pertinent here is the traditional image of the blind poet. Like Oedipus, the artist is guilty of the sin of hubris because the arrogance of his passion to create causes him to rival the Creator. In brief, eyes may give us knowledge of the surface of things, but not of their essence. From its earliest periods, the psychology of Greek culture equated eyes with the deceptiveness of the world and, according to that logic, the sage—the interpreter of the essence—had to be blind.

Thus, the self-blinding of the blindly seeing Oedipus makes him into a blind seer, and transforms surfaces into essences. Indeed, vision and blindness are analogous to the natural cycle of light and darkness and to the rhythm of waking and sleeping, in which all imaginative life begins. Hence art, which Plato called "a dream for awakened minds," seems to have as its final cause the resolution of this antithesis, the mingling of the sun and the hero. "I think," wrote Plutarch, "that the Greeks named man *phos* [light] because of the fact that in each human being there lives one essential desire to know others and to become known to himself" (*De lat. viv.*, 14.6). These words strikingly correspond to the verses by Aeschylus (*Sept.*, lines 541ff.) where the Sphinx is named *phos* as a symbol of *sophia* (wisdom). The same meaning was later assigned by the Romans to the name Lucifer and thereby passed into the European cultural tradition. The tempting devil who lives within each of us, racking our brains to seek the unknown that leads inevitably back to our inner self, bears a name that corresponds to the maxim *gnothi seauton.*

References

Badcock, C. R. 1980. *The Psychoanalysis of Culture.* Oxford: Blackwell.

Freud, S. 1900. *The Interpretation of Dreams.* In *The Standard Edition of the Complete Psychological Works,* ed. and trans. J. Strachey et al., 24 vols. London Hogarth, 1953–74, vols 4 and 5.

———. 1908. Creative Writers and Day-Dreaming. *S.E.,* 9:143–53.

———. 1910a. *Leonardo da Vinci and a Memory of His Childhood. S.E.,* 11:63–137.

———. 1910b. The Antithetical Meaning of Primal Words. *S.E.,* 11:155–61.

———. 1913. *Totem and Taboo. S.E.,* 13:1–161.

———. 1916–17. *Introductory Lectures on Psycho-Analysis. S.E.,* vols. 15 and 16.

———. 1933. *New Introductory Lectures on Psycho-Analysis, S.E.,* 22:7–192.

Höfer, J. C. F. 1842. *Histoire de la chimie,* 2 vols. Paris: Hachette.

Jung, C. G. 1959. *Archetypes of Collective Unconsciousness,* trans. R. F. C. Hull. In *Collected Works,* vol. 9. London: Routledge.

Marx, K. 1971. *The Thought of Karl Marx,* ed. D. McLellan. Harmondsworth: Penguin.

Rabinovitch, A. 1985. *Alchemy as a Phenomenon of Medieval European Culture.* Sofia: Nauka i iskustvo. (In Bulgarian.)

Robert, C. 1915. *Oidipous: Geschichte eines poetischen Stoffs im griechischen Altertum,* 2 vols. Berlin: Weidmannische Buchhandlung.

Roscher, W. H. 1909–15. *Lexicon der Mythologie,* vol. 4. Leipzig: Teubner.

Recognition in Greek Tragedy: Psychoanalytic on Aristotelian Perspectives

Bennett Simon

My aim in this chapter is to argue that psychoanalytic perspectives on Aristotle's use of recognition (*anagnorisis*) amplify the import of these terms in Aristotle; in fact, they constitute a kind of "recognition" of what is latent in Aristotle's highly compressed and terse comments in the *Poetics*. Undoubtedly Aristotle's concept itself planted a seed for the development of psychoanalytic ideas on the subject, just as his concept of catharsis was seminal for psychoanalysis (Simon 1978, 137, 140–44). Greek tragedy, especially Sophocles' *Oedipus Rex,* in turn provided an instantiation for both Aristotle and Freud of what constituted "recognition." Correspondingly, Aristotle and Freud each developed an expanded interpretation of the significance of recognition in *Oedipus Rex*.

The Role of Recognition in Aristotle.

As with any of the key terms in the *Poetics,* there is room for a great deal of controversy about the meaning and the significance of *anagnorisis*.

I thank Amelie Rorty for her considerable help, both with the substance and with organization of this chapter, particularly in regard to most effective use of the clinical material. Also, thanks to Amy and Leon Kass for an important discussion on self-recognition in Aristotle's *Ethics* and to Peter Rudnytsky for his thoughtful critique and editing.

In what follows, I will argue, based partly on my own reading of Aristotle and partly on that of Gerald Else, that *anagnorisis* constitutes a pivotal concept in the structure and argument of the *Poetics*.[1]

Recognition is one of the keys for the dramatically successful representation and resolution of the terrible events in tragedy. How do playwrights render the stories that constitute tragic plots in such a form that audiences can view and enjoy them? This is the question, I believe, that Aristotle's formal discourse on the structure and function of tragic dramas (as well as of poetry in general) implicitly addresses. The example he selects to demonstrate the pleasure we derive from *mimesis*—seeing pictures of "despised animals and of corpses"—adumbrates his position that tragedy gives us pleasure by virtue of its ability to represent (or imitate) some really awful things (1448 b, 10–11; Sinaiko 1984, 449).[2]

Aristotle discusses tragedy from the point of view of the formal devices that implement the proper function of tragedy—the *mimesis* of a significant action, the *mimesis* of a *bios* of a person. But he assumes that the stuff of which the great tragedies are made must correspond to something fundamental in our own psychology. In general, I believe he locates that which is fundamental *en tais philais,* in our family relationships and in our feelings about them. Prominent in our psychological endowment is the capacity for recognition and, as tragedy teaches us, the capacity for misrecognition and nonrecognition as well. Jocasta does not recognize that the young man who has defeated the Sphinx, married her, and begotten children with her is her own son. Even more brutally, Clytemnestra, having failed in *The Libation Bearers* to recognize that the stranger from Phocis is her own son, recognizes him as the snake-murderer only as he approaches her with an ax. And for Agave, in *The Bacchae,* the lion that she has hunted in Bacchic ecstasy and torn limb from limb proves to be her son, a sequence of misrecognition followed by recognition that is one of the most painful in literature. Heracles, too, in Euripides' *Madness of Heracles* mistakes his own children for his enemies, slays them, and converts his palace, recently besieged by his actual enemy, into the palace of an enemy that he is besieging. These recognitions and misrecognitions are powerful, horrible, and painful.

The importance of recognition for Aristotle resides not only in its power as a technical device, but in the way it overlaps with other key terms in his thought—*mimesis, hamartia,* catharsis, and metaphor. Tragic recognitions involve a form of self-recognition, an enhancement of the appreciation and awareness of who one is, especially as determined by kinship ties. Although Aristotle does not enunciate this proposition in either the *Poetics* or any other of his works, it can be shown to be compatible with his beliefs. As we shall see, a psychoanalytic interpretation of Aristotle makes this assumption explicit.

According to Aristotle, "recognition, as in fact the term itself indicates, is a shift from ignorance to awareness, pointing either to a state of close natural ties (blood relationship) or to one of enmity, on the part of those persons who have been in a clearly marked status with respect to prosperity or misfortune" (*Poetics,* 52 a, 30–32; trans. Else). As Else explicates Aristotle's meaning:

Tragic recognition is the discovery, by a person who has been in a clearly defined status of "happiness" or "unhappiness," of the identity of a naturally dear person with whom he has been involved, or is in danger of being involved, in a fatal act.... The effect of the recognition, in general, is to uncover a horrible discrepancy between two sets of relationships: on the one hand the deep ties of blood, on the other a casual or real relation of hostility that has supervened or threatened to supervene upon it.... [i]ts emotional power... depends on the tension inherent in this discrepancy; ultimately, therefore, upon the deep-seated, immemorial power of the taboo against the shedding of kindred blood.... Recognition is in fact a way in which the emotional potential inherent in certain human situations can be brought to its highest voltage, so to speak, at the moment of discharge. It is evident, then, how far Aristotle is from regarding recognition merely as a "plot-device," a matter of technique. Tragic recognition is indeed a technical device, but its *raison d'être* is its power to concentrate an intense emotional charge upon a single event, a change of awareness; for in that *metabolé* the whole depth of a human tragedy can be "contained." (1967, 352–53)

Although recognition is not a necessary ingredient of tragedy, since only "complex" but not "simple" plots contain scenes of recognition, Aristotle clearly values and praises those works where it is important, such as *Oedipus Rex, Iphigenia in Tauris,* and Homer's *Odyssey.*

Else further argues that the difficult concept of *hamartia,* which literally means "missing the mark," as in archery, but is commonly rendered "tragic flaw," is illustrated by a failure of recognition, and that such a failure may indeed be what Aristotle means by *hamartia:*

Recognition is a change *ex agnoias eis gnosin* [from ignorance to knowledge]; might not *hamartia* be the *agnoia* [ignorance] from which the change begins? Moreover tragic recognition, or the best tragic recognition, is a discovery of the identity of a "dear" person, a blood-relative; it follows that the precedent *ha-*

martia would denote particularly a mistake or error or ignorance as to the identity of that person. (1967, 379; my translations of Greek phrases)

Else realizes the boldness of the suggestion, but convincingly proposes that "the correlation of *hamartia* and recognition as interdependent parts of the best tragic plot explains everything that Aristotle says about both of them. . . . Our findings show that *hamartia* also is a part of the plot" (385). From Else's perspective, *hamartia* is organically related to the processes of recognition and nonrecognition. To expand on his discussion, it is clear that Aristotle cannot mean complete "ignorance," but rather an ignorance or nonrecognition that adumbrates grounds for the not knowing. If there is no reason for the protagonist to fail to recognize someone, then a deity must have a motive to produce that failure. In *The Libation Bearers*, chiefly human motives are suggested for Clytemnestra's nonrecognition of her son; both human and divine motives are operative in Agave's misrecognition in *The Bacchae*, while in *The Madness of Heracles* divine motives, however obscure, are more prominent than human motives. But in all these instances, from both an Aristotelean and a psychoanalytic perspective, there is enough evidence to cause the audience to suspect that there is some method to the construction of the ignorance. I would, then, read *hamartia* as referring to this sort of ignorance, a sort of which we are all perfectly capable given the proper circumstances, because it arises from a full engagement with the ambiguities, conflicts, and uncertainties of the world.

As *anagnorisis* is connected to *hamartia*, so is it also to *mimesis*, since both refer to a recognition of the essential elements that characterize a person or object. In this sense, *anagnorisis* and *mimesis* are both species of the genus of the cognitive-affective activity "defining the essentials."[3] Else argues that the recognition of an object via a *mimesis* (implicit in Aristotle's argument at 48 b, 4–24) entails the recognition "that he or she is a so-and-so," an example of the species of thus-and-thus. Though the term *anagnorisis* is not used here, this passage implies that unless the object in question has previously been seen and known to the viewer, there will be no pleasure in the act of imitation, but merely in local details of color or form. Thus, the pleasure derived from an imitation depends upon some process of *re*-cognition. In this line of argument, it is possible to see that a writer's representation of a traditional character constitutes an interpretation of a facet of that character that had hitherto not been obvious or emphasized in the myth or other versions of the drama. The form of the interpretation, were it to be stated as a proposition, might be, for example: This behavior is a species of the genus "self-deception." The fourth Stasimon of Sophocles' *Antigone* is an instance of the chorus making an *interpretation:* the chorus interprets the conflict between Antigone and Creon, especially Creon's behavior, via the myth of Danäe, as an example of the species "difficult father-daughter interactions—where the father will not give up his daughter to a marriage" (Simon 1984, 424–26). Such an analogy has broad reverberations. In fact, Creon will not allow his *son,* Haemon, to marry Antigone, but his fight with Antigone also has the emotional overtones of the typical father in Greek myth who cannot relinquish a daughter. At a deeper level of emotional reverberation, this coupling of Antigone and Creon belongs with tales of both parental and sibling incestuous binding, so that Antigone-Polyneices, Oedipus-Jocasta and their children, and Creon-Antigone all have a common denominator.

Like representations, metaphors articulate similarities. Moreover, metaphor, like *mimesis* and *anagnorisis,* can also be seen as a form of perspective, often a new perspective, and hence as a species of interpretation. Aristotle briefly comments on metaphor near the end of the *Poetics,* where he assigns it a privileged place among the poetic gifts: "but by far the most important matter is to have skill in the use of metaphor. This skill is . . . a sign of genius. For the ability to construct good metaphors implies the ability to see essential similarities (*to gar eu metapherein to to homoion theorein estin*) 1459 a; (trans. L. Golden, Golden and Hardison 1981).

As Humphrey Morris has pointed out to me, the Latinate translation of *metaphora* is "transference"; this suggests that the patient's transference experienced in analysis is a kind of metaphor. A brief clinical vignette can serve as an illustration.

A young male patient adores his male analyst, repeatedly expressing great gratitude, but occasionally and unpredictably getting surly and rebellious with the analyst. The patient exclaims that "we were swimming along so nicely and suddenly something has gone wrong between us." The analyst puts this metaphor together with the patient's history of an intense relationship with his high school swimming coach and makes the interpretation that the patient has been relating to him on the model of his relationship to that coach. Idealization, gratitude, and, apparently, fits of rebellion are part of the current picture, and they must have been all part of the relationship with the coach. The patient then realizes that the times he had gotten angry with the coach were times when the coach seemed either inattentive to him or more attentive to another swimmer. The patient continues and says how clarifying this is—he never understood how or why he got so angry with the coach. The analyst now adds that the recent occasion when the patient was suddenly surly with the analyst had to do with the analyst's having been called away unexpectedly for an emergency and having to cancel a session.

Here we may note that the psychoanalytic concepts of transference and interpretation are intrinsically connected. While the analyst's interpretation of the evolving transference is considered the psychoanalytic activity par excellence, we must add that establishing the transference involves an act of creation, of finding a similarity, on the patient's part. Transference manifestations help to capture and articulate aspects of the analyst's work or person, of which neither the analyst nor the patient had previously been fully aware. In this instance the analyst is the beloved coach, who from time to time disappoints his young athlete. The understanding of both the past history and the present situation is clarified by the several different kinds of "finding similarities" that characterize the activity both of the analyst and the patient.

For many contemporary analysts, the patient's constructing and reconstructing of his or her past is thus a form of interpretation and constitutes the basic mental activity that is scrutinized in the analysis. Freud's early idea of *Nachträglichkeit* ("after-recognition" or "deferred action," the after-processing of a trauma or a memory) implies both that the patient later reinterprets an earlier "event" as a trauma—i.e., names it, categorizes it, "recognizes" it for what it was—and also that this "after-recognition" is the method by which the early event is fully activated and experienced (Modell 1990).

Let us turn to another aspect of recognition, the question of whether or not *anagnorisis* of someone else implicitly involves some sort of self-recognition. Maxwell Anderson, writing as a playwright about recognition scenes in Greek tragedy and considering the central role that Aristotle ascribes to recognition, says:

Now scenes of exactly this sort are rare in modern drama except in detective stories adapted for the stage. But when I probed a little more deeply into the memorable pieces of Shakespeare's theatre and our own I began to see that though modern recognition scenes are subtler and harder to find, they are none the less present in the plays we choose to remember. They seldom have to do with anything so naïve as disguise or the unveiling of personal identity. But the element of discovery is just as important as ever. For the mainspring in the mechanism of a modern play is almost invariably a discovery by the hero of some element in his environment or his own soul of which he has not been aware—or which he has not taken sufficiently into account (1939, 116)

Anderson here suggests that the postclassical equivalent of recognition is to be found in self-discovery. While this is true enough, he does not take into account some of the great plots of recognition and nonrecognition in Shakespeare, especially *King Lear*. Cordelia's awakening of Lear and his simultaneous recognition of both herself and himself is one of the most powerful in all of literature, as powerful in its own way as Oedipus' recognition of who he is and to whom he is kin.

Both the truth and the distortion in Anderson's characterization of modern drama are illuminating for our purposes. Ours is a psychological age, strongly influenced by Freud, who was, in turn, part of a literary culture of growing inwardness in the second half of the nineteenth century. "Self-discovery" has been a major theme in modern literature and drama since Ibsen, just as the self has emerged as a subject of particular preoccupation in drama of the last few decades, whether in its hypertrophied presence or in its alleged disintegration and nonexistence. Indeed, some modern plays probe a literal loss of self, a complete failure of self-recognition in the form of clinical amnesia, with all the attendant consequences. Prime examples include Pirandello's *Henri IV* and Giraudoux's *Traveller without Baggage*. In the former, a young Italian aristocrat commits a murder of a rival at a historical pageant, then falls off his horse, hits his head, and becomes delusionally convinced he is Henri IV of Canossa. To protect what is left of his fragile equilibrium, he is allowed to organize a court and keep soldiers to maintain this delusion. After a number of years, the family decides to hire a doctor to try and cure him. One begins to see his delusion waver, and his struggle between renouncing and holding onto it. The doctor's strategy misfires, as "Henri" again commits a murder and announces at the end that now he must remain Henri forever. Giraudoux's play explores both the intrapsychic and the familial contexts of why and how a man with an amnesia and loss of personal identity, allegedly due to shell-shock in the

Great War, should be reluctant to regain that identity. As he recognizes the greed, betrayal, lying, and brutality in the family that probably is his, he becomes clearer about why he is better off without memory.

Plays such as these combine the literal recognition themes of Greek tragedies and the themes of discovery of something in oneself in modern drama as characterized by Maxwell Anderson. They also forge a link between Aristotelian and psychoanalytic perspectives on recognition. For these plays, using concrete scenes of recognition and nonrecognition, make explicit what is implicit in the ancient works—the motives, conscious and less than conscious, for nonrecognition. They expand upon the relatively schematic terms of Greek tragedy and Aristotelian philosophy having to do with volition and conscious knowledge, dichotomies such as willing-unwilling, knowing-not knowing (Schütrumpf 1989). Both plays make more explicit than most other modern dramas that even a failure of "self-recognition" is not an autistic act, but rather takes place in a familial and social context that is determined by who one is in relation to kin and where one belongs in the sequence of generations. The importance of events *en tais philais,* among those who are near and dear, unites ancient, Shakespearean, and modern drama, even though the more detailed examination and representation of the introspective world of the protagonists in modern drama may obscure that commonality (Simon 1988).

While modern readers of Greek tragedies take it for granted that misrecognition and nonrecognition of another person in those plays signal a failure of the protagonist to recognize a part of herself or himself, it is fair to ask whether Aristotle made a similar assumption. Although nothing in Aristotle contradicts such an assumption, explicit statments to this effect about tragedy are lacking. Martha Nussbaum calls attention to the broader implications of recognition in her discussion of Aristotle on friendship. She cites a passage from the *Magna Moralia* to show the relational basis of self-knowledge:

Now if someone, looking to his *philos,* should see what he is and of what sort of character, the *philos*—if we imagine a *philia* of the most intense sort—would seem to him to be like a second himself, as in the saying, "This is my second Heracles." Since, then, it is both a most difficult thing, as some of the sages have also said, to know oneself, and also a most pleasant thing (for to know oneself is pleasant)—moreover, we cannot ourselves study ourselves from ourselves, as is clear from the reproaches we bring against others without being aware that we do the same things ourselves—and this happens because of bias or passion, which in many of us obscures the accuracy of judgments; as, then, when we ourselves wish to see our own face we see it by looking into a mirror, similarly too, when we ourselves wish to know ourselves, we would know ourselves by looking to the *philos*. For the *philos*, as we say, is another oneself. If, then, it is pleasant to know oneself, and if it is not possible to know this without having someone else as *philos*, the self-sufficient person would need *philia* in order to know himself. (1213 a, 10–26)

Nussbaum comments:

Aristotle's argument begins from a fact of human psychology: it is difficult for each of us to see our own life clearly and without bias, assessing its patterns of action and commitment. Often we lack awareness of our own faults, because we are blinded by partiality and by involvement in our own feelings and concerns. It is therefore valuable to study the pattern of good character embodied in another good life: "It is easier for us to look at someone else than at ourselves" (*Nichomachean Ethics*, 1169 b, 33–34). This reflective look at models of goodness enhances our understanding of our own character and aspirations, improving self-criticism and sharpening judgment. For this to be so, the model in question must be a person similar to ourselves in character and aspiration, someone whom we can identify to ourselves as "another oneself" for the purpose of this scrutiny. (1986, 364)

The protagonists of tragedy more commonly come to self-recognition through collision with an enemy or opponent, whether human or divine. Aristotle's use of the proverb "a second Heracles" illuminates this aspect of recognition and self-recognition especially if it carries an allusion to Euripides' *Madness of Heracles*. Heracles, after his murderous misidentification of his own wife and children, does come to recognize at least part of himself as worthy of self-forgiveness and forswears suicide. With the help of his father and, above all, of Theseus (who can be considered a "second Heracles"), he realizes himself to be a worthy companion, a stalwart hero, loving and capable of receiving love and forgiveness.

Nussbaum's book as a whole posits that there is a significant overlap between Aristotle's view of moral stature and moral choice and the rich and complex portrayal of these issues in tragedy. But, to my knowledge, Aristotle does not himself explicitly draw the conclusion that modern writers such as Anderson and psychoanalysts do about tragedy as a means to increased self-recognition either by the protagonists or by the audience.

Psychoanalytic Perspectives on Recognition

Most discussions of Aristotle's concept of *anagnorisis* fail to make clear that not being recognized by one's own kin is an extremely painful and devastating experience. Consider the all-too-common situation of the failures of recognition associated with serious organic brain disorders, such as Alzheimer's disease. Even though we realize that a family member's failure to identify us has to do with old age and/or brain disease, and not primarily with motivated, let alone malicious, misrecognition, we can easily take this phenomenon quite personally. Relatives of patients with Alzheimer's often experience enormous pain and at times understandable anger at not being recognized by their loved one (or, worse, by their ambivalently regarded one).

But clinical psychoanalytic practice gives us an opportunity to examine and understand less florid instances of nonrecognition: the everyday embarrassment at not being able to recall the name of or to place a person whom one knows quite well and about whom one may feel quite ambivalently. " 'I did this,' says my Memory. 'I cannot have done this,' says my Pride and remains inexorable. In the end—Memory yields." Thus wrote Nietzsche, and Freud, approvingly, cites this passage several times (Simon 1978, 260–63). Remembering, thinking, perceiving, recognizing—these are all corruptible, given sufficient motive to distort and to deny.

The core psychoanalytic approach to recognition, misrecognition, and nonrecognition is to search for the unconscious motive that leads to repression or denial of the person in question, who will typically be found close to home. Failure to acknowledge the importance or existence of a significant other is a variant on the failure to recognize, a theme elegantly elaborated by Stanley Cavell in his writings, but most notably in relation to Shakespeare's *King Lear* (Cavell 1969). Sometimes we discover that a patient has a very selective amnesia concerning a period of her or his life or a particular person from that period. The discovery of the significance of such an amnesia—the acknowledgment and recognition that ensue—unfolds in the following sequence of a dream and its interpretation. The material is abstracted from the treatment of a woman by a male analyst.[4]

She was a young married woman, a scientist, who sought psychoanalytic treatment because of agoraphobia and claustrophobia that suddenly commenced several years after marriage, as well as some unhappiness in that marriage and uncertainties in her career. She was quite conflicted about whether or not to have a baby and clearly resented her family's pressure for her to "produce a grandchild." She presented herself alternately as open, curious, and eager to learn and as closed, blocked, and scrupulously compartmentalizing different areas of knowledge about the people around her. Soon after beginning treatment, she also acknowledged hatred for her next younger sister, a hatred that she sensed was either excessive or by now at least inappropriate. We learned after some time that, paradoxically, she remembered much of the mother's pregnancy with that sister and details about that sister as an infant—she was between three and four during the mother's pregnancy—but had a total amnesia for similar details of the mother's pregnancy and birth of the beloved next younger sister, born when the patient was about eight. This realization emerged in the context of discussion of her dread about having children: first, they hurt you in being born and then they take over your life.

She narrated the following dream, which occurred after a holiday gathering of her extended family:

The dream is in three parts, but I can only remember the first and the third. The middle part is missing. It is dark; there is a sphinxlike presence in the room. This "presence" asks questions. In the first part of the dream the question is, "Why were you born?" In the third part the question is, "Are you dead?" There were answers, I know, but I can't recapture them.

Both the patient and I were quite struck by the form of the dream, and the patient recalled that on the evening of the dream there had been a TV program, a detective story patterned after *Oedipus Rex,* with a sphinx-like character who posed difficult questions. She realized both from the program and from her own fund of knowledge that the riddle of the sphinx and its answer, "Man," was the frame story of the dream. But where was she as "Oedipus"? Was I the sphinx? Was she the sphinx, as she also prided herself on being enigmatic? Was she also Oedipus? Was I an Oedipus too?[5]

As her stream of associations flowed over the next few sessions, it emerged that the interactions at the family gathering converged around the question of who is having a baby, when, and why someone of the appropriate age is not having a baby. It gradually became clearer to the patient that her seemingly unresolvable conflict about whether or not to have a baby had a lot to do with the sense that she would not be acknowledged as a full human being and member of the family unless she had a child. She resented this as well as the corollary: if she had a child, she would not be acknowledged as a person in her own right, but only as the mother of another family member. It also became clearer that her struggles had to do with a long-standing awareness of difficult and perhaps intractable conflicts within the extended family. But then, over several sessions, she began to sense uncannily that something was about to emerge, something disgusting and too big for her too handle. The analyst made the interpretation that it was as if something was struggling to be born, and that the "birth" of memories associated with very unpleasant feelings was imminent. She then began to piece together puzzling fragments of memory and isolated pictures in her mind. The story that unfolded was that her paternal grandmother had died of stomach cancer and that her childhood understanding was that something bad was growing inside her grandmother's tummy, "something that eats you up and kills you." Patient and analyst gradually began to realize that the period of the grandmother's dying coincided with the patient's mother's pregnancy with the youngest sister, for which she had a near-total amnesia. Suggestions and interpretations of the analyst helped both him and the patient to recognize that memories of the sick grandmother, even memories of her body, were emerging, some for the first time.

She felt sad and helpless, recalling all the family conflict around taking care of the sick grandmother; a bitter feud between her father and his sister (her aunt) must have taken place during that period and had to do with caring for their sick mother. She then recalled, with amazement, the missing second part of the dream: the question asked was, "Are you my sister?" She surmised that an angry question like that must have been part of the arguments between her father and her aunt: "Are you my sister or not—if you are then you take care of her too!" She then recalled the answers to the questions posed in the dream: "Why were you born?"—"I don't know." "Are you dead?"—"Not yet!" She could not recall an answer to the middle question, "Are you my sister?" but went on to associate to the distressing, long-standing enmity between herself and her next younger sister. She began to realize that her own recognition and acknowledgment of that sister were deficient, that she could do better (as could the sister) in mutual acknowledgment of each other's rightful place in the family. That process of full recognition and acknowledgment had been impaired by the major rift between a sister and brother (her father and aunt), and that rift, in effect (along with other major conflicts inside the young child), helped obliterate the memory of the pregnancy and homecoming of another sister. An immediate practical result of these analytic discussions was a serious effort by the patient and her sister to deal with their ancient conflicts and rivalries. That effort did not produce a dramatic turnabout, but led to a good beginning in a new, adult relationship between them. She also then recalled the missing answer to the previously missing middle question, "Are you my sister?" "Perhaps," was the reply.

We needed to clarify further why she had had an amnesia for the birth of the beloved sister, instead for the birth of the hated sister. Her own rivalries with her mother had to be considered, as did her thwarted closeness with her father. There were numerous indications that family conflicts around the dying grandmother, and other conflicts between the mother and father, had interfered with a more ordinary resolution of her age-appropriate wishes to have a baby with the father and to have the mother play second fiddle. Sadness at the relative unavailability of both parents during that time, and the blow to her pride that she could not take the mother's place fully in the father's passions and affections, together contributed to blotting out the memories of the pregnancy. The amnesia constituted a refusal to recognize the origins of that beloved sister, because she needed to deny her own forbidden, guilt-ridden wishes and other attendant painful affects.

At bottom, this dream, its associations, the retrieved and reconstructed memories, and the interpretations constituted a form of self-recognition for the patient. She learned or, better, *realized* that she needed a new definition of herself as a sister, as a daughter, and as a potential mother. Her conflicts, her thwarted wishes, and her defenses against those wishes contributed to a complementary nonrecognition of her sister(s), her mother, her father, her aunt, and her grandmother. In the wake of the dream and its elaboration, all of these relationships and perceptions underwent subtle but significant changes.

There were other recognitions possible, some of which were actualized at various junctures later in the treatment. One such was a recognition of her fantasies and fears about the analyst and his wife, her recapitulating with the analyst the childhood tale of attempted wooing of the father, combined with wishes that the father would be a regular father and stick with his wife, her mother. Recognitions of aspects of the analyst as sphinx also emerged—mysterious, dangerous, alluring, exciting, aloof, and partly female.

There were new perceptions of herself as a woman-Oedipus: a very curious and inquisitive person, with good "detective" and investigative skills. She had allowed her curiosity to flourish in her scientific work but stifled it in her personal relationships. The analyst came to know and acknowledge aspects of the patient that he had sensed, but had not fully appreciated—such as the liveliness of her passionate emotional life as a little girl, the extent to which she keenly observed and took in everything about her family, and the extent to which she had created defensive barriers against expressing her formidable inquisitiveness and search for personal understanding. The analyst, in the course of his self-analysis, recognized pieces of himself in the patient's struggles and defenses, and recognized some of the forces and conflicts that had to some extent kept him "ignorant" of this patient. He realized that some of his own inhibitions against confronting the patient and in making important interpretations were based on his own fantasies that his interpretations were "planting a seed" in the patient, and that his own oedipal fantasies, confusing "insemination" and "seminal ideas," had been mobilized. He also realized a dimension of the Oedipus story not previously at the center of his attention, namely, how much that story was a tale of thwarted reproduction, of an interference in the generational chain. Thus, the processes of recognition and acknowledgment continued and ramified into different areas of the patient's psyche, the analyst's psyche, and the process of the psychoanalysis.

While the details of this person and her dream are idiosyncratic, the case illustrates general principles about the working through of defenses against memory and recognition. In the material presented, the experiences that were traumatic for the patient were within the realm of ones to be expected from growing up in a family and in the world. A more complete account of the woman's history would have to include a variety of externally imposed traumas, ranging from threats of nuclear destruction in her childhood to some inappropriate practices by her parents around sexual issues.

Her pain, disappointment, and poignant attempts as a little girl to work out the mysteries of birth, copulation, death, and the attendant familial relations, while not so exotic or rare, are nevertheless in their own way dramatic. They were certainly dramatic for the child experiencing them, and were again dramatic for the adult woman retrieving and reliving them. They became part of an intense drama for the analyst, a drama that included the patient and the persons in her life—living and dead—and, secondarily, persons living and dead in the life of the analyst. The audience for these dramas now includes readers of this chapter. There is, then, an analogy between the concentrically expanding analytic processes of recognition, acknowledgment, and appreciation and the processes that occur with a tragic performance. There, just as the characters within the play move to new levels of recognition, so too both the audience and actors can grow in their recognitions and self-recognitions.

This analogy leads us to a brief consideration of the way psychoanalysis has viewed tragic drama. Originally, Freud and his followers assumed that the dramas reflect the intensity of the wishes and passions of the developing child. The tragic dramas were external representations of the scenarios played out in the inner world of the child.[6] I would amend the traditional psychoanalytic assumptions about the relation between psyche and tragic drama to propose that tragic dramas portray two kinds of stories that overlap and are condensed: the internal dramas of childhood wishes and fears, and the external horrors of the world. These external horrors instantiate the internally derived nightmares of the person, and the internal wishes and dreads in turn help to construe, shape, and label the experience of the externally imposed traumata.[7]

Trauma and Recognition

Let us imagine that a papyrus with portions of a hitherto unknown Greek tragedy has recently been discovered and now translated and edited, but not as yet published. It appears that the story involves a "recognition" scene, a scene involving tokens or marks (which Aristotle considers a somewhat inferior form of recognition). Two children, a brother and sister, as infants, had been captured in war and sold into slavery. They had been separated from each other, and years later their respective owners met and decided to arrange a match between these two slaves. Of course neither owners nor slaves knew of their connection. The papyrus lacks some crucial details, but we have a scene where each realizes that a particular peculiar tattooing on her or his body, used by their owners as a basis for naming them, is a complementary part of a design that, when placed together, allows them to recognize each other as siblings. The tale seems to imply that their parents, probably the mother, had tattooed these designs on the children so that later either she or the siblings could recognize one another.

The story I've presented is a conflation of a true story from World War II with a tale (perhaps true too) from a first-century Rabbinic source about the terrible things that happened to the Jews after their defeat by the Romans and the destruction of the Holy Temple.[8] The true story involves a Jewish family in western Europe, where the mother realized that the Nazis would arrive shortly, and injected her children with the only marker at hand, some India ink. She feared that either they might not recognize her or she them or they each other if they became separated. The "happy ending" to the real-life story was that the children were separated from each other, and from the mother, but not for so long that memory faded.[9] Such stories could be multiplied many thousands of times from the Holocaust, World War II, and a painfully large number of wars since then, especially the Cambodian genocide. This mother's reflexive wish to help protect her children and do something in the face of an overwhelming threat addressed not only the actual physical dangers but also the emotional dangers of traumatic separation. It is frequently the experience of wars that parents and children who separately have been through horrendous experiences might still recognize each other physically, but emotionally they scarcely know each other (cf. the young protagonist in Jerzy Kosinski's *Painted Bird*). The tale from the Rabbinic Midrash is itself a mini-tragedy, and undoubtedly reflects the horrors of what indeed took place with the slaughter and enslavement of the defeated Jews.

It is my contention that the stuff of tragic dramas from antiquity to the present is drawn not only from the unconscious wishes and fears of childhood, but also from the horrors of the world in which the tragedians have lived—whether Greek antiquity, Elizabethan England, or postwar Europe. These traumas are presented and represented in forms whereby we can both recognize and not recognize them as parts of our own world. Classical Greece was a culture in which the horrors of war were well known (though the modern horrors could scarcely have been imagined), in which exposure of children at birth was utterly plausible,[10] and where there may well have been a certain amount of actual incest (though less than in our time), and where a certain number of mothers may have killed their children.[11] These actualities are made "presentable" first and foremost by placing them in mythological settings, and then by using all of the artistic devices of tragic drama, many of which are set forth in the *Poetics*. Aristotle's treatise is thus also a guidebook on how we should simultaneously distance ourselves from and involve ourselves in the worlds of external trauma and of internal dreads and dreaded wishes. It is, in effect, a compendium of the artistic devices by which we both recognize and fail to recognize ourselves in these fearful scenarios.

Notes

1. For a succint and balanced discussion of critical interpretations of Aristotle on *anagnorisis*, see Terence Cave's *Recognitions: A Study in Poetics* (1988), esp. pp. 27–53. Cave's book is the most comprehensive study of recognition in literature and unfortunately came to my attention after the drafting of this essay. It raises a host of intepretative questions about recognition that go beyond my present scope.

2. Else (1967, 128) argues that the imitations in question are not works of art, such as paintings, which Greek art had not yet taken up, but rather biological models and diagrams or sketches.

3. I find some textual support for this argument, again aided by Else's discussion of Aristotle's brief comments on *mimesis* (1967, 131–32).

4. The case is partly fictionalized for reasons of confidentiality. Of course, this means that we are here instantiating problems of recognition. We wish for nonrecognition, i.e., to disguise the patient in order to preserve confidentiality, but the report must also be accurate enough that it is recognizable as a true case and as a plausible dream.

5. Peter Rudnytsky draws my attention to the striking parallel to Nietzsche's questions in *Beyond Good and Evil:* "Who of us is Oedipus here? Who the Sphinx? It is a rendezvous, it seems, of questions and question marks" (Rudnytsky 1987, 91).

6. A interesting variant on this view, elaborated by George Devereux (1970), is that tragic drama represents not so much stories in the unconscious, but rather the processes of the unconscious at work. Overall, different psychoanalytic theories and schools have designated one or another conflictual schema as the central dramatic theme which fuels the great tragic dramas and makes them so appealing to an audience.

7. How would Aristotle have responded to the discoveries of psychoanalysis? What would he have made of unconscious impulses, defense mechanisms, free association, transference, slips of the tongue, infantile sexuality, and the

126   Bennett Simon

Oedipus complex? I believe he would have been quite curious and fascinated, but also cautious, even suspicious. This question deserves serious extended discussion, to which this chapter is only a preliminary contribution.

8. I learned of this tale, which is in the Midrash of the Book of Lamentations, from Prof. Galit Chazan-Rokem of the Department of Folklore of the Hebrew University; she has detailed and discussed the tale in a Hebrew publication.

9. "Happy ending" also alludes to the problem of recognition in comedy and romance. The recognitions and failures of recognitions in Shakespeare's comedies and romances typically involve story lines of rather painful and traumatic events. But I have not been able to arrive at a more general psychoanalytic theory of recognition in all genres of literature.

10. We do not have direct knowledge of exposure of children in Athens in the fifth century; B.C.E. most of our evidence (primarily concerning girls) comes from later centuries, but the fact of its existence in later centuries and the extensive mythology of exposure (mostly concerning boys) suggest strongly the existence of the practice in the fifth century as well.

11. In relation to Euripides' *Medea* Easterling (1977) raised the question of how often mothers actually kill their children. Reviewing police statistics from England and Scandinavia, she found that such killings occur much more frequently than we would care to believe.

References

Anderson, M. 1939. The Essence of Tragedy. *Aristotle's Poetics and English Literature: A Collection of Critical Essays,* ed. E. Olson. Chicago: Univ. of Chicago Press, 1965, pp. 114–121.

Cave, T. 1988. *Recognitions: A Study in Poetics.* Oxford: Clarendon Press.

Cavell, S. 1969. The Avoidance of Love: A Reading of *King Lear.* In *Disowning Knowledge in Six Plays of Shakespeare.* Cambridge: Cambridge Univ. Press, 1987, pp. 39–124.

Devereux, G. 1970. The Structure of Tragedy and the Structure of the Psyche in Aristotle's *Poetics.* In *Psychoanalysis and Philosophy,* ed. C. Hanly and M. Lazerowitz. New York: International Univ. Press, pp. 46–75.

Easterling, P. E. 1977. The Infanticide in Euripides' *Medea. Yale Classical Studies* 25:177–92.

Else, G. 1967. *Aristotle's Poetics: The Argument.* Cambridge, MA: Harvard Univ. Press.

Golden, L. and O. B. Hardison, Jr. 1981. *Aristotle's Poetics: A Translation and Commentary for Students of Literature.* Tallahassee: Univ. Presses of Florida.

Modell, A. 1990. *Other Times, Other Realities.* Cambridge, MA: Harvard Univ. Press.

Nussbaum, M. 1986. *The Fragility of Goodness: Luck and Ethics in Greek Tragedy and Philosophy.* Cambridge: Cambridge Univ. Press.

Rudnytsky, P. L. 1987. *Freud and Oedipus.* New York: Columbia Univ. Press.

Schütrumpf, E. 1989. Traditional Elements in the Concept of *Hamartia* in Aristotle's *Poetics. Harvard Studies in Classical Philology* 92:137–56.

Simon, B. 1978. *Mind and Madness in Ancient Greece: The Classical Roots of Modern Psychiatry.* Ithaca: Cornell Univ. Press.

———. 1984. With Cunning Delays and Ever Mounting Excitement; or, What Thickens the Plot in Tragedy and Psychoanalysis. In *Psychoanalysis: The Vital Issues,* vol. 2 of *Clinical Psychoanalysis and Its Applications,* ed. G. H. Pollock and J. E. Gedo. New York: International Univ. Press, pp. 387–436.

———. 1988. *Tragic Drama and the Family: Psychoanalytic Studies from Aeschylus to Beckett.* New Haven: Yale Univ. Press.

Sinaiko, H. 1984. Tragedy and Psychoanalysis. In *Psychoanalysis: The Vital Issues,* vol. 2 of *Clinical Psychoanalysis and Its Applications,* ed. G. H. Pollock and J. E. Gedo. New York: International Univ. Press, pp. 437–62.

SEVEN

Freud and Augustine

Peter L. Rudnytsky

What is the difference? Whether it is in a wife
or a mother, it is still Eve (the temptress) that
we must beware of in any woman.
—St. Augustine, Ep. 243

St. Augustine and Freud constitute indispensable points of reference in
a distinctive tradition in Western thought. This tradition is in the first
instance that of autobiography. For Augustine's *Confessions* (c. 397)
initiates the enterprise of systematic self-scrutiny in writing, whose notable descendants include Montaigne, Rousseau, and Wordsworth, and
which culminates in Freud's *Interpretation of Dreams* (1900).

But if Augustine and Freud are equally adept practitioners of the
anomalous genre in which a single self is both author and protagonist,
there is likewise a remarkable congruence between their philosophical
outlooks. Although Augustine is a theologian and Freud a psychoanalyst,
the two thinkers are at one in holding that the human race is guilty of
a primordial transgression and in their attempts to account for the human
condition through a single myth of all-embracing explanatory power. In
both *Totem and Taboo* (1913) and *Moses and Monotheism* (1939) Freud
seeks to derive the concept of original sin from his own hypothesis of
the killing of the primal father. Acknowledging the kinship between
himself and Augustine, Freud avers: "The Early Christian Father's '*inter*

urinas et faeces nascimur' clings to sexual life and cannot be detached from it in spite of every effort at idealization" (1905, 31).

Thus, together with their allegiance to autobiography, Freud and Augustine articulate definitive versions of the two dominant myths of Western culture—Oedipus and the Fall. Because of this dovetailing of form and content, their narratives refract one another. As John Freccero has remarked, Augustine's *Confessions* provides perhaps the "first literary expression" of a psychological pattern "named after Oedipus since Freud" (1986, 19). As Augustine invents the form of autobiography in a work that is structured by the oedipal paradigm, so Freud epochally interprets *Oedipus the King* in a work that consummates by its elaboration of the concept of the unconscious the paradox whereby the same individual is at once the investigating subject and the object of investigation.

Not only do Augustine and Freud frame the autobiographical tradition, therefore, but they do so in works that distill out of their personal experiences myths with a claim to universality unrivaled in the cultural repertoire of Athens or Jerusalem. But the assumption of universality implicit in both the Christian and the psychoanalytic master-myths constitutes at once their greatest appeal and greatest danger. If "In Adam's fall, we sinned all," and if every person is subject to the Oedipus complex, then there is no place outside the frameworks provided by the theories themselves from which they may be called into question. Thus, although it is unquestionably true that human beings die, it need not follow that mortality must be regarded as punishment for a primal act of disobedience, as the story of the Fall would have it. Similarly, although all human beings incontrovertibly experience sexual and aggressive urges in early childhood, these impulses need not be accorded the centrality that have been given by Freud or lead to the tragic consequences that they did for Oedipus. And, as both Augustine and Freud are men, and patently cast their theories from a masculine point of view, the suspicion arises that the introspective tradition I am delineating is at bottom one of male misogyny and sexual anxiety. Indeed, the cultural heritage of which Augustine and Freud are such conspicuous landmarks is ultimately that of patriarchy. Until the final section of this chapter, I shall largely take the points of view of Augustine and Freud for granted and seek to expound them, as it were, from within, but it is salutary to imagine from the outset the possibility of feminist and other critiques.

To explore the conjunctions between Augustine and Freud, I shall first undertake a psychoanalytic reading of the *Confessions* as a whole, paying special attention to patterns of repetition in Augustine's life. Next, I shall dwell on the famous episode of his theft of the pears, which marks the point of convergence between the Oedipus myth and the Fall and thereby discloses also the subjective dimensions of Augustine's account of the Fall in *The City of God*. In conclusion, I shall contrast the pessimistic conception of knowledge held by both Freud and Augustine with the more optimistic attitude espoused by Aristotle and, within a psychoanalytic framework, by Heinz Hartmann and D. W. Winnicott, the leading representatives, respectively, of ego psychology and object relations theory. Through this multifaceted procedure, I hope to show how the Fall assumes the lineaments of the Oedipus complex and why Freud and Augustine are so closely in accord as theorists of forbidden knowledge.

I

Nowhere are both Augustine's psychological acuity and his affinity with Freud more clearly in evidence than in Book I of the *Confessions,* where he contemplates infancy. Seeking to substantiate his hypothesis that "no man is free from sin, not even a child who has lived only one day on earth" (I.7),[1] Augustine presents a view of human nature in the cradle that is distinctively "Freudian." One cornerstone of Freud's outlook is his conviction that human behavior is motivated by the pleasure principle, a drive to fulfill wishes through tension-reduction. Augustine likewise emphasizes how, as an infant, he strove "to make my wishes known to others, who might satisfy them" (I.6). But, he continues, "because my wishes were inside me, while other people were outside," adults often failed to understand him, "so I would toss my arms and legs about and make noises, hoping that such few signs as I could make would show my meaning, though they were quite unlike what they were meant to mime" (I.6). In this anatomy of preverbal communication, Augustine distills not only Freud's thesis concerning the primacy of inner drive-states but also his later elaboration of the "two principles of mental functioning" (1911), according to which the reality principle achieves by indirect means the aims of the pleasure principle.

Like a developmental psychologist, Augustine utilizes infant observation to corroborate conclusions reached by introspection: "By watching babies I have learnt that this is how they behave, and they, quite unconsciously, have done more than those who brought me up to convince me that I behaved in just the same way myself" (I.6). Unlike many contemporary psychoanalysts, however, Augustine shares Freud's assumption that an infant's primary needs are physiological and not emotional. He writes: "But in those days all I knew was how to suck, and how to lie still when my body sensed comfort or cry when it felt pain" (I.6). But, as John Bowlby has cogently argued in opposition to Freud, the overriding need in infancy is not for nourishment but for *attachment* (1982, 211–14). Thus, both the Augustinian and the Freudian accounts of infancy are founded on a model of the drives that is highly suspect, and which in turn provides a basis for a critique of their respective theories of original sin.

The Freudian overtones of Book I of the *Confessions* deepen when Augustine turns to the theme of sibling rivalry. Affirming that he has witnessed "jealousy in a baby," Augustine cites the example of an infant who, "whenever he saw his foster-brother at the breast, . . . would go pale with envy. Mothers and nurses," Augustine adds, "say that they can work such things out of the system by one means or another, but surely it cannot be called innocence, when the milk flows in such abundance from its source, to object to a rival desperately in need and depending for its life on this one form of nourishment" (I.7). This description is memorable, but again one might wonder whether it is the mother's *milk* that is the object of envy, or rather the love of the mother herself who may be insufficiently generous with her affections. The allusion to foster-brothers is a curious detail. Augustine expressly states that this incident is one that he has observed and not experienced. And yet, as we shall see, he himself exhibits the symptoms of acute sibling rivalry. Thus, the possibility cannot be discounted that this memory possesses a veiled autobiographical dimension. Appositely, sibling rivalry likewise played a formative role in Freud's personal history, as is shown by the way that the birth and death of his brother Julius, before Freud himself was two years of age, continued to haunt him during adult life and reinforced the guilt over the death of his father that led to his discovery of the Oedipus complex (Rudnytsky 1987, 18–23).

As is true of Freud, many of Augustine's specific ideas about infancy can be challenged, but both thinkers are surely justified in their general premise that early experience provides a prototype for everything that follows it. Augustine, for his part, staunchly upholds what is known in psychoanalysis as the *genetic* principle of explanation. He writes: "For commanders and kings may take the place of tutors and schoolmasters, nuts and balls and pet birds may give way to money and estates and servants, but these same passions remain with us while one stage of life follows another" (I.19). The paradigm of the infant at the mother's breast, moreover, continues to reverberate throughout the *Confessions*. Augustine equates God's mercy with "the comfort of woman's milk" (I.25), and implores: "Let us scent your fragrance and taste your sweetness" (VIII.4). By summoning these infantile memories, Augustine delivers his religious appeal to the reader in the most powerful emotional terms.

Augustine's commitment to a genetic outlook is especially evident in the portraits he draws of his mother and father, Monica and Patricius, which enable us to follow the process whereby internalized images of his parents are projected onto individuals he meets throughout life. This pattern, familiar to psychoanalysts as *transference,* stands out in the case of male figures, who outnumber and—with the notable exception of his mother—overshadow female ones in the *Confessions*.

Augustine's characterization of his father is marked by a combination of affection and criticism. Although he converted on his deathbed (IX.9), Patricius was not a Christian, and Augustine reports that Monica "did all that she could to see that you, my God, should be a Father to me rather than he" (I.11). He was unfaithful to his wife and had a "hot temper," but could also be "remarkably kind" (IX.9). Despite his limited means, Patricius "was ready to provide his son with all that was needed" for travel and study, but "took no trouble at all to see how I was growing in your sight or whether I was chaste or not" (II.3). When, in an incident to which I shall return, Patricius one day in the public baths "saw the signs of active virility coming to life" in Augustine, he responded affirm-atively to his adolescent son's sexuality, though Augustine adds that his delight in the thought of grandchildren "was due to the intoxication which causes the world to forget you, its Creator" (II.3).

Augustine subsequently encounters two contrasting father figures—Faustus and Ambrose. As a young man in Carthage, he awaits Faustus, the Manichean sage, with "keenest expectation" (V.6) and is at first impressed by his polished manner. Upon seeking to know his teacher better, however, Augustine is disappointed by the poverty of his scholarship. Faustus' inability to resolve Augustine's intellectual doubts causes the latter to begin questioning Manichean doctrines. But though his final judgment is negative, Augustine lauds Faustus for recognizing his limitations and adds that "modesty and candour are finer equipment for the mind than scientific knowledge of the kind that I wished to possess" (V.7). With this ambivalent verdict, Augustine clearly casts Faustus in the mold of Patricius.

Whereas Faustus is Augustine's pagan father figure, Ambrose is his surrogate Christian father.[2] Augustine makes explicit the filial dimension of his relationship to Ambrose: "This man of God received me like a father and, as bishop, told me how glad he was that I had come" (V.13). The trajectory of Augustine's attitude toward Ambrose is the obverse of that toward Faustus. At first, despite the bishop of Milan's kindness and erudition, Augustine is "uninterested" and even "contemptuous" of his sermons, which he fails to deliver in a "soothing and gratifying manner" (V.13). Only gradually does the young man begin to listen seriously to Ambrose's arguments in defense of the Catholic faith.

Ambrose's role as paternal ideal for Augustine is confirmed by an incident involving Monica, who had journeyed to Milan to be with Augustine. Although it had been her custom in Africa to bring offerings of bread and wine to the shrines of saints, she immediately ceased doing so in Milan upon learning that the practice had been prohibited by Ambrose. (This ritual permitted Monica to partake of the wine herself, though Augustine insists that she did so only out of noble motives.) As Augustine surmises, Monica's "pious submission" (VI.2) to this edict would not have been forthcoming had it been issued by anyone whom she venerated less deeply. For Augustine, Ambrose thus reinstates a strong paternal principle, which had been lacking in his own early upbringing.

In evaluating his parents' marriage, Augustine stresses that Monica never openly disobeyed Patricius in any way. Indeed, she would reproach other wives who complained about being beaten by their husbands for the looseness of their tongues: "Her manner was light but her meaning serious when she told them that ever since they had heard the marriage deed read over to them, they ought to have regarded it as a contract which bound them to serve their husbands, and from that time onward they should remember their condition and not defy their masters" (IX.9). Monica defines her identity within the limits placed on women's roles in late classical culture, but her subservience to Patricius and defense of patriarchy are offset by the force of her personality and by her evident grip on the reins of power within the family.

The chain of Augustine's transference substitutions is less easy to follow in the case of Monica than in that of Patricius precisely because her overwhelming presence in her son's life made it impossible for him to replace her with any other woman. In a pattern typical of patriarchal societies, the absence of any extrafamilial outlet for Monica's energies caused her to dedicate herself to the rearing of her children. As Ian Suttie has observed, in a culture where the woman is accorded respect and autonomy she normally will be able "to terminate [her children's] dependency" and to "repress infantile sexuality in a permanently and completely effective manner." However, if the woman has no status apart from her maternal role, she becomes "dependent on the child, will cling to it and cultivate its dependency on herself, with contrary effects upon the Oedipus wishes" (1935, 122).

Suttie's analysis delineates the way that the intensity of Augustine's Oedipus complex is itself a function of his mother's unduly passionate and possessive love for him. Because Patricius was not a Christian, as we have seen, Monica sought to make Augustine feel that God was his father, thereby creating a bond between mother and son from which the rival parent was excluded. Monica thus reared Augustine in an analogue to the Holy Family, in which—as innumerable pictorial representations attest—the infant Jesus shares an intimacy with the Virgin Mary to which his human father Joseph is not privy.

As this comparison suggests, moreover, the triangulation that structures so much of Augustine's experience is superimposed on an underlying mother-son dyad. Indeed, Monica, who shared Patricius' ambitions for Augustine (II.3), evidently induced in her son intense anxieties concerning separation. This anxiety was acted out in Augustine's attempt—in imitation of Aeneas, about whose wanderings he had read as a schoolboy (I.11)—to escape from her influence by sailing at night secretly from Carthage to Rome (V.8).[3] Augustine expressly interprets this journey as a means by which God used Monica's "too jealous love for her son as a scourge for her own just punishment. For as mothers do, and far more than most, she loved to have me with her" (V.8). Even though he deceived his mother, Augustine notes that God "did not punish me for it" (V.8), since the sea-journey passed without incident. One may infer that Augustine expected to be punished, and he adds without further comment: "At Rome I was at once struck down by illness" (V.9). This unexplained illness seems to be at least in part psychosomatic, as though Augustine succumbed upon arrival to the guilt-feelings he had temporarily withstood in venturing to sail away from Monica in the first place.

Unlike Dido, however, who yielded to despair and anger following her abandonment by Aeneas and impaled herself on a sword, Monica refused to concede defeat and followed her son on his epic journey (VI.1). Thus, Augustine never fully separated himself from her, and because of Monica's intransigence he may be said to have become a Christian and not a classical hero. The battle of wills between mother and son is symbolized by Monica's dream of the wooden rule in Book III, in which she and a young man in a "halo of splendour" (III.11) stand at either end of a plank, the interpretation of which—underscored in a conversation with Augustine—hinges on the detail that *he* shall come to where she is, and not vice versa. The young man in the dream is not explicitly identified as Augustine, but it is clear that he represents Augustine in a state of glory. After her dream, when the disconsolate Monica talks to a priest about her wayward son, he reassures her with the words: "It cannot be that the son of these tears should be lost" (III.12). As Augustine's eventual conversion to Christianity goes to show, Monica did indeed get her way, but at the cost of depriving her offspring of a normal process of separation and individuation.

One consequence of Monica's possessiveness may be seen in Augustine's relations with his mistress, the mother of his child, who was "torn from my side" when he contemplated marriage, "a blow which crushed my heart to bleeding" (VI.15). As Augustine was unable to escape from his mother, so he paid the price by being forcibly separated from the woman he loved. The anonymity of this woman is a further telling measure of the shadow cast by Monica across Augustine's life.

Not only did Augustine abandon his mistress, only to form another liaison in short order, but he could not bring himself to marry anyone. Although there was no external obligation that he renounce sexuality—Christians were permitted to marry—Augustine consistently equated his struggle to convert with a subduing of the flesh: "Though you did not forbid me to marry, you counselled me to take a better course" (X.30). This preoccupation with the issue of celibacy—epitomized by Augustine's oft-echoed prayer, "Give me chastity and continence, but not yet"

(VIII.7)—must be ascribed to psychological factors. Indeed, after being betrothed to a girl so young that he would have to wait two years until she came of age, Augustine describes himself as "exhausted by the canker of anxiety, because there were other reasons too why I found it irksome to be forced to adapt myself to living with a wife" (VIII.1). Augustine does not specify why he found the prospect of marriage so "irksome," but his "canker of anxiety" goes deeper than the typical enjoyment of sexual freedom that might be expected in a young man of late antiquity and stems in all likelihood from an unconscious incestuous fixation. A notorious libertine obsessed by sexuality—going so far in adolescence as to gratify his lust "within the walls of your church during the celebration of your mysteries" (III.3)—Augustine conforms to the pattern of the Don Juan who strives through promiscuity to replace the mother on whom he remains emotionally dependent.

The theme of celibacy comes to a head at the moment of Augustine's conversion. Just prior to his final breakthrough, Augustine sees before him, standing on the other side of a "barrier," "the chaste beauty of Continence in all her serene, unsullied joy" (VIII.11). He envisions Continence not as "barren," but as "a fruitful mother of children, of joys born of you, O Lord, her spouse" (VIII.11). This personification is deliberately allegorical and depicts the "unity of self" he had dissipated by the pursuit of a "variety of pleasures" (X.29). But in addition to its religious meaning, the fusion of chastity and fecundity in the figure of Continence can be interpreted psychoanalytically as a representation of the mother, who, in her son's eyes, is at once a nonsexual and sexual being. As Augustine's earlier promiscuity was a symptom of his incestuous attachment, so the "barrier" between himself and Continence stands for the incest taboo, which is paradoxically at once restored (in that Augustine renounces sexuality) and violated (in that he takes possession of the mother) when Augustine crosses to the other side. Indeed, the first thing that Augustine does, after his conversion and that of his friend Alypius, is to go in and tell his mother, who is "overjoyed" that her son no longer "desired a wife," but, in fulfillment of her dream, is rather prepared to join her upon the "rule of faith" (VIII.12).

The death of Monica, recorded in Book IX, prompts Augustine to look back on her life as a whole. He recalls a conversation on the night before Monica's death, in which he and she together contemplated the superiority of heavenly joys to any earthly pleasures: "And while we spoke of the eternal Wisdom, longing for it and straining for it with all the strength of our hearts, for one fleeting instant we reached out and touched it. Then with a sigh...we returned to the sound of our own speech, in which each word has a beginning and an ending" (IX.10). This highly charged evocation of a transcendence beyond language is suffused with sexuality, as mother and son attain a mystical ecstasy, a communion of souls that is Augustine's most intense religious experience.

A further striking feature of the description of Monica on her deathbed is that it elicits Augustine's sole reference to a sibling. While Augustine struggles to hold back his tears, his brother (who, like the women in Augustine's life, remains anonymous) remarks how unfortunate it is that Monica has to die abroad instead of in her own country. To this, she responds with a reproachful glance and says to Augustine: "See how he talks!" (IX.11). Augustine seems to introduce his brother for no other purpose than thus cruelly to demolish him, and it is this passage that suggests that his discussion in Book I of sibling rivalry at the maternal breast is subjectively motivated.

From his brother, Augustine's narrative reverts to his father. With her dying breath, Monica renounces the "vain desire" of being buried beside her husband. Whereas earlier she had "always wanted this extra happiness," at the end Monica no longer sought such worldly consolations, and Augustine admits that he was "both surprised and pleased to find that this was so" (IX.11). Despite Patricius' own conversion to Christianity, he and Monica remain apart after death, and this separation of his parents seals Augustine's triumph over his father. (In a gesture of reparation, Augustine prays, "Let her rest in peace with her husband. He was her first husband and she married no other after him" [IX.13]. But this afterthought does not undo his act of symbolic patricide.) Thus, through his mother's death Augustine simultaneously vanquishes both his sibling and oedipal rivals. Monica's last wish ratifies for eternity her devaluation of her conjugal duties in favor of her spiritual intimacy with her son. Fittingly, although Augustine consecrates most of a book to his mother's death, he mentions that of his father only in passing (III.4).

In Book XII, Augustine offers a hymn of praise to his "beloved mother" Jerusalem and to God: "And I shall remember you her Ruler, you who give her light, you her Father, her Guardian, and her Spouse" (XII.16). That Augustine should celebrate God and Jerusalem as partners in a mystic marriage, where the husband "rules" his wife, is readily comprehensible in theological terms. But, like the personification of Continence, this metaphor takes on additional meaning when it is interpreted as the culmination of Augustine's family romance. God here replaces Ambrose as the ultimate husband-father who can reassert authority over the feminine principle embodied in Jerusalem.

II

The theft of the pears that Augustine recounts in Book II of the *Confessions* disquiets both him and the reader because of its apparent lack of motivation: "For of what I stole I already had plenty, and much better at that, and I had no wish to enjoy the things I coveted by stealing, but only to enjoy the theft itself and the sin. . . . Perhaps we ate some of them, but our real pleasure consisted in doing something that was forbidden" (II.4).

In anatomizing a crime whose horror consists in its absence of a rational motive, Augustine is the precursor of Dostoevsky in *Crime and Punishment*. Through his theft of the pears Augustine confronts as an emotional reality the puzzle of the nature of evil with which he also struggles intellectually in the *Confessions:* "Where then is evil? What is its origin? How did it steal into the world?" (VII.5). Augustine's Christian answer to these questions is that evil is not a substance (as the Manichees claimed) but rather a privation of good, arising from the choice of the perverted will to disobey God. Looking back on the transgression, committed at the age of sixteen (II.6), Augustine declares: "I am quite sure that I would not have done it on my own" (II.8). Kenneth Burke has illuminated this collective aspect of the episode by proposing that Augustine and his band form a blasphemous counterpart to the fellowship of the Christian church, in that the *gratuitousness* of the sin that binds them together is balanced and redeemed by Christ's gift of *grace* to all who accept the offer of salvation through his blood (1961, 93–101).

From a theological standpoint, therefore, Augustine's theft of the pears signifies an ontogenetic reenactment of the Fall. Noting that Augustine refers to the pears as *poma,* the same word used in the Vulgate to mean "fruit" in the Garden of Eden, Freccero proposes a typological relation between the pear tree, redolent of sexuality, and the fig tree, associated with maternity, beneath which Augustine (like Nathanael in John 1:45–48) is sitting when he experiences his conversion (1986, 25–28). This correspondence between Adam's sin and that of Augustine can only be approximate rather than exact, because it is precisely the consequence of Adam's disobedience that none of his descendants can recapture his freedom of the will, which would once again make it possible to choose *not* to sin. But the parallel is unmistakable nonetheless, for, as Augustine remarks in *The City of God,* not only was Adam's sin "committed about food," but the lure of Adam's tree, no less than his own, arose from the fact that it was "not bad nor noxious, except because it was forbidden" (XIV.12).

The lack of motivation that is the essence of Augustine's, as of every, sin constitutes an attempt on the part of a creature to deny contingency and dependence on its Creator. In Freccero's words, "the appropriation of the pears is a self-appropriation, an illicit assertion of one's selfhood and one's autonomy" (1986, 24). But this theological understanding of the *causa sui* project may be reinterpreted psychoanalytically as a manifestation of the oedipal fantasy of usurping the place of the father and begetting oneself.

The oedipal aspects of Augustine's theft of the pears are further illuminated when his insistence on the triviality of the occurrence is subjected to psychoanalytic scrutiny. For, as I shall argue, this symbolic transgression serves Augustine as a *screen memory* for other forbidden wishes. Freud defines screen memories as the recollection of "everyday and indifferent events" in place of disturbing "serious and tragic" ones from the same or a different period (1899, 305). He unexpectedly maintains that earlier memories can serve to conceal later ones, as well as the reverse; etiologically significant events thus continue to take place in adolescence and beyond.

The "serious and tragic" determinants of Augustine's screen memory lie concealed in plain sight. In Book II, Augustine discloses two psychologically significant memories concerning his parents. The first of these, to which I have already alluded, is his father's witnessing of "the signs of active virility coming to life" (II.3) in Augustine in the public baths. The second involves his mother, who, "alarmed and apprehensive" that Augustine might stray from the path of virtue, "most earnestly warned me not to commit fornication and above all not to seduce any man's wife" (II.3). Monica conspicuously enjoins Augustine not merely from fornication but also from adultery. But, since the first and prototypical wife of another man for whom a boy experiences sexual desire is his mother, Monica's warning against adultery is ultimately an admonition *not to violate the incest taboo*. From all that we have seen of the exceptional intimacy between mother and son, moreover, this prohibition must itself be viewed as a reaction formation, which paradoxically intensifies the very repressed incestuous longings it is designed to defend against— Monica's as well as those of the overstimulated Augustine.

Either of these incidents would likely have been formative on its own, but their impact is compounded by their convergence. In Book II, Augustine reaches adolescence, "the age at which the frenzy gripped me and I surrendered myself entirely to lust" (II.2), and these memories concerning his parents distill the emotional impact of his arrival at puberty and initiation into genital sexuality. What is more, Augustine reports these two highly charged experiences in the section of Book II *immediately prior* to that in which he commences his narrative of the pear-stealing episode.

The disproportion between the triviality of Augustine's offense and the extreme importance he imputes to it may thus be explained psychoanalytically as a displacement of the sense of guilt properly attaching to the former events onto the latter. It is this displacement of affect from something serious onto something trivial that makes the theft of the pears truly a "screen memory." And since, as I have contended, Monica's warning against fornication and adultery rests on the incest taboo, Augustine's stealing of the forbidden fruit is at once a reenactment of the Fall and a symptom of his Oedipus complex as it is revived in adolescence.[4]

But just as the oedipal patterns in Augustine's life as a whole are superimposed upon preoedipal ones, so his theft of the pears is open to interpretations on multiple psychological levels. A crucial insight into the earlier determinants of Augustine's deed is provided by D. W. Winnicott:

But a child who, say, regularly goes and steals apples, and quickly gives them away without himself enjoying them, is acting under a compulsion, and is ill. He can be called a thief. He will not know why he has done what he has done, and if pressed for a reason he will become a liar. The thing is, what is this boy doing? ... *The thief is not looking for the object that he takes. He is looking for a person. He is looking for his own mother, only he does not know this.* (1964, 163; italics in original)

Winnicott does not mention St. Augustine, and the compulsiveness of the behavior he describes contrasts with the apparently isolated nature of Augustine's theft. Nonetheless, his comments read as though they were intended as an exegesis of the *Confessions*.[5] For Augustine does not enjoy the fruit that he steals, just as he cannot provide a motive for his actions. The incestuous component of Augustine's fixation on his mother is not contradicted by this underlying theme of dependence. Indeed, from a Winnicottian standpoint, Augustine's sexual promiscuity may itself be construed as an attempt to compensate for a lack of emotional security, for a sense of having been cheated of his mother's love through the birth of a brother. And just as Freud resembles Augustine in his intertwining of oedipal and sibling rivalry, so, too, in his early childhood Freud stole coins from his mother's purse when she was pregnant with his sister Anna in a characteristic response to deprivation that likewise exemplifies Winnicott's ideas (Rudnytsky 1991, 101).

This conjunction between the Oedipus complex and the Fall in the *Confessions* forged by the theft of the pears in turn sheds light on Augustine's exegesis of the Fall in *The City of God*. For he there loses no opportunity to magnify the sexual component of Adam's transgression. The prize exhibit of Augustine's great law of retribution, "that they who do evil should suffer evil" (XIV.15), is the (male) sexual organs, "for the insubordination of these members, and their defiance of the will, are the clear testimony of man's first sin" (XIV.20). As Adam disobeyed God, so disobedience is now lodged within the human body, subjected both to lust and death.

Augustine's appeal in the *Confessions* to infant observation to substantiate his bleak view of human nature is buttressed in *The City of God* by his empirical case that the shame attached to sin is fundamentally sexual in nature:

Who does not know what passes between husband and wife that children may be born? ... And yet, when this well-understood act is gone about for the procreation of children, not even the children themselves, who may already have been born to them, are suffered to be witnesses. ... And rather will a man endure a crowd of witnesses when he is unjustly venting his anger on some one, than the eye of one man when he innocently copulates with his wife. (XIV.18–19)

Had Adam and Eve remained unfallen in the Garden of Eden, Augustine speculates, their acts of generation would have been prompted by the will and not by lust, and "the male semen could have been introduced into the womb of the wife with the integrity of the female genital organ being preserved, just as now, with that same integrity being safe, the menstrual flow of blood can be emitted from the womb of a virgin" (XIV.26).

From the evidence of the *Confessions,* it is clear that—whatever other cultural and historical factors may be involved—Augustine's sexual reading of the Fall is based on his personal experience. Adam is Augustine writ large, just as Augustine suffers the effects of Adam's sin. In this dialectic between subjective and objective truth, Augustine traces the circle that hermeneutic philosophers have argued is constitutive of self-reflective knowledge (Hoy 1978). And as a hermeneutic circle structures Augustine's rendering of the Fall, so, too, it subtends Freud's articulation of the Oedipus complex (Rudnytsky 1987, 64–65). Not only does Freud in *The Interpretation of Dreams* fuse the autobiographical quality of the *Confessions* and the doctrinal quality of *The City of God* (Schorske 1980, 183), but, as Augustine does with Adam, he invokes the mythological figure of Oedipus to universalize the insights arrived at in the course of his own self-analysis.

The principal intellectual source for Augustine's theology of the Fall is St. Paul, and above all his epistle to the Romans.[6] When Augustine in the garden hears the voice of a child telling him to take up and read the Bible, a quotation from Romans (13:13–14) provides the final catalyst for his conversion to Christianity (VIII.12). Passages from Paul are interspersed with verses from the Psalms—Augustine's favorite biblical quarry—with increasing frequency as his narrative builds to its climax. Paul, however, is indispensable for Augustine not simply because of his ideas, but also because he provides the prototype for Christian spiritual autobiography.

When Augustine writes of himself, prior to his conversion, that "it was I who willed to take this course and again it was I who willed not to take it....So I was at odds with myself" (VIII.10), his indictment paraphrases the "Pauline paradox" set forth in Romans: "For the good that I would, I do not: but the evil which I would not, that I do" (7:19). What is more, Paul's expostulation, "O wretched man that I am! who shall deliver me from the body of this death?" (7:24), makes it plain that his "captivity to the law of sin which is in my members" (7:23) is no less urgently and personally felt than that of Augustine. That Adam's transgression has universal significance is never asserted in the Hebrew Bible, though the assumption seems to inhere in Genesis. Not until Paul's typological pairing of Adam and Christ is this idea made explicit: "For

as by one man's disobedience many were made sinners, so by the obe-
dience of one shall many be made righteous" (5:16). And, as Paul's
subjective experience of the conflict between sin and grace prompted him
to posit the universality of the Fall, so Augustine's reliving of Paul's
spiritual struggle allowed him to carry the latter's theology to its logical
conclusion by formulating the doctrine of original sin.

III

For both Freud and Augustine, all knowledge is at bottom forbidden
knowledge because, as Freud writes, "the thirst for knowledge seems to
be inseparable from sexual curiosity" (1909, 9). Although this point of
view is a powerful one, it needs to be balanced against that expounded
by Aristotle at the outset of the *Metaphysics:* "All men by nature desire
to know. An indication of this is the delight we take in our senses; for
even apart from their usefulness they are loved for themselves; and above
all others the sense of sight" (1941, 689). Like Heinz Hartmann (1939),
Aristotle regards the pursuit of knowledge as an "autonomous ego function" that is intrisically motivated and not necessarily contaminated by
sexual or aggressive drives.

As my references to Hartmann and Winnicott suggest, the larger debate
in the history of ideas between Freud and St. Augustine on the one hand
and Aristotle on the other is reenacted within the domain of psychoanalysis. In a searching meditation on these questions, Victoria Hamilton
has drawn a contrast between the "tragic vision," which is tied to a
model of the infant as "a need-orientated, autistic creature who does not
wish to know about his reality or to relate to the beings who inhabit it,"
and a "holy curiosity," in which "the varieties of mental functioning
develop in the context of [maternal] presence and minimal frustration
and are linked to the emergence of transitional objects and phenomena"
(1982, 255–56). For Hamilton, the former position is represented in
Britain by the Kleinian school, notably by W. R. Bion, and the latter by
the Independent group, led by Winnicott.

A glimpse of the outlines of an alternative perspective on human
development and the acquisition of knowledge helps to set the claims of
universality propounded by both Freud and Augustine into critical relief.
In accentuating archetypal patterns, the danger always lies in underes-
timating the degree to which the form they take is subject to modification

by environmental influences. As I have already urged, the fact that death is universal need not be explained as a punishment, as the doctrine of the Fall would have it, and death is surely experienced differently by different individuals and cultures. By the same token, Freud's theory of innate drives of sexuality and aggression overlooks that human beings are never isolated monads but rather exist, from infancy on, in a state of interconnectedness to others, and that it is these personal relationships that largely determine the quality of a person's emotional life.

Whereas the defense of "holy curiosity" by Aristotle and his psychoanalytic allies may be termed *philosophical*, the vision of Freud and Augustine is indeed quintessentially *tragic*. For, again and again, it is the lesson of the tragic poets that wisdom comes through suffering, that knowledge is acquired only through the violation of a taboo. Aristotle's equation of knowledge with vision hearkens back to Plato's similes of the sun and the cave in the *Republic*. But precisely this priority given to the sense of sight is exploited by the tragedians, for whom the act of witnessing a spectacle on the stage is not an innocent pastime. Sophocles' *Oedipus*, with its agon between Oedipus and Teiresias, immediately comes to mind for its thematization of the dialectic of blindness and insight. But no less relevant in this connection is Euripides' *Bacchae*, the last Greek tragedy, which circles back to the myth of Dionysus that presides over tragedy's birth. For, in Pentheus' succumbing to Dionysus' temptation to see the rites of the Bacchantes, which leads to his dismemberment by his mother, Euripides furnishes a parable of what it means to come to watch a play being performed in the theater. The spectator, initially secure in the illusion of Apollonian detachment, comes to find that he is implicated in what he gazes upon, and ends up being cast in the role of hero and victim, destroyed by the Dionysian forces he has unwittingly unleashed.[7]

In Book X of the *Confessions*, after expatiating on the temptations posed by the bodily appetites, Augustine comes to the "more dangerous" peril of the mind's use of the senses to satisfy its own inquisitiveness: "This futile curiosity masquerades under the name of science and learning, and since it derives from our thirst for knowledge and sight is the principal sense by which knowledge is acquired, in the Scriptures it is called *gratification of the eye*" (X.35). Not only does Augustine agree with the Greek tragedians on the subversive implications of the equation between vision and knowledge, but he uses the concept of "lust of the eyes" to launch an attack on scientific inquiry in general: "It is to satisfy this unhealthy curiosity that freaks and prodigies are put on show in the theatre, and for the same reason that men are led to investigate the secrets of nature, which are irrelevant to our lives" (X.35). Augustine's anti-intellectualism—a strand of Christian theology not openly challenged until Bacon—is not likely to appeal to most modern readers, but it follows logically from his insistence on the instinctual roots of even seemingly innocuous activities.

Augustine provides an illustration of scoptophilic lust in action in the story of Alypius, who detested the gladiatorial displays in Rome, but on one occasion allowed himself to be led thither by friends, convinced that he could remain unmoved by the atrocities. He kept his eyes tightly shut until, thrilled by the roar of the crowd, he could no longer contain his curiosity: "So he opened his eyes, and his soul was stabbed with a wound more deadly than any which the gladiator, whom he was anxious to see, had received in his body. He fell, and fell more pitifully than the man whose fall had drawn the roar of excitement from the crowd" (VI.8). Alypius experiences a Christian version of the fate of Pentheus and becomes the tragic protagonist of a spectacle by which he was consciously repelled but unconsciously fascinated, and which he thought he could safely witness.

With his customary psychological acuity, Augustine traces this "lust of the eyes" to its roots in childhood. He writes of his own early love of the theater: "As time went on my eyes shone more and more with the same eager curiosity, because I wanted to see the shows and sports which grown-ups enjoyed" (I.10). In a restatement of the genetic outlook, he recognizes the continuity between the games played by children and adults: "However, grown-up games are known as 'business,' and even though boys' games are much the same, they are punished for them by their elders" (I.9).

Through his iteration of the verb "fall" (*cadere*) in the tale of Alypius, moreover, Augustine makes plain that all such "futile curiosity" is a repetition of the sin of Adam. In his analysis of the Fall in *The City of God*, Augustine stresses the visual component of the shame visited upon Adam and Eve as a consequence of their transgression: "that their disobedience might be punished by fit retribution, there began in the movement of their bodily members a shameless novelty which made nakedness indecent: it at once made them observant and made them ashamed"

(XIV.17). And, as I have noted, Augustine offers as proof of the shame attendant on all sexual intercourse the fact that "not even the children themselves... are suffered to be witnesses."

Since the counterpart to parents' attempts to conceal their sexual activity is the "eager curiosity" of children to pry into these mysteries, Augustine's exegesis of scoptophilia converges with Freud's conviction that the ultimate object of infantile sexual curiosity is a view of the primal scene. No analyst has more forcefully championed this concept, and the importance of infantile fantasy in general, than Melanie Klein:

The first object of this instinct for knowledge is the interior of the mother's body, which the child first of all regards as an object of oral gratification and then as the scene where intercourse between its parents takes place.... At the same time as it wants to force its way into the mother's body in order to take possession of the contents and to destroy them, it wants to know what is going on and what things look like in there.... Thus the instinct for knowledge becomes linked at its source with sadism when it is at its height, which makes it easier to understand why that bond should be so close, and why the instinct for knowledge should arouse feelings of guilt in the individual. (1932, 174)

In a critical review of Klein's thought, Edward Glover maintains that her view of the infant's relation to its mother "is a variant of the doctrine of Original Sin" (1945, 117). But one may agree with Glover's assessment without concurring that Klein's coupling of the "instinct for knowledge" with sadism and guilt is therefore incompatible with psychoanalysis. Indeed, her position is simply a more extreme version of that espoused by Freud, who averred that psychoanalysis "is no more than confirming the habitual pronouncement of the pious: we are all miserable sinners" (1913, 72); and it is rather environmentally oriented theorists, such as Winnicott and Hartmann, who face the challenge of grafting their more flexible outlooks onto Freud's pessimistic legacy.

Book X serves an important function in the structure of the *Confessions* as a whole, for in it Augustine confronts the ineradicability of sin in his own life even after he has embraced Christianity. (In the final three books, Augustine abandons autobiography altogether in favor of an extended allegorical exegesis of the opening verses in Genesis, as the *Confessions* undergoes a narrative "conversion" from personal to impersonal themes that parallels the trajectory of Augustine's own life.) Augustine observes that the images of his former habits—above all, fornication— which remain feeble during his waking hours, return with full force while he is asleep: "But when I dream, they not only give me pleasure but are very much like acquiescence in the act" (X.30). Unlike sex, however, which he was at least able to relegate to the realm of dreams, the appetite for food and drink is not one that he can altogether repudiate. What Augustine finds most insidious is that the "snare of concupiscence" lurks even in such biologically ordained activities: "although the purpose of eating and drinking is to preserve health, in its train there follows an ominous kind of enjoyment" (X.31). Himself prone to overeating, Augustine asks rhetorically: "But is there anyone, O Lord, who is never enticed a little beyond the strict limit of need?" (X.31).

Augustine vividly exemplifies the dangers of this temptation in his narrative of the life of his mother. As a child, Monica's upbringing had been entrusted to an aged female servant, who, except at mealtimes, would not allow Monica or her sisters "to drink even water, however great their thirst, for fear that they might develop bad habits" (IX.8). This severe discipline seems initially to have backfired, however, for Monica "developed a secret liking for wine." When she was sent by her parents to draw wine from the cask, "she would sip a few drops, barely touching it with her lips, but no more than this, because she found the taste disagreeable. She did this, not because she had any relish for the liquor and its effects, but simply from the exuberant high spirits of childhood" (IX.8). Each day, Monica took increasingly larger sips until "it soon became a habit, and she would drink her wine at a draught, almost by the cupful" (IX.8). Only when a quarrelsome servant-girl called her a drunkard did Monica realize the despicableness of her fault and put a stop to it.

Augustine's tale of Monica forms a pendant to his own youthful theft of the pears. For, like Augustine, Monica at first drinks the liquor "not because she had any relish" for it, but simply out of "high spirits." This symmetry between the paradigmatic sins of mother and son suggests that Augustine's reenactment of the Fall is determined by the bond between himself and his mother at an even deeper level than Monica's warning against adultery. Freud observes that "a child's super-ego is in fact constituted on the model not of its parents but of its parents' super-ego" (1933, 67), and his insight is borne out by the way that Augustine's strict conscience, transmitted by Monica, may be further traced back to her maternal nursemaid, who "was conscientious in attending to her duties, correcting the children when necessary with strictness, for the love of

God, and teaching them to lead wise and sober lives" (IX.8). Monica's secret drinking likewise helps to explain her submission to Ambrose's prohibition against bringing libations to the shrines of the saints in Milan, although Augustine never makes explicit this connection between her childhood and adult life.

Augustine's commentary on the "ominous kind of enjoyment" that accompanies eating again highlights the affinity between his thought and Freud's. For both theorists, as we have seen, the infant is a fundamentally selfish creature impelled to discharge instinctual tensions. Freud writes of infants' proclivity to sucking: "The baby's obstinate persistence in sucking gives evidence at an early age of a need for satisfaction which, though it originates from and is instigated by the taking of nourishment, nevertheless strives to obtain pleasure independently of nourishment and for that reason may and should be termed *sexual*" (1940, 154). For both Augustine and Freud, the taking of nourishment arouses a pleasure that exceeds "the strict limit of need," and this surcharge of excitation contaminates the whole of life with a residue of sexuality that resists all efforts at sublimation.

The emphasis placed on oral experience by both Augustine and Freud conforms to what Hamilton with respect to Bion has called the "feeding model" of human knowledge, which generates the tragic vision because "the knower oscillates between hunger and satisfaction, neither of which extremes is acceptable" (1982, 243). Bowlby, on the other hand, would dissent from the proponents of inevitable tragedy by arguing that attachment, and not the "secondary drive" of the oral zone, is the paramount desire of human life. Hamilton's collocation of the "feeding model" with a tendency to oscillate between extremes is vindicated by Augustine and Freud. Ernest Jones has drawn attention to Freud's "obstinate dualism," his "difficulty in contemplating any topic unless he could divide it into two opposites, and never more than two" (1955, 469–70), and Augustine exhibits the same penchant for contraries. Just as each incarnation of Freud's instinct theory employs one or another pair of antithetical terms, so Augustine's entire scheme of the universe is founded on the dichotomy between love of self (*cupiditas*) and love of other (*caritas*) or the City of Man and the City of God.

The majestic power of the Freudian and Augustinian tragic visions is beyond dispute, but, as with their reliance on master-myths, one ought to ask what is lost as well as gained by such exclusive fidelity to a binary model. The dualistic systems of both men find a concomitant in their zealous devotion to a cause, in whose service each could be a passionate hater as well as a lover. Augustine writes contemptuously of the practitioners of astrology, "By now I was eager to move to the attack and reduce these people to silence by ridicule" (VII.6), and Freud similarly spares no quarter in his controversies with the opponents of psychoanalysis. In light of their aggressive temperaments, it is not surprising that many of the works of both defenders of the faith should be *polemical* in character and bear the impress of the occasions by which they were called into being.

But whatever one's qualms about their ideas or characters, there can be no doubt that both Augustine and Freud possessed—together with intellectual and administrative powers of the highest order—the introspective genius that allowed them to immortalize their personal histories in works that epitomize the Western traditions of autobiography and patriarchy. As Peter Brown has observed, Augustine "takes up a position analogous to that of Freud" in maintaining that a "dislocation in human consciousness" makes self-knowledge inherently imperfect and language always in need of interpretation (1967, 261). As is true of Freud, moreover, Augustine simultaneously expounds a theory of repression—in his view, a result of the Fall—and encounters it at every turn in his self-analysis: "But while he [Ponticianus] was speaking, O Lord, you were turning me around to look at myself. For I had placed myself behind my own back, refusing to see myself" (VIII.7). According to Freud, dreams, slips, and neurotic symptoms are all *compromise formations,* in which both repressing and repressed agencies of the mind find partial expression. Confronting the paradox of inhibition, Augustine reaches the same conclusion a millennium and a half earlier: "It [the mind] gives the order only in so far as it wills, and in so far as it does not will the order is not carried out" (VIII.9).

Masud Khan has persuasively argued that Freud's "greatest invention" will always be "the unique human situation where a person can explore the meaning and experiential realities of his life, through a relationship with another, and yet not be intruded upon or manipulated in any way that is not true to his own self and values" (1972, 127). The roots of the analytic setting lie in the form of autobiography, in which the self takes itself as its own object in order to recover integrity through dialogue with an imagined other, whether that other be the transcendent deity of

St. Augustine or the human interlocutors of Montaigne, Rousseau, and Freud (Khan 1970). In Winnicott's (1958) view, the prototype of psychoanalytic treatment is the relationship between the infant and mother, in which the mother permits the infant to be alone in her presence. Augustine reveals the same space to be essential to his dialogue with God. He confesses his anguished response to the Psalms of David: "this cry came from my inmost heart, when I was alone in your presence" (IX.4).

That a child should wish to strike those who know better than he, including his own parents, Augustine contends, "shows that, if babies are innocent, it is not for lack of will to do harm, but for lack of strength" (I.7). This unsparing judgment on human nature in the cradle anticipates the passage from Diderot's *Rameau's Nephew* invoked by Freud as an illustration of his own teachings: "If the little savage were left to himself, preserving all his foolishness and adding to the small sense of a child in the cradle the violent passions of a man of thirty, he would strangle his father and lie with his mother" (1916–17, 338). What Augustine called original sin, Freud renamed the Oedipus complex; and both theologian and psychoanalyst wrote from personal experience of the sense of guilt that they deemed the bedrock of civilization and the price of forbidden knowledge.

Notes

1. Quotations from the *Confessions* are to the translation of R. S. Pine-Coffin. For the sake of convenience, I will give parenthetical references by book and section number. The same holds for the translation from *The City of God* by Marcus Dods.
2. Commenting on this pattern, whereby Augustine replaces his pagan father with Ambrose, Freccero argues that the psyche revealed in the *Confessions* is "not that of St. Augustine the individual but rather that of Latin Christianity" (1986, 27). But it is not necessary to choose between individual, cultural, and universal levels of meaning, all of which are at play in Augustine's oedipal drama of salvation.
3. On Augustine and Aeneas, see Kligerman (1957), to whom I am indebted on the oedipal configurations in Augustine's family.
4. In a previous paper (1988) I have attempted to show that the Oedipus complex functions as the "latent content" of Milton's rendering of the Fall in *Paradise Lost*.

5. My collocation of Winnicott's ideas and Augustine's theft of the pears has been anticipated by Hopkins (1981).
6. See Pagels (1988), who, however, exaggerates the novelty of Augustine's interpretation of the Fall. Quotations from the Bible are to the King James Version.
7. For a profound meditation on these "metatragic" dimensions of *The Bacchae*, see Segal (1982, 215–71) and Spitz (1991, 178-201).

References

Aristotle. 1941. *Metaphysics*. In *The Basic Works of Aristotle*, ed. R. McKeon. New York: Random House, pp. 689–926.
Augustine, St. 1950. *The City of God*, trans. M. Dods. New York: Modern Library.
———. 1961. *Confessions*, trans. R. S. Pine-Coffin. Harmondsworth: Penguin Books, 1969.
Bowlby, J. 1982. *Attachment*, 2d ed. New York: Basic Books.
Brown, P. 1967. *Augustine of Hippo*. Berkeley: Univ. of California Press, 1969.
Burke, K. 1961. *The Rhetoric of Religion: Studies in Logology*. Boston: Beacon Press.
Freccero, J. 1986. Autobiography and Narrative. In *Reconstructing Individualism: Autonomy, Individuality, and the Self in Western Thought*, ed. T. C. Heller, M. Sosna, and D. E. Wellbery. Stanford: Stanford Univ. Press, 1988, pp. 16–29.
Freud, S. 1899. Screen Memories. In *The Standard Edition of the Complete Psychological Works*, ed. and trans. J. Strachey et al., 24 vols. London: Hogarth Press, 1953–74, 3:303–22. (Hereafter *S.E.*)
———. 1900. *The Interpretation of Dreams. S.E.*, vols. 4 and 5.
———. 1905. *Fragment of an Analysis of a Case of Hysteria. S.E.*, 7:7–122.
———. 1909. *Analysis of a Phobia in a Five-Year-Old-Boy. S.E.*, 10:5–147.
———. 1911. Formulations on the Two Principles of Mental Functioning. *S.E.*, 12:218–26.
———. 1913. *Totem and Taboo. S.E.*, 13:1–161.
———. 1916–17. *Introductory Lectures on Psycho-Analysis. S.E.*, vols. 15 and 16.
———. 1933. *New Introductory Lectures on Psycho-Analysis. S.E.*, 22:5–182.
———. 1939. *Moses and Monotheism: Three Essays. S.E.*, 23:7–137.
———. 1940. *An Outline of Psycho-Analysis. S.E.*, 23:145–207.
Glover, E. 1945. Examination of the Klein System of Child Psychology. *Psychoanal. Study Child*. 1:75–118.
Hamilton, V. 1982. *Narcissus and Oedipus: The Children of Psychoanalysis*. London: Routledge and Kegan Paul.
Hartmann, H. 1939. *Ego Psychology and the Problem of Adaptation*, trans. D. Rapaport. New York: International Univ. Press.

Hopkins, B. 1981. St. Augustine's *Confessions:* The Pear-Stealing Episode. *Am. Imago,* 38:97–104.

Hoy, D. 1978. *The Critical Circle: Literature, History, and Philosophical Hermeneutics.* Berkeley: Univ. of California Press, 1982.

Jones, E. 1955. *The Life and Work in Sigmund Freud,* vol. 2. London: Hogarth Press, 1967.

Khan, M. M. R. 1970. Montaigne, Rousseau, and Freud. In Khan (1974), pp. 99–111.

———. 1972. The Becoming of a Psycho-Analyst. In Khan (1974), pp. 112–28.

———. 1974. *The Privacy of the Self.* London: Hogarth Press, 1986.

Klein, M. 1932. *The Psycho-Analysis of Children. The Writings of Melanie Klein,* vol. 2, ed. R. Money-Kyrle et al., trans. A. Strachey and H. A. Thorner. London: Hogarth Press, 1986.

Kligerman, C. 1957. A Psychoanalytic Study of the *Confessions* of St. Augustine. *J. Am. Pschoanal. Assn.* 5:469–84.

Masson, J. M., trans. and ed. 1985. *The Complete Letters of Sigmund Freud to Wilhelm Fliess, 1887–1904.* Cambridge, MA: Harvard Univ. Press.

Pagels, E. 1988. *Adam, Eve, and the Serpent.* New York: Random House.

Rudnytsky, P. L. 1987. *Freud and Oedipus.* New York: Columbia Univ. Press.

———. 1988. "Here Only Weak": Sexuality and the Structure of Trauma in *Paradise Lost.* In *The Persistence of Myth: Psychoanalytic and Structuralist Perspectives,* ed. P. L. Rudnytsky. New York: Guilford, pp. 153–76.

———. 1991. *The Psychoanalytic Vocation: Rank, Winnicott, and the Legacy of Freud.* New Haven: Yale Univ. Press.

Schorske, C. E. 1980. *Fin-de-Siècle Vienna: Politics and Culture.* New York: Knopf.

Segal, C. 1982. *Dionysiac Poetics and Euripides' "Bacchae."* Princeton: Princeton Univ. Press.

Spitz, E. Handler. 1991. "Meditations on the Smile of Dionysus : Representations of Perverse Fantasy in Euripides' *Bacchae*" in *Image and Insight.* New York: Columbia Univ. Press, 178-201.

Suttie, I. 1935. *The Origins of Love and Hate.* London: Free Association Books, 1988.

Winnicott, D. W. 1958. The Capacity to Be Alone. In *The Maturational Processes and the Facilitating Environment.* London: Hogarth Press, 1966, pp. 29–36.

———. 1964. *The Child, the Family, and the Outside World.* Harmondsworth: Penguin Books, 1978.

EIGHT

The Architecture of Sexuality:
Body and Space in *The Decameron*

Richard Kuhns

Cognominato Prencipe Galeotto.
—Boccaccio, *The Decameron*

All paintings that metaphorize the body receive
some part of their authority to do so from the
way they engage with primitive phantasies
about the body.
—Richard Wollheim, *Painting as an Art*

In an earlier study (1989) I told the story of the poet who would also
be, and regarded himself as, the painter. Boccaccio—for he is the poet
as painter I referred to—explored all of the arts in the book which might
be regarded as the first *Gesamtkunstwerk* of a long tradition we know
well in our own time of opera and "happenings." As *The Decameron*
grows in its one hundred stories, it plots out and establishes the boundaries of many architectural and physiological spaces. Nor does it neglect
to set them in time, the other fundamental parameter of human consciousness.

Running as a sinew of articulation throughout the ten days of storytelling that make the corpus of *The Decameron* there are repeated
descriptions of buildings and bodies. It is at once obvious that they

metaphorize one another, and that in the representation of architectural settings and human bodies symbolic references to space and time, parts, and wholes, create a latent foundation for the manifest entertainments. That buildings and bodies stand as metaphors for one another has been noted by many psychoanalysts and art historians. Richard Wollheim (1987, 305–54) has analyzed those realizations in painting through a study of Titian, Bellini, Bellotto, and De Kooning.

Of course, we are familiar from literature with the many ways in which human bodies metaphorize space and time, and objects metaphorize bodies. In *The Decameron* Boccaccio found subtle, and for his purposes essential, ways to endow bodies with meanings well beyond the literal and to use mere physical presences as metaphors for the body. As the ten days of storytelling unfold, there is a developing complexity in the architectural and physiological interconnections. They begin at the beginning: the *brigata* meets in Santa Maria Novella; they return to that church at the conclusion of their storytelling stays in three different gardens outside of Florence. Santa Maria Novella housed frescoes whose narrative content establishes forms and themes for the succeeding stories, and the paintings offer obvious interpretative suggestions to the reader. I mention only two of the frescoes: the representation, in an anthill-like cross section, of Dante's *Inferno,* by Nardo di Cione; and the colorful, heavily populated paintings in the Spanish Chapel depicting the glory of St. Thomas Aquinas (Santa Maria Novella is a Dominican center of worship and learning), and on another wall, an allegory of the Dominican order. A full analysis of *The Decameron* would reveal affinities between it and Dante's *Divine Comedy,* and would open up to our inquiries the presence of Thomas Aquinas in many of the stories.

Gardens, both open and enclosed, courtyards, and walled vestibules— the last of which are often given anatomical specifically sexual suggestiveness as chambers that serve as entrances to an inner or adjacent cavity—appear over and over again in *The Decameron.* The readings I offer below serve as examples. The book's use of a common garden-enclosure *topos* has been well understood through many studies of the history of such structures and spaces (Doob 1990). Yet with this tradition, as with everything else he represents, Boccaccio works wonderful transformations and creates witty analogues as well as profound interconnections. It is my interest here to explore some of these spaces and to climb around upon some of the structures. I imagine myself in the (momentarily) happy condition of Guiscardo on his way to meet Ghismonda, in Day IV, Story 1. I only hope I do not end as he did, in having my heart cut out and sent to my object of desire as a punishment.

The sad tale of Ghismonda is preceded by rather detailed descriptions of women, their place in family life, their minds, and their bodies as well as of the consolation and philosophical instruction this book as Galeotto (or go-between) will provide for them. *The Decameron* as a whole opens with an address to women who are in danger of falling into melancholy because of the sequestered and lonely lives they are forced to lead, yet who hide within their breasts a fiery passion which drives them to seek objects—not just of sexual gratification, but of insight and understanding. They are like Plato's aspiring youths who need direction and a means of ascent to the proper object of their driving erotic desire. And they are also, we learn in the introduction to Day IV, Muses, *real* Muses, who inspire the poet, Boccaccio, to feats of linguistic excellence in storytelling. Flesh and blood ladies are inspirations; the mythic Muses are not!

Once one has given thought to these declarations on the part of the author who bestows the cognomen of "Prencipe Galeotto" upon his book, one will be ready to understand the deep hidden meaning in that delightful first story of Day III which I shall read as an introduction to the story of Ghismonda.

This is the story of Masetto of Lamporecchio, who pretends to be dumb and takes a job as a gardener in a convent where all the nuns use him as their bedfellow. To be sure, the story is usually read as an indictment of the lascivious life of women denied their necessary sexual pleasures. But here, as with almost every other story in *The Decameron*, there is a "secret" to be excavated by the perceptive reader. There are nine nuns (including the Mother Superior), just as there are nine Muses. Intercourse with the Muses is the poet's avenue to song, and indeed sexual intercourse with the nuns leads the "dumb" Masetto to break into speech when the Mother Superior exhausts him in sexual play. "A miracle," she shouts. Indeed it is a miracle he hasn't cried "Uncle" long before; but the miracle is, as we readers know, the miraculous move across boundaries when the simple man becomes a poet. As the text says, "when his tongue ligament was cut" he broke into words (rotto lo scilinguagnolo, cominciò a dire); he is now truly tempered in the service to his Muses, and thereafter devotes himself to fathering "babies," i.e., his works. Indeed, moving into deserved retirement, Masetto calls the readers' attention to his function as a surrogate for Boccaccio: "And this, he maintained, was the way that Christ treated anybody who placed a pair of horns upon his [Christ's] crown" (che cosí trattava Cristo che gli poneva le corna sopra 'l cappello) (1972, 234–41; 1984, 81–86). *The Decameron* slyly points out its own incommensurability with the beliefs and doctrines of Christianity. This story belongs to a whole set of stories which are explicitly concerned with artists, such as Giotto, Buffalmacco, Calandrino, and others who appear in various disguises (VI, 5; VIII, 3; VIII, 6; VIII, 9; IX, 3; IX, 5).

The cuckolding of Christ puts the poet in a particular relationship to both the Muses of the pagan world and the Savior of the Christian world: to *be* a poet not only must one seduce and lie with the Muses (till exhausted), but one must also be a sexual traitor to Christ himself, bedding down his own brides. By depriving Christ of their ministrations, one declares oneself forever freed from the hold of Christianity upon poetry's creative thought.

This lovely tale stands as a paradigm for every one in the book in that it hides deep and yet deeper meanings; they are for us to ferret out, to dig down to, to lift up into consciousness. And thus the simple gardener of Lamporecchio not only works the soil in an enclosed place, but explores with his Muses the bodies they intertwine within a fertile garden. Space and the body now begin to fill out the many suggestive implications of the cognomen of the book, Prince Galeotto.

The book, we begin to understand as we interpret the individual stories, and most emphatically the *author* of the book, Boccaccio, Mr. Badmouth, he who pulls faces, he who wears masks—for all those meanings are hidden in the name Boccaccio bestowed upon himself—is the Prince of Pimps, the go-between, the one who leads his characters into their sexual-linguistic interchanges and communions of body and of mind, and the one who takes the reader into his confidence if the reader only knows how to read, which means, as with Masetto, how to commune with the Muses, the lovely ladies.

Of course, such communions have their risks; as with all sexual-artistic play, one may fall over the edge, one may descend from art to pornography, or one may beget bathetic tales. Worse, one may end up dead. That is the fate of poor Guiscardo, who became the lover of the philosophically and sexually adventurous Ghismonda. Here, in the first story of Day IV, the architecture of sexuality is fully explored: the space without and within the body, the room designed for love, the danger of being discovered, and the penalties attached to women's explorations of both their own bodies and their sexual relations with men are closely represented in a complex set of metaphors and arguments. Here philosophy and poetry join forces in a revelation that is at once shocking and enobling.

The philosophically subtle and physically deprived Ghismonda selects the unaffected Guiscardo as her lover-to-be. She hands him a note hidden in a reed, and says to him, "Turn it into a bellows-pipe for your serving wench, so that she can use it to kindle the fire this evening" (1972, 333). One need not seek far for the sexual meaning of this exchange. And Ghismonda has, we quickly learn, been exploring both her own body and the architecture of the place in which she lives: flesh and earth metaphorize each other, as we philosophically know they in fact do.

This interanimation is represented in the following description:

Inside the mountain on which the Prince's palace stood, there was a cavern, formed at some remote period of the past, which was partially lit from above through a shaft driven into the hillside. But since the cavern was no longer used, the mouth of the shaft was almost entirely covered over by weeds and brambles. There was a secret staircase leading to the cavern from a room occupied by the lady, on the ground floor of the palace, but the way was barred by a massive door. So many years had passed since the staircase had last been used, that hardly anybody remembered it was still there; but Love, to whose eyes nothing remains concealed, had reminded the enamoured lady of its existence.

For several days she had been struggling to open this door by herself, using certain implements of her own as picklocks so that no one should perceive what was afoot. Having finally got it open, she had descended alone into the cavern, seen the shaft, and written to Guiscardo, giving him a rough idea of the distance between the top of the shaft and the floor of the cavern, and telling him to try and use the shaft as his means of access. . . . [T]he following night . . . he made his way to the shaft, wearing a suit of leather to protect himself from the brambles. Firmly tying one end of the rope to a stout bush that had taken root at the mouth of the opening, he lowered himself into the cavern and waited for the lady to come. (1972, 333–34)

But the envy of Fortune brings their pleasure to a tragic end; Ghismonda's father, Tancredi, an oedipal Pa if ever there was one, observes his daughter and her lover in their sexual exertions. Tancredi has Guiscardo killed, and conveys his heart to Ghismonda with the cruelest words uttered in the whole book: "Your father sends you this to comfort you in the loss of your dearest possession, just as you have comforted him in the loss of his" (1972, 339).

Ghismonda's detailed account to her father of the purposes, necessities, and elevating powers of love gives the impression that Boccaccio had read Plato's *Symposium*. He of course knew of it indirectly, but manuscripts of the *Symposium* became available only in the next century. Nonetheless, *The Decameron* is throughout a deeply philosophical book, and in this story of Guiscardo and Ghismonda the hierarchy of body-mind-spirit and the linking of rational argument with corporality is very like the twin themes of the *Phaedrus* in which Socrates unites (in a very sexual way—one must recall that Phaedrus initially seeks out Socrates in order to receive instruction on seduction) myth and argument, body and soul, earthy physicality and ethereal spirituality in the story of the chariot drawn by black and white steeds. Indeed, Socrates, like Boccaccio, is a Prince Galeotto. But then that is the very nature of philosophy itself, and of *The Decameron*. Socrates referred to himself as a pimp (*Mastropos; Theaetetus*, 150a).

Day VIII, Story 7, the longest tale of *The Decameron,* is at once the most difficult to interpret and the most complex in its exploration of body and mind, sexuality and thought. The characters—Elena the widow and Rinieri the philosopher—represent body and mind, and the mind-body problem was never so delicately yet so harshly and cruelly set forth.

In the collection of stories, this one is number 77, and since every number is meaningful in *The Decameron*, the reader is expected to understand that 77 suggests completion twice over. (Seven is the day on which God rested after creating the universe.) The double here, I suggest, refers to the twinship and total interdependence of body and mind. I shall explain the underlying narrative strategy that it seems to me Boccaccio slyly invokes.

This is the story in which the poet-pimp brings together ambiguously defined "lovers" in what appears to be deep misogyny, in a book that up to this point has been devoted to the lovely ladies. The would-be lovers in this story can, it appears, only destroy each other. Yet there lies beneath the cruel surface depths of calm understanding and even, I believe, biblical wisdom.

The story begins with Rinieri, the philosopher, just returned from studying in Paris, eagerly seeking to win the widow Elena. She already has a lover and finds pleasure in forcing Rinieri to stand outside in the courtyard of her house on a bitterly cold night while the lovers desport themselves inside. Shortly thereafter Elena loses her lover and seeks out Rinieri, to whom she attributes magical powers—he being a philosopher—and he promises to help her. In midsummer heat she stands naked on a tower in the belief that magical charms will bring her lover back to her. The ladder by which she might descend has been removed. As Rinieri nearly died of the cold, she nearly dies of the heat.

I shall seek the inner hidden plot of this story through the "argument" given by Rinieri to the lady he has finally trapped on the tower where she is being tortured by exposure, in her nakedness, to the sun.

And even supposing that all my little schemes had failed, I should still have had my pen, with which I should have lampooned you so mercilessly, and with so much eloquence, that when my writings came to your notice, as they certainly would, you would have wished a thousand times a day that you had never been born. The power of the pen is far greater than those people suppose who have not proved it by experience. (1972, 636)

The philosopher then delivers a lecture on the sexual potency, staying power, and technique of older lovers, for "they will shake your skin-coat with greater vigor, the older man, being more experienced, has a better idea of where the fleas are lurking" (637). The older man does not go off at a gallop, but conveys the lady with a gentle trot to their destination. Conversely, in Day VI, Story 1, Madonna Oretta is given a bad ride by the incompetent "storyteller" and suffers sexual arousal without full gratification. So she who has little time—"Oretta" meaning "little hour"—suffers from the youthful knight's inability to use his "pen" to the full, and with it to create a satisfying story. In all the stories there are close metaphoric affinities between horses, horseback riding, story-telling, and the power of the pen, whose phonetic likeness, in Italian as in English, to another instrument is only too obvious.

However, I am puzzled about the complex inner structure of Story 77, of which I have uncovered but a small part. My still evolving interpretation goes like this: Elena represents the body; Rinieri, the mind. Each must be "educated" in the powers of the other and their need for interdependence. Elena teaches Rinieri the coldness of intellect and philosophy if pursued without attention to the needs of the flesh; Rinieri teaches Elena the destructive force of bodily passion without mind or attention to truth and thought. Thus Elena believes philosophy to be black magic, and Rinieri plays on that deficiency to lead her into self-destruction.[1] If left isolated, body and mind destroy each other; neither can survive without the other. Attendant upon body and mind, and essential to their fullest development, are two powers—sight and speech. The hero and heroine of this story learn how to use and control their eyes and voice, the ability to see clearly and truthfully, and Rinieri possesses the ability to write powerfully as storyteller. To suggest to us the essential nature of these two gifts which in their interdependence define humanity—that is, the eye and the pen—the story tells us how it should be read and understood. The gift of sight and its powers are represented in the figure of Saint Lucy, for it is in Santa Lucia dal Prato that Elena and Rinieri meet when Elena turns to her "magician" for help.

Saint Lucy was the virgin martyr of Syracuse, in the reign of Diocletian. She was denounced and condemned as a Christian, but no power could move her from the place where she stood. The order was given to burn her, but the flames did not touch her. She was slain by a sword, thrust into her neck. A curious story is attached to the life of the saint; it is recounted that a young man was so moved by the beauty of her eyes that he could find no rest. She, to requite his passion, tore out her eyes and sent them to him. Thus, she is represented holding a plate with her eyes on it.[2]

The story emphasizes the power of language through Rinieri's arguments hurled at Elena and his boasting about the power of his pen. Mind will always win over body, but body must be given its due and the salvation of body depends on mind, because only through mind (thought) does body achieve immortality. This is both theological doctrine and psychological insight, a pairing that is characteristic of Boccaccio's power as a writer.

Day VIII, Story 7 explores the mind-body problem in terms that go beyond theological and philosophical sophistries. In the process it explores the ways in which the interdependence of mind and body becomes known to us and the means whereby we explore each side of the self. Sexual life brings two bodies together. That was the original goal of Rinieri, and he almost gives into lust when he sees Elena naked; but he controls his body on behalf of the chastening of body he will impose on Elena. She imposes a chastening upon his body in her turn, but it was on behalf of those passions that interfere with philosophy—greed, envy, anger, and petty narcissistic boasting to her lover.

The model of Saint Lucy should be a guide for Elena, and for those of us who use eyes to read. The insights of philosophy should be a guide for Rinieri, who had gone to Paris to study, and for us the life of the saint and the teachings of philosophy should be entertained in connection with Saint Lucy's purity of body. The highest exercise of mind (philosophy) and the most severe chastening of the body (religious fervor) come together in a story that teaches us how to place body and mind in their proper order.

When Elena and her maidservant are finally freed from the tower, it is recounted that the maid broke her thigh while climbing down the ladder. The breaking of the thigh is, I believe, a reference to Gen. 32:25–33, where Jacob wrestles the angel, and connects also with the vision of Jacob, i.e. Jacob's Ladder. To break the thigh is, by analogy, to sustain the injury inflicted by the angel upon Jacob. This I interpret as a symbol of the danger that one's soul may be alienated from the whole and thus reduce the self by half.[3]

The servant of Elena suffers an injury that represents what has happened to her mistress: the soul is no longer present in the body, and the physical and the spiritual realms have been split. The person is reduced to an animal form. This interpretation is metaphorized in the description of Elena who, suffering extreme sunburn, is like a snake shedding its skin. Elena is a snake, that is without a soul, and the incarnation of sheer carnality. In contrast, Rinieri, by means of mind and thought—that is philosophy—controls his sexual impulses sufficiently to suppress the physical. The hoped-for sexual union was to take place on the day after Christmas, the great feast day of the *incarnation* of the Lord. But that incarnation occurs every moment in which mind and body couple and create further mind-bodies. Boccaccio as Prince Galeotto works on the levels of both physical-bodily and spiritual-aesthetic reality. Art is the product of the pen-brush-penis as it inseminates the Muses, and they in turn give birth to pimping imagination's images and narratives. They gain their power over us through their wisdom in beauty. The beautiful—that which we respond to as aesthetic—enfolds, encloses, shrouds the deepest thought, for through the beauty of art the way is gained first into the enclosed garden or courtyard, and then into the womb of creativity.

Notes

1. There are, I believe, hidden references to Boccaccio himself in the theme of magic. The biographer of Boccaccio, Henri Hauvette, makes a strange comment about the way in which Boccaccio was remembered by his neighbors in Certaldo:

   The good people of Certaldo, whose intelligence Boccaccio never boasted of, preserved only a memory of him as a kind of magician or sorcerer. The devil, it was said, at Boccaccio's bidding joined together by a bridge of glass his house to the strange hill which faced it, since he had a longing to walk there at night. It is told that a woman, whose work as a weaver shook the wall that separated her house from that of the story teller, saw [through] a break in the wall an avalanche of papers and conjuring books that he had devotedly and with haste cast into the fire. (1914, 464)

2. Boccaccio's tale contains frequent references to the putting out of eyes. Elena says: "I've been crying so much over the trick I played on you...that it's a miracle I have any eyes left in my head" (1972, 633). Rinieri boasts of the power of his pen: "you would have been so mortified by the things I had written that you would have put out your eyes rather than look upon yourself ever again" (636).

3. The thigh (*coscia*) has a multitude of meanings in all languages, so the references here are comlex. The thigh is often a metonymy for the genitals, and the breaking of the thigh therefore suggests castration. In the Vulgate, "femur" is the thigh, and the passage in Gen. 32:25 states: "Qui [the angel] cum videret quid eum [Jacob] superare non posset, te tigit nervum femoris eius, et statim emarcuit" (And when he saw that he prevailed not against him, he touched the hollow of his thigh; and the hollow of Jacob's thigh was out of joint.) "Femur" is often translated "loins," the source of fertility and future generations. See Gen. 46:26; Exod. 1:15. (I am indebted to Eugene Rice for these references.)

References

Boccaccio, G. 1972. *The Decameron*, trans. G. H. McWilliam. Hamondsworth, England: Penguin Books.
———. 1984. *Decameron*, ed. C. Segre. Milano: Mursia.
Doob, P. R. 1990. *The Idea of the Labyrinth*. Ithaca: Cornell Univ. Press.

Hauvette, H. 1914. *Boccace: Étude biographique et littéraire.* Paris: Armand Colin.

Kuhns, R. 1989. The Writer as Painter: Observations on Boccaccio's *Decameron.* In *Malerei und Stadtkultur in der Dantezeit,* ed. H. Belting. Munich: Hirmer Verlag, pp. 65–69.

Wollheim, R. 1987. *Painting as an Art.* Princeton: Princeton Univ. Press.

On Hamlet's Madnesses and the Unsaid

André Green

Why does Hamlet delay? The problem invites too many answers, proof, unfortunately, that none of them is convincing. When we ask, however, "Why does Shakespeare have Hamlet delay?" and link this question to the theater, and to the fact that the theater represents itself in Hamlet, we are tempted to connect the theater's mise-en-abîme with the over-turning of its mainspring—action. Shakespeare constructs his play by inverting the signs of the theatrical project of his time, opposing to action its negative—inaction, or diverted action. In this the theater in *Hamlet* becomes mimetic of the psyche, which defers, displaces, and condenses by representation. In being represented, the theater is negativized, in-verting its aims and catching the conscience of the spectator through the nonrealization of desire.

Although one can explain this nonrealization in psychopathological terms, these terms will always be inadequate because what is in question here is not the content of the representation but rather the structure of representation[1] itself or, more precisely, the subject's relation to his rep-

This chapter is a translation by Joshua Wilner of excerpts from André Green, *Hamlet et Hamlet; une interprétation psychoanalytique de la représentation* (Paris: Balland, 1983). The chapter has previously appeared in *Hebrew University Studies in Literature and the Arts* 14 (Autumn 1986):18–39 and is reprinted here by permission of the editors and Dr. Green.

resentation. In psychopathology, one can separate the subject from his representation, one even conceives of him as using his representation not merely to disguise or to deceive himself but to efface himself, so that we will look for him someplace else. In the theater, this separation is impossible; the excess of representation saturates consciousness, fascinates it, and bars the thought of a separable subject. As the representation of a situation, of a character or of several characters joined in solidarity, as the representation of their own representation, *Hamlet* is exemplary. *Hamlet* is a *pièce de théâtre* about theater, which is to say, about the subject's (author and/or actor) relation to representation. But to understand this piece of theater, it is not enough to be present at its staging; one must rethink it by a reading which situates the representation retrospectively.[2]

As with language, so with representation. Unceasingly, the deepened analysis of representation sends us back to itself, to the container which it constitutes, and which one seeks to apprehend independent of all content; and unceasingly, in delimiting its formal framework, we become aware that we are unable to grasp it apart from its content, without which we are unable to conceive it. We try in vain to think the frame without the picture, the container without the content: the frame relegates us to the picture, which in its turn sends us back to the frame. There is no way to separate this frame from the representation of parricide and incest. The symbolic efficacy of the one depends on the symbolizing power of the others.

We have dwelt on the analysis of the frame in order to make it clear that a tragedy which might seem like any other of Shakespeare's tragedies is, in fact, of a formal complexity which precludes the possibility of understanding it simply in terms of a theme approachable with the tools of consciousness. All the more so in that parricide and incest are bound up here with the question of Hamlet's madness.

The limits of psychological interpretation are never better revealed than when critical commentary tries to say something about the question of madness in *Hamlet* and more particularly the question of Hamlet's madness. For madness is not one aspect of this tragedy among others. It is bound up with the theme of parricide and incest and with the hero's obscure problematic. And not his alone, since Ophelia is also stricken, suffering definitively the fate that might have been Hamlet's. What must be recognized is the existence of interdependent relations between the problematic of the theater—representation—that of incest and parricide, and finally that of madness. What we lack is the representation of this totality and its articulations, which would call for a conception of the representational function in and of these three orders. No other tragedy more clearly shows that it is the haunting of representation which drives one mad and it is by working through representation that one is saved from madness, be it only by shifting its burden to another. Parricide and incest hold the key to the power of representation; their structuring power may nevertheless be a screen for something unrepresentable which must at all costs be exorcised.

To address, even if only in a few words, the enigma of madness in *Hamlet* and in Hamlet's case is to kill two birds with one stone: on the one hand, to try to respond in another way—by means of psychoanalytic interpretation—to its *raison d'être;* on the other hand, to demonstrate why only a psychoanalytic interpretation is capable of bringing us close to this conception of the whole, since two of its three aspects belong to a domain which, though transposed onto the theatrical stage, nonetheless belongs to the area of competence of psychoanalysis.

What seems at first sight to be outside its interpetative field—theater— will enter into its orbit by way of an analysis of the function of representation. This will address, in the case of the author, the relations between madness and the thematic of parricide and incest.

Let us turn then to madness since we have left this subject in abeyance.

Hamlet's Madnesses

Rivers of ink have been flowing now for centuries on the subject of Hamlet's madness. Those who believe in it and those who don't have by turns deployed the arsenal of their arguments and quibbles, which range from the most convincing to the most conjectural, the best-supported to the most fragile. Examining these controversies in the light of the text, one quickly comes to the conclusion that the debate is completely misguided. It seems as though both fiction and its theatrical representation— in the final analysis Shakespeare's creation—are being denied the resources of ambiguity that fiction turns to its advantage, clinical description being out of place on the stage. One cannot schematize in accordance with the terms of the debate: either he's mad, or he's playing at being mad while sane. This would be a strange position to take since alienation presupposes a duality, all madness arising from some kind of rationality and coexisting with it, and all rationality being able to construct itself only on the basis of a repressed madness to which a certain field of play has been allowed alongside with rationality. The problem seems to become distressing when fiction forges the figure of a plural madness, alienation being located then not in the relations between madness and reason but between different madnesses, within a single subject. Whether it is a matter of madness or of reason, we are always sent back to meaning and its strategy: the method, as Polonius says—in relation to the *cause*. One is compelled to admit, if one reads *Hamlet* with the eyes of desire, rather than of reason, that there are at least three madnesses where its hero it concerned, coexisting under the same mask.

The first, most evident and most openly avowed, is that which serves cunning's cause; it works through dissimulation. It is only after having seen the Ghost that Hamlet announces for the first time his intention of playing at madness. It is not in order to protect himself that Hamlet dissimulates. On the contrary, his inner needs compel him to play the fool not in order to hide himself, but rather to show himself, to realize his project by never ceasing—if only by equivocation—to speak his truth. Madness is the game by which he reveals himself, while unsettling his enemies, who are unable to decide if he knows, what he knows, and to what degree he knows. This madness makes use of the resources of semantic ambiguity, playing with the signifier as Yorick did once at the court. When Hamlet plays mad [*fait le fou*—i.e. plays the fool,], his madness is histrionic, in the sense in which Yorick is the king's fool, with the difference that the jester is only partially his model. As a prince, he doesn't know how to be mad except by being truly mad. This madness gives the desire to exhibit oneself precedence over the desire to succeed in one's action, which would dictate discretion for the sake of success in one's enterprise. Hamlet wants to resolve the conflict between the desire to show himself and the desire to hide by showing himself as a way of hiding. But in fact, unable to relinquish his comedic self-exhibition, he reveals himself far too much so that the thrust of his exhibitionism is masochistic. This is hysterical madness.

The second madness, less evident because on the borders of that which one agrees to call normality, is Hamlet's melancholy passion. It is born from mourning for the father who has been monumentalized by the ego ideal and from the collapse of the idealized image of the mother, the support of the ideal ego. It is perceived as excessive by others, particularly those who fear the unpredictable consequences of a mourning that threatens to drive Hamlet to extremes. But it is remarkable that the work of mourning and the inhibition which afflict Hamlet are enigmatic to himself. Madness here is hidden from itself. What is more comprehensible than the pain of a son in mourning for a murdered father, and who can say what limits such a work of mourning must not cross in order to remain normal? Mourning or melancholia? The distinction is difficult. Perhaps it would be better to say mourning *and* melancholia.[3] What leads one to see in Hamlet a pathological mourning process is not its excessiveness, but rather its ambivalence, which is not unrelated to his procrastination. The internal object in relation to the dead father is under too much suspicion of being the devil's messenger for this mourning to be brought to its conclusion in an ordinary way. As regards the image of the departed king, its idealization testifies to Hamlet's intolerance of the feelings of unconscious hostility that inhabit him, feelings that make themselves felt in his deferral of vengeance. If one recalls that along with mourning his dead father Hamlet is also living out the separation that he must achieve from his living mother, from whom he has withdrawn his love in consequence of her remarriage, this double loss drives him to a narcissistic regression in which the danger of suicide inclines us toward a diagnosis of melancholia. The second madness, the melancholic one, is thus the wound inflicted by his feelings for the dead father, and the resentment he feels toward a mother who has fallen to the level of whore-actress.

There is a final madness, resulting from the other two, which totally eludes the subject's control. It is Hamlet's true psychosis, and one that escapes the spectator's notice, because it is not translated into the language of unreason. This is amorous madness. Originating in the other's— that is to say, his mother's—incest, it is propped up by the dutiful madness of mourning. It is a sexual and murderous madness legitimated by the filial love that we see at work in the bedchamber scene. The madness that is most secret, the one that is most hidden, even from Hamlet himself, is in the final analysis his sexual madness regarding Ophelia, a madness that aims at rendering the other mad, not guilty as in the case of Gertrude whom he wishes would admit her guilt, but mad to the point of suicide. Hamlet thus exorcises his truest madness in driving Ophelia to madness and suicide, which is his own greatest temptation.

Having differentiated these three madnesses, we are now going to reunite them in revealing their common cause—femininity. For when Hamlet plays the fool, his exhibitionism and clowning give him a pleasure that he experiences as guilty. He is unable to resist this tendency because of his love of the theater. Thus if one says that Hamlet plays at being mad, one should not place the emphasis on the madness, but on its theatricality. What matters is not that he has chosen to play the role of a madman, but that his madness finds no outlet other than in acting. It is not the choice of madness as a ruse that should claim our attention, but the compulsiveness with which he gives his madness a theatrical turn. Now, as the whole tragedy has shown, the actor is, by essence, a woman. This simulated madness is thus the weapon of a woman-whore-actress, three words which, for Hamlet, mean the same thing.

Let us now consider Hamlet's second madness—his melancholia. Here again we will find femininity on our way. For both Hamlet's idealization of the dead father and the reproaches that he directs at himself for failing to act are explainable in terms of a homosexual feminizing submission to a paternal image. In relation to Claudius, this feminization is evident. Claudius is spoken of as a woman, a whore, or an actor on several occasions, and Hamlet directs the same accusations at himself, likening himself to what he abhors. Here what is involved is defeated rivalry with the paternal image. But the same holds true of the love-relation with the idealized dead father. When the son compares himself to his father, he never ceases to underscore his smallness, his mediocrity, his inadequacy in the face of the grandeur, excellence, and majesty of the dead king. When Hamlet condemns his mother's weakness, attributing it to the power of the flesh over her entire being, he ends up recognizing himself in his depiction of her, feeling himself incapable of breaking the tie that binds him to her and subjects him in spite of himself, to the feminine identification.

The madness of Hamlet's that is most generally recognized as such—the only one capable of turning his melancholy into paranoia—reveals in him a boundless sadism and cruelty where Gertrude and even more where Ophelia are concerned. This is because the love he has for them is so strongly misogynistic that he is forced to repel them violently and to hate them, fearing that the defilement he sees in them will through contact invade him. Yet it is only because he expels it from himself that he sees this defilement in them. His disgust with the flesh and with sexuality merely translates his refusal of a femininity that he can neither accept nor integrate and that is going to find expression in an inability to act when the action demanded of him leads him to confront the person who has realized his own desires, the treacherous Claudius, a king of "shreds and patches."

Thus it is the femininity of the man that drives him to the various madnesses played out in him by turns—hysteria, melancholy, persecution. Shakespeare undoubtedly had his reasons for understanding the forces behind this masculine madness, at once unitary and threefold, each of its manifestations tempering the action of the others; and it is thanks to their reciprocal play that he keeps Hamlet from succumbing to one or another of their outcomes, so that his hero can live out the time of the tragedy. And so that he himself can see his work through to its end. For Shakespeare, to play is to allow the performance to go on, without interrupting it, as with the too explicit "Murder of Gonzago."

What he will teach us is that it is representations and not events that make Hamlet go mad. And that the only means of escaping the total invasion of madness is the representation of these representations. In the final analysis, it is theater that saves Shakespeare from madness, the tragedy's development that saves Hamlet from madness, and the representation to us both of this thematic of incest and parricide and of the threat menacing our reason that saves us at the same stroke from madness.

The Unsaid of the Tragedy

Behind the madness that assails the hero—and not just him—another madness, one suspects, is at work, haunting his author. One could see the work of the tragedy as the latter's attempted cure, one that permits the threat to be conjured while refusing to cede to it. Where is one to find its traces if not in something unsaid against which Shakespeare struggles with more or less success?

The failure of traditional criticism to explain the difference of *Hamlet* stems perhaps from its refusal to take into consideration the stimulus to creation to be found in Shakespeare's mental turmoil prior to its writing. The birth of this work was not a creation *ex nihilo*. If *Hamlet* marks a break in the Shakespearean corpus, this splitting results from a mutation effected in relation to himself and his predecessors.

By the time he began work on *Hamlet,* Shakespeare had already written all of his historical dramas.[4] Regicide is a problem with which he is familiar, the fate of some of England's kings having provided him with material for reflection. There are numerous situations in these plays that offer the psychoanalyst an opportunity to show the oedipal relations at work between monarchs and their sons. Sovereigns cloaking themselves in virtue in order to conceal the grave crimes that weigh on their consciences and that they confess to their inheritors at the moment of extreme unction, a prince donning his father's crown even before his death has been officially announced—these are matters he has already spoken of (II *Henry IV*). Assassin-kings who do away with their brothers to reach the throne, who seduce the wife of the one they have murdered—these he has encountered (*Richard III*). Despoiled princes who will do anything to reign he has described (*King John*). Monarchs doomed to failure and death by excessive shyness we find at the periphery of his work (*Henry VI*). And some have seen in Richard II an early prototype of Hamlet.

It is not only the history of England, as seen through Holinshed's eyes, that inspires Shakespeare in preparation for *Hamlet*. Ancient Rome, to which this tragedy makes such frequent allusion, also came to occupy the author's thoughts with *Julius Caesar* immediately preceding the turn to Denmark.[5]

These facts only bring out more clearly the extent to which Shakespeare, having already taken on all these situations, does something else with *Hamlet*. Far from providing antecedents for *Hamlet*, they underscore what sets it apart. *Hamlet* is Shakespeare's first true tragedy, the first to take only its pretext from history, like *Macbeth* or *King Lear*, for in all of these cases, the historic framework recedes behind the interiorization of the character.

The same movement characterizes Shakespeare's treatment of the *Hamlet* theme itself, a theme that was already in the repertory, since, from 1589 on, a now-lost *Hamlet* of Thomas Kyd had been performed on the London stage, and was undoubtedly followed by many others. Although we know nothing about Kyd's play, the comparison of Shakespeare's *Hamlet* to related works, such as *The Spanish Tragedy* (c. 1588; Büchner 1878, 133–36), also by Kyd, opens on to an abyss of differences. A German play, *Der bestrafte Brudermord* (The Fratricide Punished) *oder Prinz Hamlet aus Doenemark*, which originated with Kyd or another author, but in any case followed a very old version anterior to Shakespeare was performed in Germany early in the seventeenth century.[6] Whatever the case may be, all these works "practice to the point of excess the cult of the horrible mixed with burlesque."[7] It is difficult to say how much knowledge Shakespeare and his predecessors had of the legend of Hamlet arising from the *Historia Danica* of Saxo Grammaticus[7] or of the adapted translation by Belleforest in his *Tragic Histories*. But many details in *Hamlet* from which Shakespeare derives intense dramatic effects are to be found in the Danish myth.

The movement from Saxo Grammaticus to Shakespeare is a cultural one from myth to tragedy. The legend recounted in the *Historia Danica* is agglomerate, diffuse, and complicated, the myth lending itself to developments in which the principal theme is waylaid in secondary episodes. There is no point in relating it here despite the interest it offers and the surprises it holds for the reader who recognizes in this primitive source features that will later find a place in Shakespeare's work. Even though we know nothing about Kyd's 1589 *Hamlet,* what we do know about the other tragedies with which *Hamlet* can be compared shows that the representation of the myth on the stage led to a narrative reduction, to a tightening of the plot in general, to a search for ways to dramatize the story. But until we get to Shakespeare we find ourselves in a genre that remains considerably indebted to melodrama, making of *Hamlet,* or rather the *Hamlet*s, a target for the jibes of his contemporaries, who did not fail to smile at theatrical excesses that smacked more of a Punch-and-Judy pastime than of high tragedy.

The mutation that Shakespeare has Hamlet undergo is connected above all with the reversal of the theatrical perspective; that is to say, the principal aim of the theater is no longer to show on stage the story of the protagonists' actions. It is no longer a question of moving toward an externalization of the mythic narrative. Up to this point its theatrical materialization had facilitated the visibility of actions arranged in such a manner as to arouse the spectator's emotion by giving him the illusion that he was present not at a mythic narrative but at the reproduction before his very eyes of the reality of which the myth speaks, expressed in the language of the stage. Shakespeare takes the opposite track. What he puts on the stage, what he is going to try to show, is not a semblance, but rather that which cannot be shown. Whence the importance of Hamlet's response to his mother's question:

Queen: ... Why seems it so particular with thee?
Hamlet: Seems, madam? Nay, it is. I know not "seems."
'Tis not alone my inky cloak, good mother,
Nor customary suits of solemn black,
Nor windy suspiration of forc'd breath,
No, nor the fruitful river in the eye,
Nor the dejected havior of the visage,
Together with all forms, moods, shapes of grief,
That can denote me truly. These indeed seem,
For they are actions that a man might play,
But I have that within which passes show;
These but the trappings and the suits of woe. (1.2.75–86)[8]

The whole passage, with its theatrical allusion to "actions that a man might play," reflects one of the many condemnations of the theatrical style of the period from which Shakespeare sets himself off. "But I have that within which passes show." That which is within cannot be externalized in a spectacle or "show." It is this very impossibility that *Hamlet* is going to make possible through an interiorization of the tragic in both Hamlet and *Hamlet,* the entire tragedy bearing the mark of its hero.

It is not by chance that the lines I have just cited speak of mourning as an experience in which the whole psyche undergoes a narcissistic withdrawal subsequent to the loss of the object, and in which the subject, paralyzed by sorrow and suffering cruelly from what he experiences as a painful anesthesia, finds that he is stricken by inhibition. This being the case, it is logical that the movement of internalization the tragedy undergoes should invert the canons of the genre, which exploit the dramatic resources of action, by substituting for them a contrary dramatic value—inaction.

It is here that one must locate the decisive influence of the personal event that contributed to Shakespeare's mutation—the death of his father. This mourning was not a simple matter, no more than was Hamlet's. It is probably not a point of departure, but the end result of a psychic process that was perhaps as complicated at the start as were the theatrical plots of the pre-Shakespearean *Hamlets.* I am assuming here that the mourning itself was the resolution of a state of madness arising from the resurgence of early childhood fantasies and giving rise to a host of quasi-delirious representations of which the unsaid is the trace. Shakespeare's melancholy will absorb these representations in order to yield itself entirely to the double interiorization that presided simultaneously over the work of mourning and the work of literary creation.

Shakespeare's work of mourning will effect an extraordinarily fruitful chiasmus. For if the work is going to gain in depth through an interiorization of tragedy, the process of artistic creation is going to compel the author to give the work of personal mourning an opposite turn. That is to say, it will force Shakespeare to exteriorize through representation the internal psychic work, thus wresting it from its unrepresentability.

Public representation is going to give us access to the private world of the protagonists while the private world of the author is going to be given over to the publicity of theater.

The work of theater and the work of mourning are going to combine forces and tend toward a single goal—representation. Behind the reproduction of events, which it endows with the palpitation of life, setting the protagonists before us "body and flesh," caught in the net of the conflictual ordeals that govern their relationships, representation reveals its own structure. No longer the mirror of an external action, it allows us to rediscover at its heart the reflexive relationships that all subjective organizations disclose, especially when they plunge so deeply into the unconscious. In other words, it is the mirror of the mind that representation brings to light rather than the mind as the mirror of the world. Better still, the mirror of the mind that the tragedy holds out to the spectator assigns language the function of representing that which no mirror can reflect because it does not belong to the order of representation. Language will be accorded primacy, in so far as it is the highest realization of the work of representation, the only mode of representation that can say what cannot be shown, the only one that is capable, if not of expressing affect, at least of creating in poetry the vehicle of its transmission. It takes up the challenge of pronouncing the unpronounceable, of articulating the inarticulable—be it as cry or as silence—and all of this enclosed within the strict limits of the theater.

This elaboration is based on a double refusal—not only the one that takes its distance from the theatrical tradition of the moment, but also that refusal in the mourning process which keeps at a distance everything of the imaginary relations between the dead and the living that the personal fantasized of the past causes to reemerge. All the same, however radical this rupture may be, it leaves the trace of its scar. It is impossible to know if Shakespeare willed this repression in a deliberate manner;

still it remains the case that the work gained additional power in leaving something unsaid whose pattern we have guessed at, for the author could not avoid leaving behind him the signs by which the unsaid escapes the forgetfulness in which he would have wished to imprison it. Unless the unsaid was never clearly formulated in his mind.

The ruse of the tragedy is to make us believe that the story that has gained currency about the king's death contains no more secrets for us. In other words, that we, the spectators, like Hamlet, *know*. And that there is nothing else to know.[9] But the disclosure of something unsaid may well serve as a screen for something else unsaid that has been reduced to silence. Or almost. The myth worked its way through the play, compelling the latter to free itself. But another myth, this time a personal one, filled the void left by the first even before Shakespeare decided to turn his back on it. It is this crossing that engenders *Hamlet,* the hybridization being consigned to the scrapheap so as to leave the field to the auditing of a debt owed a dead father, who has been washed clean of all suspicion. Or almost. For "how his audit stands who knows save heaven?" (3.3.82).

Despite everything, the unsaid weighs on the tragedy, as it weighs on us. From within the silence that contains it, it works in the shadows. It works through us, forcing us to penetrate its secret, to risk forging in our turn a crude, improbable story, which will lead the tragedy back to the primitive material of the unconscious from which it issued in order to become what it is. In rediscovering the madness from which Shakespeare extricated himself, it is we ourselves who might pass for mad.

What we are going to relate takes off from our reading of *Hamlet* in order to construct the plot of the play that Shakespeare *did not write,* but about which he would have dreamed before writing the tragedy which bears its mark. One would have found in it traces of the reworked Danish myth and the exteriorization of personal reveries unearthed by mourning. This version involves incoherences and absurdities that in no way impede the fantasmatic construction.

Three families are present: the Hamletides, the Polonides, and the Fortinbrasides. This triangulation is Shakespeare's creation. They represent three nations: Denmark, Poland, and Norway. Although Shakespeare at no moment suggests a connection between Poland and Polonius, one cannot attribute the choice of this name to chance.[10] Intermediaries between the principal adversaries, the Danes and the Norwegians, they are vassals of the former. Everything began, as in the legend, with old Fortinbras' challenge to a younger adversary, Hamlet the Valiant, whose exploits endangered the reputation of his Nordic neighbor. But in Shakespeare's myth, one must suppose that Gertrude was also the stake of this duel. Like Claudius later, King Hamlet, not wishing to risk his crown and his queen, chose to resort to cunning. He obtained the services of Polonius, who proposed to him the same stratagems as those which Shakespeare will use for the duel between the Prince of Denmark and Laertes. Fortinbras is vanquished the day of Hamlet's birth, which is also the day the gravedigger begins to practice his trade. This coincidence indicates that the prince is doomed to die, perhaps in order to pay for his father's sin, perhaps, as well, because his birth is illegitimate. Claudius, who is jealous of his brother and who doesn't like war, profits from the king's absences to woo Gertrude, who yields to his advances. A suspicion hangs over this birth. Is the prince the son of Hamlet the Valiant or of Claudius the traitor? Gertrude presents Claudius to Hamlet as his father—a suggestion that Hamlet energetically rejects with his very first reply, "A little more than kin, and less than kind." Claudius multiplies his displays of affection for Hamlet, and not solely for the purpose of deception:

> for let the world take note
> You are the most immediate to our throne
> And with no less nobility of love
> Than that which dearest father bears his son
> Do I impart toward you.

> (1.2.108–12)

He explicitly calls himself Hamlet's father (4.3.50). But the uncertainty of this paternity drives Claudius at the moment of danger to resolve on infanticide.

Does Hamlet suspect this in the least? The insistence with which he deepens the distance between father and uncle and detects in himself the same faults that he condemns in Claudius may support this unconscious fantasy. What equivocal words has he heard from Yorick in their games? Yorick observed all and mocked all, his insolent words hardly mattering. Thus one sees that Hamlet had two reasons to die, in consequence of both his father's and his mother's faults.

But this does not explain the extermination of the Polonides. As for Polonius, whose behavior under Claudius allows us to guess what he might have been like under his predecessor, there is hardly any need to look further for the cause of his death. But his children? Laertes' sharp words upon his return to Denmark, his vehemence, seem like a denial:

> That drop of blood that's calm proclaims me bastard,
> Cries cuckold to my father, brands the harlot
> Even here between the chaste unsmirched brow
> Of my true mother.
>
> (4.5.118–21)

The words that delirium wrests from Ophelia, "It is the false steward, that stole his master's daughter," (4.5.173), seem to point to her father. Polonius' children would be the work of the late king and their mother. This would explain the conspiratorial behavior of Polonius, who must wreak vengeance on the Hamletides. He has allied himself with Claudius in order to get rid of the late king, since Claudius is tired of waiting and wants the crown and the queen. Polonius, for his part, dreams of setting up his children on the throne after Claudius. That Laertes should be proclaimed king by the crown on his return shows that he is a potential successor, as beloved of the people as Hamlet. And if Polonius fails in this, he can always hope that Ophelia, whom he turns away from Hamlet only to force the prince's hand, will be queen. Her father's death and Hamlet's recklessness will drive Ophelia mad, permitting Shakespeare to show us that she knows much more than one might have thought. Not only about the death of the king, but also, no doubt, about her own parentage.

Here it is not the clown's folly that tells the truth, but true folly, that madness which Hamlet and Shakespeare eluded and that calls forth what foreclosure had totally annihilated. For while one may pose questions about what Hamlet knows and doesn't know, Ophelia's innocence is certain. The sum of traumatisms created by Hamlet's assassination of Polonius and perhaps even the child that she is bearing by him are needed to bring back into the domain of the real something of the past that seemed totally abolished. That Gertrude is distrustful of the consequences of this madness and the words that might come from her mouth explains why she refuses to see her. For Ophelia's delirium is terribly accusatory and the truth that it reveals will be heard by one who can understand ... Gertrude is too much a woman not to divine it. It is only at this point that she expresses some anxiety:

To my sick soul, as sin's true nature is,
Each toy seems prologue to some great amiss,
So full of artless jealousy is guilt,
It spills itself in fearing to be spilt.

(4.5.17–20)

Ophelia will kill herself because her discourse was heard by no one, because she has come up against the wall of denial that those who are guilty and who, to the end, want to see in her nothing but the innocent, the charming, the sweet, the poor Ophelia, have erected. With Ophelia, Shakespeare redeems all his misogyny. He seems to evoke through her a young girl of very long ago who has been loved and lost.

At the end of the tragedy, the Last Judgment has pronounced its sentence. It has brought about the punishment, throughout the tragedy, not just of the one guilty party, but of all who are guilty of crimes, both revealed and unrevealed. It has proceeded to the destruction of the children issued from these impure races. It has established the rights of an unknown from elsewhere, victim of the first wrong—Fortinbras.

This is the essence of the unsaid that works the tragedy from within.[11]

It appears in places in the thread of the text like a series of islands that I have sought to link together, from Horatio's first remark on the trembling of the Specter, to Fortinbras' final affirmation claiming rights over Denmark. I have constructed the link that might unite the islands of this archipelago in order to explain Hamlet's conclusion. A certain boldness is needed to unearth this quasi-delirious construction and ridicule can kill it. I remain nonetheless convinced that *Hamlet* emerged from this mad reverie or *from another of the same kind* before knowing the destiny of its definitive form. From where does it come?

The construction I have proposed is not unlike a mythic narrative. Sexuality, feminine betrayal, the treachery of kings—all these occupy a large place in Saxo's legend, which is marked by the harshness of the old narratives. Thus Shakespeare would be building a myth upon a myth. This story, one not of his own devising, would have served as a core of excitation, to become invested with the projections with which he would have enriched it in drawing on the delusional trends of his most inner psyche.

It must be acknowledged that no erudite or rational commentary will ever get to the bottom of *Hamlet*. That requires the poetic imagination of the writer. In some stunning and all the same delusional pages, James Joyce delineates through the intermediary of Stephen Dedalus, the portrait of a Shakespeare beaten and betrayed by women, by his wife as well as his mother, both unfaithful spouses seduced by their brothers-in-law. For the theme of the false, usurping, and adulterous brother is everywhere in his work. When the Ghost speaks to Hamlet, Joyce thinks, Shakespeare is speaking to his own son Hamnet to tell him that his mother is guilty. And yet, Shakespeare is also Hamlet and the Ghost his own father bringing the same accusation against his wife. Shakespeare writing *Hamlet* is the Father of all his race. Another version of a family romance, in which the fantasm of bastardy is explicit. One must read these pages, which show more insight into Shakespeare than anything else one could read.[12]

Dedalus's Christian ravings deal with the problem of Hamlet in terms of the mourning that reunites the son and the dead father betrayed by maternal love. Our hypothesis concerning the unsaid speaks of a phase prior to the institution of mourning in which the father is the object of a criminal accusation in a delirious network of conspiracies and adulteries that stir the memory of enshrouded fantasms concerning a primeval father who knows no other law than that of his desire.

Had Shakespeare ceded to the promptings of these fantasms he would have written a mediocre melodrama altogether within the theatrical tradition of the period. And he would have spared himself a good deal of mourning. But he plunged into it, and the writing of *Hamlet* takes on the function of a mise-en-scène that brings about a recasting of the family romance in order to rescue the memory of the dead father.

Now we behold his lofty and noble figure imbued with spirituality, coupled with a mother who is a prisoner of the flesh. All the guilt will be borne by the bad brother, a distant echo of the treachery of all the fathers of the primitive construction.

What then is the function of the unsaid? Repressed by the author, it will become the scheme behind the work, its silent motor, the hidden demon that leads to the structuring of the manifest plot. Working against it, Shakespeare will use it as a foil by means of which to effect an inward deployment of the work. The unsaid will be the support against which the theatrical work and the work of mourning are built up. In other words, Shakespeare will use what is unsaid as a kind of unconscious operator, the object of a permanent anticathexis compelling the tragedy to weave itself in order to cover it over. The cohesion of this structure depends on something being crossed out, on an unfilled blank compelling it to construct itself as a way of conjuring the "delirium" tied up with the family romance and its dark indictment of the parental images. This is why the tragedy's unfolding is far from uniform, but rather constantly strives to sustain a coherence that must overcome the work's contradictory tensions, its excursions into side-plots whose necessity will be revealed only at the tragedy's end.

Nonetheless, the unsaid, which, out of its repression, leads to a structuring, organizes the hiatus that bars all totalization. It becomes generative of richly uncertain relations and productive of incomplete meanings *of* which we will never have our fill.

What have we done in constructing it? Filled in what is missing? Certainly not. We have invented a simulacrum of that which might have been at the origin of the *refusal* from which *Hamlet* arises. A pure conjecture. What is most fictive in this fiction, this unsaid, becomes a fiction of fiction, and thus verges on truth. But this fiction is in limbo; it never came into existence. On the other hand, it allowed the theatrical fiction to come into being, which is no small accomplishment.

Out of a group of chaotic representations, gathered together by a thread of precarious rationalization like a piece of clothing made of "shreds and patches—that minimal binding of which madness is yet capable—representation brought something into being. Representation and its mise-en-abîme as articulation, network, faceted diamond or palace of mirrors, whose maddening internal power transmutes itself and becomes, but this time by force of richness, infinitely revelatory of connections leading to other connections, of reverberations between space and time, of crossed identifications...The tragedy became a symbolic structure, but this structure remains invisible, as yet to be discovered, carried away on the surge of poetic writing that keeps us from catching our breath so that we might contemplate its architecture and attempt to grasp its composition. Its greatest accomplishment will have been to contain psychic space within the limits of the stage, to bring this other scene with its infinite prolongations onto the strict space of the boards, where it must be confined. It has organized its network around the fictive being that radiates at its center. The theater has become a symbolic matrix, a reflector of our own minds[13] and of our heroic double.

This is *Hamlet* containing Hamlet.

Notes

1. The French *représentation*, while similar in meaning to its English cognate, is also used to speak about a theatrical performance. Since I have consistently rendered *représentation* as "representation," the reader should bear this range of meaning in mind [Translator's Note].

2. The text in the original uses the psychoanalytic expression *après-coup (Nachträglich)*, for which there is no appropriate translation. Deferred action has been proposed to designate the mechanism by which an event becomes meaningful only when it is reactivated by memory after a certain delay.

3. In the psychiatric sense.

4. With the exception of *Henry VIII*, in any case a collaborative work.

5. Belleforest had already noted the analogy between Hamlet and Brutus. Cf. A. Büchner (1878, 61). (1878, 61).

6. In 1603 according to Büchner, in 1626 according to Bernhardy; cited by Jones (1949, 107).

7. Büchner, p. 103. Hamlet belonged to the group of "revenge tragedies."

8. All quotations from *Hamlet* are to the text of *The Riverside Shakespeare* (Evans et al. 1974).

9. Lacan remarks that in *Hamlet* the father knows how he died and makes this known to Hamlet—in which he differs from Oedipus who doesn't know, and wants to.

10. In an earlier version, Polonius is called Corambis, which has been attributed to an interpretation of the copyist, who would have completed the abbreviation "Cor." for courtier.

11. This construction has much in common with Nicolas Abraham (1978, 447–74). His text, which dates from 1974–5, was known to me from the time it was written. I will not conceal that it elicited from me at that time a total rejection. I was greatly surprised when, years later, in the process of working on this essay, I realized that I had arrived in my own way at many conclusions in which he had preceded me. Nonetheless I am far from sharing all of Abraham's deductions; I understand quite differently the function of the unsaid.

12. James Joyce (1922, 184–214). It is remarkable that when Dedalus, having come to the end of this dazzling construction, is asked "Do you believe your own theory?" can only answer "No," as if the unsaid—even though different from ours—must, once unearthed, be annihilated again.

13. This is what Mallarmé understood so well: "Shakespeare's work is so well made, according to the only theater of our mind, prototype of the rest.... His solitary drama! And which at times, so much did this wanderer in a labyrinth of troubles and sorrows prolong their circuits with the suspense

182   André Green

of an uncompleted act, seems the very spectacle for which the stage exists, as does the gilded quasi moral space which it guards" (1887, 300).

References

Abraham, N. 1978. *L'Écorce et le noyau*. Paris: Flammarion.
Büchner, A. 1878. *Hamlet le Danois*. Paris: Hachette.
Evans, G., et al., eds. 1974. *The Riverside Shakespeare*. Boston: Houghton Mifflin.
Jones, E. 1949. *Hamlet and Oedipus*. New York: Norton, 1976.
Joyce, J. 1922. *Ulysses*. New York: Modern Library, 1961.
Mallarmé, S. 1887. Crayonné au théâtre. In *Oeuvres complètes,* ed. H. Mondor and G. Jean-Aubry. Paris: Bibliothèque de la Pléiade, 1945, pp. 293–351.

Index